British Theatre Since The War

British Theatre Since The War

Dominic Shellard

Yale University Press
New Haven and London

Set in Simoncini Garamond by Northern Phototypesetting Co. Ltd, Bolton, Lancs.
Printed in Great Britain by Redwood Books, Trowbridge, Wilts.

Library of Congress Cataloging-in-Publication Data
Shellard, Dominic.
    British theatre since the war/by Dominic Shellard.
    Includes bibliographical references and index.
    ISBN 0–300–07684–3 (hbk.)
    ISBN 0–300–08737–3 (pbk.)
    1. Theater—Great Britain—History—20th century.   I. Title.
PN2595.S42   1999
792'.0941.0945—dc21   98–53505
                                                        CIP

For permission to reprint extracts from copyright material the author and publishers gratefully acknowledge the following: Faber and Faber for *Look Back in Anger* (1986) by John Osborne; Methuen for *Separate Tables* in *Plays* (1985) by Terence Rattigan; Faber and Faber for *Waiting for Godot* (1965) by Samuel Beckett; Penguin Books for *The Good Person of Setzuan* by Bertolt Brecht translated by Eric Bentley in *Parables for the Theatre* (1982); Methuen for *The Room* (1959) by Harold Pinter; Faber and Faber for *The Entertainer* (1990) by John Osborne; Hodder & Stoughton for *Knight Errant* (1995) by Robert Stephens; Marion Boyars for *Marat/Sade* (1991) by Peter Weiss, translated by Geoffrey Skelton; Methuen for *Orton – 1 The Complete Plays* (1987) by Joe Orton; Methuen for *The Orton Diaries* (1987) edited by John Lahr; Penguin Books for *Empty Seats* (1984) by Michael White; Methuen for *Saved* by Edward Bond in *Plays One* (1995); Redburn Productions Ltd for *Absurd Person Singular* (1997) by Alan Ayckbourn; Methuen for *Our Country's Good* (1988) by Timberlake Wertenbaker.
    The author and publishers would also like to thank the Estate of Kenneth Tynan for kind permission to quote extracts from letters by Kenneth Tynan: Jocelyn Herbert and the Estate of George Devine for kind permission to quote from a letter by George Devine; Joan Plowright and the Estate of Laurence Olivier for kind permission to quote from a letter by Laurence Olivier; and Crown Copyright for kind permission to quote from the Lord Chamberlain's Papers.

A catalogue record for this book is available from the British Library.

10 9 8 7 6 5 4 3 2

For my nephew, Ross

Contents

Preface

Over recent years I have been frustrated by the absence of a book that provided an overview of significant developments in the evolution of British theatre since the Second World War. In an age where modularisation at universities has decreased the amount of time students have available for research and reflection, the need for such a work has become ever more pressing. So, spurred on by my students at the University of Sheffield, I decided to write one myself.

Given the vast amount of material that deserves to be covered, I have inevitably had to prioritise some topics over others. On re-reading my manuscript, I was surprised at the extent to which London recurs throughout the narrative, but then London has been *the* site of theatrical activity throughout the period. A debate about the advisability of such centralisation is long overdue.

The book, therefore, is not intended to be definitive but introductory. If it succeeds in providing useful signposts that help orientate the reader towards further investigation, it will have achieved its aim. The writing of history is, like the very process of creating drama itself, fluid. Subsequent historians will advance different perspectives on the period, and my conclusions will necessarily be challenged. Given the vacuum of works that provide an account of the history of post-war British theatre, I hope that I have created a first and useful map.

I would like to acknowledge the help and support of the following: Jack Reading, whose advice has been invaluable; Fiona Kavanagh Fearon for permission to read and refer to her unpublished thesis; Professor David Lewis and the University of Sheffield Research Fund; Sally Brown and Kathryn Johnson at the British Library; John Walker; Mum, Dad, Sonya, Bobby and Jessica; my Editor at Yale University Press, Robert Baldock; Pete and Carol Lilleker; and, inevitably, QPR.

Table of Significant Events

Date	Theatrical events in the UK	Other events in the UK	Other international events
	CHAPTER 1: 1945–54		
1945	(*1944* Old Vic Company opens at New Theatre *Aug.* **Peer Gynt**) *Jan.* **Uncle Vanya** *Sept.* **Henry IV Parts 1 and 2** (Richardson's Falstaff) *Oct.* **Oedipus** (Olivier)	*Jul.* General Election. Labour wins with majority of 146. Clement Attlee becomes Prime Minister	*7 May* Germany surrenders *6 Aug.* Atomic Bomb dropped on Hiroshima *9 Aug.* Atomic Bomb dropped on Nagasaki *14 Aug.* Japan surrenders, Second World War ends
1946	*Apr.* SMT **Love's Labour's Lost** (dir. Brook) *May* Rattigan, **The Winslow Boy** *Aug.* Foundation of the Arts Council *Sept.* **King Lear** (Olivier) *Oct.* Priestley, **An Inspector Calls** First issue of **Theatre Notebook** Creation of first university drama department at Bristol		
1947	*Jan.* Old Vic Theatre reopens *Apr.* **Oklahoma!** *Jul.* Harold Hobson becomes theatre critic of the *Sunday Times* *Aug.* First Edinburgh Festival		*Aug.* Britain grants independence to India

Year	Theatre	Britain	International
1948	*Mar.* Fry, **The Lady's Not for Burning** *Sept.* Jean-Louis Barrault and the Comédie Française at the Edinburgh Festival *Sept.* Rattigan, **The Browning Version** Foundation of the Society for Theatre Research	*Jul.* National Health Service inaugurated	*Sept. to May 1949* Berlin blockade
1949	*Aug.* Eliot, **The Cocktail Party** *Oct.* Williams, **A Streetcar Named Desire** (Vivien Leigh)		
1950	*Jan.* Fry, **Venus Observ'd** *Feb.* Fry, **Ring Round the Moon** *Jun.* Rodgers and Hammerstein, **Carousel**	*Feb.* General Election. Labour wins with majority of 5	*Mar.* USSR announces it possesses the atom bomb *Jun.* North Korea invades South Korea
1951	*Apr.* **Henry IV, Part One** (Richard Burton) *Apr.* Hunter, **Waters of the Moon** *May* **Antony and Cleopatra** (Olivier and Leigh) *Oct.* Claudel, **Partage de Midi** (Edwige Feuillère)	*May* Festival of Britain *Jun.* Burgess and Maclean defect to the USSR *Oct.* General Election. Conservatives win with majority of 17. Winston Churchill becomes Prime Minister	*Oct.* Renewal of Korean Armistice talks
1952	*Mar.* Rattigan, **The Deep Blue Sea** *Oct.* Gershwin, **Porgy and Bess**	*Feb.* George VI dies	*Nov.* General Eisenhower elected US President
1953	*May* **Guys and Dolls** *Nov.* Rattigan, **The Sleeping Prince** *Dec.* Hunter, **A Day by the Sea** First issue of **Plays and Players** Theatre Workshop takes up the lease of the Theatre Royal, Stratford East	*Jun.* Coronation of Elizabeth II	*Jun.* Korean Armistice signed *Sept.* Khrushchev becomes First Secretary of the Communist Party, USSR

Date	Theatrical events in the UK	Other events in the UK	Other international events
1954	*Mar.* Whiting, **Marching Song** *Sept.* Rattigan, **Separate Tables** *Sept.* Kenneth Tynan becomes theatre critic of the *Observer*	*Jul.* Food rationing ends	*Dec.* US senate 'condemns' McCarthy 'witch-trials'

CHAPTER 2: 1955–62

Date	Theatrical events in the UK	Other events in the UK	Other international events
1955	*Jan.* Theatre Workshop's **Richard II** *Mar.* Ionesco, **The Lesson** (Arts) *Jul.* Brecht, **Mother Courage** (Joan Littlewood) *Aug.* Beckett, **Waiting for Godot** (Arts) *Aug.* **Titus Andronicus** (Olivier, dir. Brook)	*May* General Election. Conservatives win with majority of 60. Anthony Eden becomes Prime Minister *Jul.* Execution of Ruth Ellis spurs campaign to end capital punishment *Sept.* Commercial TV introduced	*Jul.* European Parliament holds first meeting in Strasbourg
1956	*Apr.* Opening season of the English Stage Company (ESC) at the Royal Court 8 *May* Osborne, **Look Back in Anger** *May* Behan, **The Quare Fellow** *Aug.* Berliner Ensemble's **Mother Courage** (Helene Weigel) *Nov.* ESC's **The Good Woman of Setzuan** Foundation of the National Youth Theatre	*Apr.* Khrushchev visits Britain	*Jul.* Nassar nationalises the Suez Canal *Oct.* Soviet troops invade Hungary *Nov.* British and French troops land at Port Said; intervention aborted two days later *Nov.* Re-election of President Eisenhower
1957	*Apr.* Osborne, **The Entertainer** *Apr.* Beckett, **Fin de Partie**	*Jan.* Eden resigns as Prime Minister following Suez debacle, Harold Macmillan succeeds him *Jul.* Macmillan 'Most of our people have never had it so good' *Sept.* Wolfenden Report on homosexuality	*Mar.* EEC established with the Treaty of Rome *Oct.* Sputniks launched

1958	*Jan.*, Wesker, **Chicken Soup With Barley** *May* Pinter, **The Birthday Party** *Oct.* Behan, **The Hostage** *Nov.* Delaney, **A Taste of Honey** *Dec.* Bernstein, **West Side Story** Belgrade Theatre, Coventry, opens Lord Chamberlain's secret memorandum on homosexuality	*Feb.* Campaign for Nuclear Disarmament launched	*Jan.* Common Market comes into force
1959	*Jul.* Wesker, **Roots** *Oct.* Arden, **Serjeant Musgrave's Dance** Royal Court Nottingham Playhouse opens	*Feb.* Macmillan visits Moscow *Oct.* General Election. Conservatives win with majority of 100	*Jan.* De Gaulle proclaimed President of the Fifth Republic
1960	*Jun.* Pinter, **The Caretaker** Peter Hall appointed Director of the Royal Shakespeare Company	*Feb.* Macmillan in South Africa: 'a wind of change is blowing through the continent'	
1961	*Jul.* Osborne, **Luther** RSC takes out lease on Aldwych Theatre		Cyprus granted independence from UK *Aug.* East Germany seals border with West Berlin and begins construction of the Berlin Wall
1962	*May* Wesker, **Chips With Everything** (ESC) Formation of National Theatre Company Chichester Festival Theatre opens Victoria Theatre, Stoke, opens	Commonwealth Immigration Act	*Oct.* Cuban missile crisis

Date	Theatrical events in the UK	Other events in the UK	Other international events
	CHAPTER 3: 1963–68		
1963	*Mar.* Chilton, **Oh, What a Lovely War!** *Jul.* Barton/Hall, **The Wars of the Roses** *Oct.* **Hamlet** (Inaugural NT production) *Nov.* **Uncle Vanya** *Dec.* **The Recruiting Officer** (NT, dir. Gaskill) Traverse Theatre, Edinburgh, opens	*Jul.* Kim Philby named 'the third man' *Oct.* Macmillan resigns as Prime Minister citing ill health *Oct.* Alec Douglas-Home becomes Prime Minister	*Jan.* De Gaulle rejects first British application to join the EEC
1964	*May* Orton, **Entertaining Mr Sloane** *Aug.* Weiss, **Marat/Sade** (dir. Brook) *Dec.* Shaffer, **The Royal Hunt of the Sun** Theatre of Cruelty season at LAMDA First World Theatre Season (Peter Daubeny)	*Oct.* General Election. Labour wins with a majority of 4. Harold Wilson becomes Prime Minister	
1965	*May* **The Three Sisters** (Actors' Studio) *Jun.*, Pinter, **The Homecoming** *Jul.* Osborne, **A Patriot for Me** *Nov.* Bond, **Saved** Jenny Lee becomes Minister of the Arts	*Jan.* Sir Winston Churchill dies aged 90 *Nov.* Capital punishment abolished	
1966	*Sept.* Orton, **Loot**	*Mar.* General Election. Labour wins with majority of 97 *Jun.* Abortion Bill permits abortion 'where the woman's capacity as a mother would be severely overstrained' *Jul.* Sexual Offences Bill decriminalises homosexuality between consenting adults over the age of 21	

Year		
1967	*Mar.* Ayckbourn, **Relatively Speaking** (Duke of York's) *Apr.* Stoppard, **Rosencrantz and Guildenstern Are Dead** Octagon Theatre, Bolton, opens	*May* 'Les evenments' – student uprisings in Paris and worldwide *Nov.* Assassination of President Kennedy
1968	*Sept.* **Hair** Theatres Act removes power of Lord Chamberlain to censor plays	*Mar.* Riots in Grosvenor Square following protests against the Vietnam War
1969	**CHAPTER 4: 1969–79** *Oct.* Shaffer, **The National Health**	*Aug.* British troops deployed on the streets of Londonderry, Northern Ireland
1970	*Mar.* **The Merchant of Venice** (Olivier, dir. Miller) *Jun.* Storey, **Home** *Aug.* **A Midsummer Night's Dream** (dir. Brook)	*Jun.* General Election. Conservatives win with majority of 31. Edward Heath becomes Prime Minister
1971	*Sept.* O'Neill, **Long Day's Journey Into Night** (Olivier) *Sept.* Bond, **Lear** *Nov.* Tabelak, **Godspell** *Nov.* Storey, **The Changing Room** Trevor Nunn succeeds Hall as director of the RSC Crucible Theatre, Sheffield, opens	
1972	*Feb.* Stoppard **Jumpers** *May* Sheridan, **The School for Scandal** (NT) *Aug.* **Jesus Christ Superstar** *Oct.* Portable's **England's Ireland** Hall to succeed Olivier as director of NT	*Jan.* First Miners' strike (Government concedes claims on *19 February*) Unemployment passes one million *Mar.* Suspension of Northern Ireland Parliament at Stormont; Direct Rule begins

Date	Theatrical events in the UK	Other events in the UK	Other international events
1973	*Jul.* Shaffer, **Equus** *Jul.* Ayckbourn, **Absurd Person Singular** *Sept.* Brenton/Hare, **Brassneck** *Dec.* Griffiths, **The Party**	*Jan.* Britain joins EEC *Nov.* Miners begin overtime ban *Dec.* Because of fuel shortages, government announces a three-day week	*Oct.* Yom Kippur War; oil prices escalate
1974	*Jun.* Stoppard, **Travesties** Foundation of Joint Stock The Other Place, Stratford, opens	*Feb.* General Election. Labour wins the largest number of seats but falls short of an overall majority *Mar.* Harold Wilson becomes Prime Minister *Oct.* General Election. Labour wins with majority of 3	
1975	*Jul.* Ayckbourn, **Absent Friends** *Sept.* Griffiths, **Comedians** *Sept.* Hare, **Fanshen** Gay Sweatshop formed	*Feb.* Margaret Thatcher elected leader of the Conservative Party	
1976	*Aug.* Brenton, **Weapons of Happiness** *Sept.* Churchill, **Light Shining in Buckinghamshire** *Sept.* **Macbeth** (RSC, dir. Nunn) Royal Exchange Theatre, Manchester, opens	*Mar.* Harold Wilson resigns as Prime Minister. James Callaghan elected his successor on 5 *Apr.*	
1977	*Jan.* Hampton, **Tales from the Vienna Woods** *Aug.* Brenton, **Epsom Downs** *Aug.* Ayckbourn, **Bedroom Farce** (NT)	*Jun.* Grunwick disputes, mass picketing begins	
1978	*Apr.* Hare, **Plenty** *Apr.* **Henry VI** trilogy (RSC)	*Summer* Saatchi and Saatchi advertising slogan for the Conservatives: 'Labour Isn't Working'	

CHAPTER 5: 1980–97

Year		Britain	World
1979	*Feb.* Churchill, **Cloud Nine** *May* Sherman, **Bent** (McKellen) *Nov.* Shaffer, **Amadeus**	*Winter* Winter of Discontent (mass industrial unrest) *May* General Election. Conservatives win with majority of 43. Margaret Thatcher becomes the first female Prime Minister	*Dec.* Soviet Union invades Afghanistan
1980	*Feb.* Berkoff, **Greek** *Jun.* **Nicholas Nickelby** (RSC) *Aug.* Brenton/Brecht, **The Life of Galileo** *Oct.* Brenton, **The Romans in Britain**	*May* SAS storms Iranian embassy, London *Oct.* Thatcher: 'The lady's not for turning' *Oct.* First Maze hunger strike begins	*Sept.* Iran/Iraq War begins *Nov.* Ronald Reagan elected American president
1981	*May* Lloyd Webber, **Cats** *Nov.* **Oresteia** (NT dir. Hall)	*Apr.* Brixton riots *Jul.* Toxteth and Moss Side riots *Oct.* Second Maze hunger strike, begun by Bobby Sands, ends following 10 deaths	*Dec.* Martial law begins in Poland
1982	*Feb.* Frayn, **Noises Off** *Aug.* Churchill, **Top Girls**		*Apr.* Argentina invades the Falkland Islands *Apr.* British task force recaptures South Georgia *Jun.* Port Stanley recaptured; Argentinians surrender
1983	*Sept.* Hampton, **Tales from Hollywood**	*Jun.* General Election. Conservatives win with majority of 144	*Oct.* US invades Grenada
1984	*Mar.* Lloyd Webber, **Starlight Express** *Jun.* **Richard III** (Sher)	*Mar.* Miners Strike begins *Oct.* IRA bomb attempts to assassinate Margaret Thatcher	*Nov.* Ronald Reagan re-elected American President
1985	*Jan.* **The Mysteries** (NT) *May* (Brenton/Hare) **Pravda** (NT, Hopkins) *Sept.* Hampton, **Les Liaisons Dangereuses** **Les Misérables**	*Mar.* Miners return to work	*Mar.* Mikhail Gorbachev becomes the new Soviet leader

Date	Theatrical events in the UK	Other events in the UK	Other international events
1986	Whitemore, **Breaking the Code** Lloyd Webber, **The Phantom of the Opera** Cartwright, **Road** The Cork Report: An Inquiry into Professional Theatre		*Apr.* US raid on Libya
1987	*Mar.* Churchill, **Serious Money** *Apr.* **Antony and Cleopatra** (Hopkins and Dench, dir. Hall) *May* Ayckbourn, **A Small Family Business** (NT)	*Jun.* General Election. Conservatives reelected.	*Oct.* 'Black Monday'
1988	*Apr.* **Titus Andronicus** (RSC, dir. *Warner*) *Sept.* Wertenbaker, **Our Country's Good** *Oct.* Hare, **The Secret Rapture** *Dec.* Bennett, **Single Spies** *Dec.* **Electra** (RSC, Shaw, dir. *Warner*)	*Mar.* Budget cuts income tax to 25% and 40% *Dec.* Lockerbie air disaster	*Nov.* George Bush elected American President
1989	*Dec.* **Coriolanus** (Charles Dance) Eyre suceeds Hall as Director of NT	*Oct.* Nigel Lawson, Chancellor of the Exchequer, resigns	*Jun.* Tiananmen Square massacre, Peking *Nov.* East Germany announces opening of border with West Germany *Nov.* demolition of Berlin Wall begins
1990	*Feb.* Hare, **Racing Demon** (NT) *Jul.* **King Lear** (RSC, John Wood) *Jul.* **Richard III** (NT, Mckellen) *Oct.* Friel, **Dancing at Lughnasa** (NT) *Oct.* Bennett, **Wind in the Willows** (NT)	*Mar.* Trafalgar Square riot against the Poll Tax *Nov.* Margaret Thatcher resigns as Prime Minister	*Aug.* Iraq invades Kuwait *Oct.* reunification of Germany
1991	*Jun.* **Henry IV Parts 1 & 2** (RSC, Stephens, dir. Noble) *Oct.* Hare, **Murmuring Judges** *Nov.* Bennett, **The Madness of George III**		

1992	*Jan.* Kushner, **Millennium Approaches** (NT) *Aug.* Marlowe, **Tamburlaine** (Sher) *Sept.* Priestley, **An Inspector Calls** (NT, dir. Daldry) *Nov.* Pinter, **Mountain Language** *Dec.* **Carousel** (NT)	*Apr.* General Election. Conservatives reelected.	*Nov.* Bill Clinton elected President of the United States
1993	*Apr.* Stoppard, **Arcadia** *Oct.* Hare, **The Absence of War** (NT) *Oct.* Treadwell, **Machinal** (NT) *Nov.* Kushner, **Perestroika** (NT)		
1994	*Feb.* Wesker, **The Kitchen** (dir. Daldry) *Apr.* Elyot, **My Night With Reg** Harvey, **Beautiful Thing** Daldry succeeds Max Stafford-Clark as director of the Royal Court		
1995	*Jan.* Kane, **Blasted** *May* Hare, **Skylight** (NT) *Jul.* Butterworth, **Mojo**		
1996	*Sept.* Pinter, **Ashes to Ashes** *Oct.* Ravenhill, **Shopping and F***ing**		*Nov.* Bill Clinton reelected President of the United States
1997	*May* Marber, **Closer** *Jun.* Hare, **Amy's View** (NT)	May General Election. Labour wins with majority of 179. Tony Blair becomes Prime Minister.	

Chapter 1

1945–1954

Post-War Uncertainty

As the Second World War was drawing to a close in Europe in the early months of 1945, people's thoughts in Britain began to turn to the impending post-war period. On returning to England after active service in Italy, Anthony Quayle, the future director of the Shakespeare Memorial Theatre at Stratford, was struck by the stoicism of the past, the hardship of the present and the potential for the future:

> Spread out before me was the devastation of London, the unimaginable tons of masonry that had come blazing and crashing to the ground. Less obvious, but almost tangible, was the stubborn courage of the people in every city of the land who had endured the storm, and held fast. Until America was drawn into the battle, they had had no hope of winning the war; but they had held on, and held on, and never for a moment contemplated the possibility of defeat. Now they were shabby, ill-fed and tired, but bonded together in the crucible.[1]

In many walks of life the characteristic mood was one of optimism at the prospect of peace, mixed with uncertainty as to how the peace was to be shaped. The exuberant VE and VJ day celebrations, the unexpected election of a Labour government by a landslide majority of 146 seats on a manifesto entitled 'Let Us Face the Future',[2] the prospect of a welfare state providing free medical treatment and even the freshness and youth of the future queen, Princess Elizabeth, all added to the elation at the cessation of hostilities and the feeling that a new era was dawning. Against this weighed the country's exhaustion following six years of war, the trauma of bereavement that touched almost every family, the problem of reintegrating service personnel into civilian life and the economic and political weakness of a country that had been one of the four western allies, but which was quickly to discover that its world position was far less significant in a post-war context of superpower rivalry.

The theatre world too was affected by this uncertainty. Although the radio bulletin that had carried Prime Minister Neville Chamberlain's declaration of war on 3 September 1939 had also contained the news that all places of entertainment were to be closed for fear of German air-raids – a move that was quickly rescinded as an overreaction – and the blitz of 1940 had temporarily curtailed almost all theatrical activity in the capital, the London theatre had staged a remarkable recovery by 1945. Revues, light comedies, revivals of classics by noted actors including John Gielgud, Laurence Olivier and Ralph Richardson, and the occasional highly successful new work, such as Noel Coward's *Blithe Spirit* (1941), had all proved an appealing mix for audiences. By July 1945, for example, *Blithe Spirit* had achieved 1,716 consecutive performances, *Charley's Aunt* 1,466 and *Arsenic and Old Lace* 1,057.[3]

Warning Voices

For some, however, this popularity was illusory, in that it masked the problems that the theatre world would soon have to address. During the war cinema-going had become a national obsession, with three-quarters of the adult population seeking entertainment from films and information from newsreels and between twenty-five and thirty million seats being sold each week.[4] The 'talkies' were a very real rival to the theatre and they would soon be joined by the nascent medium of television, which had already broadcast its first play direct from a theatre – J.B. Priestley's *When We Are Married* – as long ago as 20 November 1938. In addition to the threat posed by these media were four very real concerns: the paucity of new serious work of quality by British playwrights, an issue that was to dominate British theatre over the next ten years; the fallacy of equating war-time popularity with post-war strength; the dominance of London theatre over theatrical activity in the regions; and the question of how to fund any renaissance of drama.

One concerned observer was the drama critic of the *Christian Science Monitor* (and from 1947 of the *Sunday Times*), Harold Hobson. In March 1945 he supplied a status report that reflects the ambivalent feelings of many theatre professionals at this time. 'The London theater is beginning tentatively to consider its position when the war with Germany is over', he began. 'For the past year, except during the worst of the flying bomb attacks last summer and autumn, London theaters have enjoyed enormous popularity. They have been crowded at most performances'.[5] This did not allow for complacency, however, since it was due partly to the large numbers of troops on leave and partly to the greatly reduced number of theatres available. Before the war the Lyceum and Gaiety theatres had been closed by the London County Council because of the inadequate nature of their exits, Drury Lane had become the national headquarters of the Entertainments National Service Association (mischievously renamed as 'Every Night Something Awful' by many), the Shaftesbury and Queen's theatres had been badly damaged by bombs, and several other venues, including the Criterion and the Old Vic theatres, were all out of action.

In essence, Hobson was arguing that in the short term it was easy to fill a diminished number of venues – there were 12 per cent less theatres at the end of the war than at the beginning[6] – but in the long term something more substantial than revues and farces would be needed to stimulate the post-war theatre-going public. The artistic value of an institution, he later claimed, should 'not be confused with the economic well-being of its workers'.[7] He was thereby articulating an opinion that would be voiced periodically during the subsequent debate about state subsidy of the arts.

A Congested West End

The congested nature of the West End, which severely restricted the opportunity for new productions, became increasingly apparent in the second half of 1945, the early months of peace. The monopolising of the London stage by long-running productions led to the introduction of an experiment at the Whitehall Theatre where one play, *Worm's Eye View*, started as a late matinée at 5.45pm and a second, *Fit for Heroes* starring Dame Irene Vanbrugh, began at 8.15pm as the evening show. This arrangement barely lasted a month, however, because audiences complained that, although they disliked plays 'starting just after tea-time', current transport arrangements made it very difficult for them to return home after a play that had begun at the pre-war starting time (8.15pm).[8] This clash between audience expectation, economic considerations and the imperative to provide a diverse mix of theatrical entertainments was to become a recurring theme of the entire post-war period.

Olivier, Richardson and the Old Vic Company

If the war-time London stage could not boast many notable new works by indigenous writers, it was undoubtedly graced by some fine acting performances. In 1944 Laurence Olivier and Ralph Richardson were allowed to leave the Fleet Air Arm and the Admiralty respectively in order to lead the Old Vic company, which was temporarily based at the New Theatre (now the Albery). The first three productions in which they appeared – *Peer Gynt*, *Arms and the Man* and *Richard III* – were remarkable not just for their artistic quality or their rapturous reception, but for the fact that they were performed in a near approximation of true repertory (the staging of plays in rotation). *Peer Gynt* opened on 31 August 1944 and was followed by the London openings of the two other productions within the next fourteen days. The company quickly became an emblem of national consciousness second only to Shakespeare, and as the Old Vic's historian, George Rowell, points out, its success was 'partly due to the spirit of the times' since there 'was real hope for a nation that could mount *Peer Gynt* and *Richard III* concurrently with the return to Europe, and mark Victory in Japan (VJ) day by the two parts of *Henry IV*'.[9] The production of the *Henry* plays again imbued many with hope for the future, as the comments on Part One made by the *Observer*'s Ivor Brown confirm:

> These two portraits [Olivier as Hotspur and Richardson as Falstaff], aligned in a notable production, give one high pride in the English theatre, which, amid all the difficulties of our time, is offering, in several quarters, presentations of the classics worthy of a National Theatre with every resource of staging and casting at its disposal.[10]

Brown was even more enthusiastic about the production of *Henry IV*, *Part Two*, which he saw in October 1945, and he provides both a salutary reminder that for many observers Ralph Richardson's Old Vic performances were equal, if not superior, to those of Laurence Olivier, and a testimony to the revivifying effect that this company achieved:

> Mr Richardson's Falstaff continues, even grows, in its own magnificence, which is that of a surging mind above a sagging paunch. ... Without entering on those comparisons with old giants, which lead, as a rule, to bickering without evidence, we can fairly claim that these are years of genuine greatness in acting and production of the classics.[11]

Following encomia such as this, it is unsurprising that the company was swiftly despatched after the end of its London run as cultural ambassadors to Hamburg, the Comédie Française and even Belsen.

Olivier's Oedipus

The first post-war season of the Old Vic, 1945–6, was to supply one of the earliest icons of post-war British theatre, and certainly 'the most sensational success of the Olivier–Richardson years': Olivier's performance as Oedipus in *Oedipus Rex*.[12] Initially, his decision to pair the Greek tragedy with Sheridan's comedy *The Critic* had caused internal dissension, with the director Tyrone Guthrie resigning over what he perceived to be an incongruous double-bill. This controversy quickly diminished, however, in the light of Olivier's realisation of the pathos of the doomed King of Thebes. What elicited particular admiration was Olivier's terrifying cry of anguish, when Oedipus, realising that he has fathered his children on his own mother, stabs out his eyes with Jocasta's brooch. This moment was allegedly inspired by an account Olivier had heard of how ermine are captured by licking salt placed on the ice by trappers, their tongues becoming frozen to the surface and their wails of terror sounding increasingly harrowing as the hunters approach with their clubs.[13] Kenneth Tynan described this in one of his earliest reviews:

> The thick, intolerant voice syncopated perfectly with the lithe, jungle movements of the man: intellectually and physically he was equipped for the heaviest suffering: his shoulders could bear disaster. I know that from the first I was waiting breathlessly for the time when the rack would move into the final notch, and the lyric cry would be released: but I never hoped for so vast an anguish. Olivier's famous 'Oh! Oh!' when the full catalogue of his sin is unfolded must still be resounding in some high recess of the New Theatre's dome: some stick of wood must still, I feel, be throbbing from it. The two cries were torn from beyond tears or shame or guilt: they came from the stomach, with all the ecstatic grief and fright of a newborn baby's wail.[14]

Again, it is important not to undervalue Richardson's role in this production. According to one member of the first-night audience, Richardson acted Olivier off the stage as the blind seer Tiresias whenever they both appeared together.[15]

The Foundation of CEMA and the Arts Council

Whilst the Old Vic company was lighting up the capital, important plans were being laid to ensure that theatre could flourish in the regions of

Britain, too. The insatiable appetite for theatrical diversion during the war was not confined to Londoners, and the value of the arts in maintaining national morale had been quickly recognised with the creation in January 1940 of the Council for the Encouragement of Music and the Arts (CEMA) by the Pilgrim Trust, an American-financed organisation dedicated to supporting cultural activity. By April 1940, the government had acknowledged the merit of this new body and awarded it a large grant of £50,000, one of the earliest examples of state assistance for the arts.[16] As far as CEMA's theatrical remit was concerned, its initial aim was to send touring companies to areas of Britain previously bereft of theatre, such as South Wales and the North-East,[17] but its eventual metamorphosis into the Arts Council of Great Britain on 9 August 1946 was an event of even greater significance for the theatrical health of the nation as a whole, in that it established the principle of state subsidy of the arts that was to underpin so much theatrical activity for the next fifty years. Receiving its funds from the Treasury on an annual basis, the Arts Council was structured so that it was required to answer to parliament for its expenditure, but the allocation of individual grants was devolved by the government to the organisation. This arms-length principle lead to both the size of the Arts Council's annual income and its distribution of grant-aid becoming a source of constant debate during the eighties and nineties.

Early Arts Council grants encouraged, amongst other things, the foundation of the Bristol Old Vic in February 1946 and the emergence of repertory theatres in Guildford (1946), Ipswich (1947), Leatherhead (1951), Canterbury (1951) and Derby (1951).[18] This renaissance of venues outside London provided a tremendous stimulus for regional theatre and, in turn, created a new training ground for actors, directors, designers and technical staff, previously restricted to employment in the commercial sector. It also conferred greater freedom on producers to experiment with the programme, since the commercial imperative to stage safe and money-spinning works had to some extent been alleviated.

Institutions 1

A substantial part of the history of post-war British theatre is the history of institutions, both literal and metaphorical. If the Arts Council and the related entities of regional theatre and subsidy are the first such institution, then the next ten years (1945–54) invite a consideration of West End theatre and the Shakespeare Memorial Theatre (to evolve into the Royal Shakespeare Company in 1961), in addition to less palpable concepts such as theatre criticism and censorship.

H.M. Tennent Ltd

Prior to the advent of state subsidy, London and, in particular, West End theatre had been controlled by entrepreneurs dedicated to creating viable financial concerns. Pre-eminent amongst these was Hugh 'Binkie' Beaumont, the managing director of H.M. Tennent Ltd, who, on the day of the war ending in Europe, 8 May 1945, was responsible for 12 'Tennent' productions in 8 of the 36 West End theatres and who had staged 59 plays during the 6 years of the war.[19] During the forties, Beaumont's domination of the West End was scarcely challenged. Purveying a house style that his biographer, Richard Huggett, defines as employing 'the greatest stars in gorgeous classic revivals amidst the most sumptuous settings which taste and money could devise'.[20] Beaumont was responsible for some spectacular events: *Lady Windermere's Fan*, lavishly designed by Cecil Beaton (August 1945); Terence Rattigan's *The Winslow Boy*, starring Emlyn Williams (May 1946); the hugely popular American musical, *Oklahoma!* (April 1947), that so lit up the post-war gloom; Jean Cocteau's *The Eagle Has Two Heads*, starring Eileen Herlie (1947), which, along with Christopher Fry's adaptation of Anouilh's *Ring Round the Moon* (1950), confirmed the increasing obsession that British theatre was to have with all things French; and the highly controversial production of Tennessee Williams' *A Streetcar Named Desire*, directed by Laurence Olivier and starring Vivien Leigh (1949), to name just a few. Much of the polemic that was to sustain the new realist theatre after the advent of *Look Back in Anger* (1956) was predicated on an impassioned rejection of this very commercial success and, in particular, of the values that Tennent's was alleged to embody: an obsession with glamour, a refusal to stage works that glanced at contemporary life or political concerns, a blind adherence to favoured house dramatists, such as Terence Rattigan, and a continual representation of upper-middle-class (and for realists, irrelevant) milieus. Coupled to the perception that Beaumont maintained a blacklist of actors who had crossed him that made it near impossible to obtain further work, the belief that Tennent's domination of the West End stifled new creativity and the erroneous conviction that Beaumont, a discreet homosexual, employed only homosexual actors, it is easy to see how Beaumont was to become an important and inevitable Mephistopheles, fiendishly leading British theatre astray and memorably described by John Osborne as 'the most powerful of the unacceptable faeces of theatrical capitalism'.[21] A more objective assessment of this important figure is necessarily less clear-cut. He undeniably paid poverty wages to all but his stars – Vivien Leigh received ten per cent of the gross weekly box-office receipts and a minimum of £175 per week for playing Blanche Dubois in the 1949

production of *A Streetcar Named Desire*,[22] against the £5 per week offered
to Frances St Barbe-West for being the understudy to the part of Eunice
and taking a walk-on role.[23] Similarly, Diana Wynyard was paid ten per cent
of the takings and a minimum of £100 per week for the role of Catherine
de Troyas in John Whiting's *Marching Song* (1954), whilst the stage-man-
ager, Ann Robinson, had to make do with £7 per week during initial
rehearsals, rising to a paltry £14 per week when the show went on tour
before reaching the West End.[24] But for all his infamous parsimony Beaumont was nevertheless responsible for shows that still live in the memory,
on account of the quality of their execution and the unparalleled lavishness that made them so diverting. This lavishness – which often embraced
importing the latest Dior fashion from Paris for his leading ladies – necessarily contrasted strongly with post-war austerity and simultaneously
enthralled and provoked. The ambiguity of theatrical attitudes in this
period, an ambiguity encapsulated by Beaumont's productions, can be
seen in the surprisingly flattering description by the young Kenneth Tynan
– later to become the most vigorous champion of 'Kitchen-Sink' drama,
the antithesis of H.M. Tennent panache – of the impresario at the height
of his power. In his 1953 'anthology of unique human beings' (compiled
with Cecil Beaton) entitled *Persona Grata*,[25] Tynan was to write:

> With simple intentness, like a child setting out a doll's house, Beaumont
> enjoys arranging the theatre's affairs. Call him, if you like the image, an
> agile gnome with a genius for calculated risk. ... His basic gift repels
> definition. If questioned how he manages to bring the right men and the
> right moment into such unfailing theatrical collaboration, he raises an
> eyebrow, smiles a small, arcane smile, and says: 'I hear curious drums
> beating...' Apart from a tendency to revive and overdress bad Victorian
> plays at the drop of a box-office receipt, he has been righter, on a higher
> level, than anyone else in the theatre of his time.[26]

How views would change.

The Lord Chamberlain and Censorship

If 'Binkie' Beaumont was to prove an important shaping force in the story
of the evolution of British theatre, theatrical censorship was to have a similarly catalytic, and longer-running, effect. It is customary to consider this
particular institution in relation to the 1960s, when successive playwrights
and theatres became increasingly aggressive in their stand against the Lord
Chamberlain. This stridency ultimately lead to the abolition of his powers
to censor drama in 1968. However, a consideration of the Lord Cham-

berlain's papers, recently deposited at the British Library, suggests that it is instructive to consider the effects of censorship from the beginning of the post-war period rather than merely from the end.

The most recent guidelines that the first post-war Lord Chamberlain, Lord Clarendon, could call upon were those issued by the Parliamentary Joint Select Committee in 1909, under the heading 'Proposals with respect to the Licensing of Plays'. These decreed that the Lord Chamberlain, the most senior member of the Royal household, should license a play, unless he considered that it might be reasonably held:

a) To be indecent
b) To contain offensive personalities
c) To represent in an invidious manner a living person, or a person recently dead
d) To do violence to the sentiment of religious reverence
e) To be calculated to conduce to crime or vice
f) To be calculated to impair friendly relations with a Foreign Power
g) To be calculated to cause a breach of the peace.[27]

In addition to these catch-all provisions, successive Lord Chamberlains and their readers from 1945 onwards referred to both past precedent and personal whim to reach their decisions.

If a theatre manager in the immediate post-war period wished to stage a play on a public stage, he first had to apply for a licence from the office of the Lord Chamberlain – the granting of a licence being a legal requirement for a public performance (and hence a handy way of periphrastically asserting that the Lord Chamberlain never suppressed drama, since he merely withheld a licence). On the payment of a fee of one guinea for a one-act play, or two guineas for a play of two acts or more, the submitted script would be vetted by the Lord Chamberlain's readers – mostly ex-military men – at Stable Yard, St James's Palace, and either returned unamended with a licence attached, returned with a request for modifications before a licence could be granted, or, on occasions, returned with the message that (after either some or no discussion with the managers) a licence could under no circumstances be granted. The only way to stage a work that had been refused a licence was to produce it in an invariably small and financially constrained club theatre, which could only perform shows to its members.

In 1945 the number of plays that fell into the category of being banned from public performance was 4, in 1946 5, in 1947 2, in 1948 3, in 1949 1, in 1950 8, in 1951 7, in 1952 3, in 1953 6 and in 1954 3 – 42 plays in ten years, a significantly higher number than it is normally realised to be, since the general perception has been that the Lord Chamberlain and respective managers usually managed to reach some form of compromise.[28] The reasons given for this outright suppression – and the deliberate creation of a whole generation of lost plays – are both familiar and surprising. Of the 42 banned works, 18 were refused a licence on account of alleged sexual impropriety; 14 because of their treatment of what the Lord Chamberlain was to refer to in 1957 as 'the forbidden subject', homosexuality;[29] 4 because they included representations of Queen Victoria; 3 for referring to living people; 2 because of political objections (a criterion for censorship not widely remarked upon by theatre historians); and 1 for being deemed offensive to christianity.

The largest category of banned plays, those which contained references to sex unacceptable to the readers, seem from a late twentieth-century perspective to have suffered a harsh and almost comic fate – until one realises that people's livelihoods were being threatened by this crude process. Inevitably the personal whim of the readers sealed these plays' suppression. *First Thing*, for example, was refused a licence in 1945 for being a 'black-out sketch ... implying an over-indulgence of sexual intercourse';[30] *Patricia English* (1946) would have been permitted a licence if the eponymous heroine's seven inherited brothels had been transformed into night-clubs (the refusal of the management to accede to this request meant that the work never saw the light of day);[31] and *Getting a Flat* (1946) was suppressed on account of its central premise, a 'vulgar ... misunderstanding over the words "lavatory" and "laboratory".[32]

As the war receded, the readers became increasingly taxed by what they perceived to be the 'nasty play',[33] a work construed to offer, as in *Street Girl* (1950), 'pornography' that was 'salacious and disgusting'.[34] *If He Came*, presented for licensing in 1948, was a particular trial for one reader, since it not only presented 'blasphemous effrontery', but constituted the 'silliest and smuttiest Welsh play I have ever read'. The smut centred on a 'puerile double entendre' where Lisa the Gossip is discussing with Jonathan his preparations for the 'monkey gland operation'. The reader cites two lines to illustrate the baseness of the work –

LISA: And take your instrument with you.
JONATHAN: Instrument?

– followed by the pious observation: 'As there has been no previous mention of Jonathan in connection with any band, the coarseness of the implication is unmistakeable'.[35]

The subjectivity of this whole process is self-evident but it took on an intriguing dimension in 1947 when one reader, H.C. Game, made some significant observations about post-war audiences in his report on Ernst Toller's work, *Hinkemann*, submitted for presentation at the Rudolf Steiner Hall in 1947 in a translation by Vera Mendel. In his opening paragraph, Game informs the Lord Chamberlain of the historical background to the work, which was published in 1924 and deals in a morbid and cynical fashion with the plight of the demobilised soldier returning from the First World War:

> This play was submitted in 1935 and was refused a licence, no doubt inevitably in those days. But public opinion has since then become very much more sophisticated, and what would have shocked many people in 1935, in 1947 is accepted as a legitimate subject for the dramatist's pen. But even in 1935 I do not think I should have agreed with Mr Street [the earlier reader] in describing Toller's play as 'a mixture of obscenity and raving', though I would certainly agree that Toller was an 'over-rated German', and I might add, a bore!

The racism and stiff humour is a familiar call-sign of the Lord Chamberlain's readers, but the move into assessing the artistic validity of a work is clearly straying beyond the remit – however ill-defined – of the licensing authorities. Game now attempts to apply dramatic criticism to the play and concludes with a surprisingly liberal verdict:

> Certainly the dramatist's theme is an embarrassing one, but his aim is obviously not obscenity. What the play is about is the mental torture suffered by a hefty working class type, who has been sexually mutilated in the war and who believes that in his fellows' eyes he has in consequence become an object of ridicule, and the psychological effects of that mental distress. Given the theme, I do not think the treatment – European Expressionism of the early twenties – can be considered extravagant or unjustifiable. The play is now a museum piece of a bad and rather bogus period of dramatic art; but apart from the likely embarrassment of those who still believe in reticence, I personally see little against the play except the meanness of the tragedy. One may not care for this sort of thing, I do not myself; but I don't think one can argue that anybody is going to suffer moral degradation by seeing it acted.

What is most intriguing, however, is his subsequent segregation into hierarchies of the immediate post-war audience:

> The Rudolf Steiner Hall has by this time, I expect, the reputation of housing high-brow plays, and it is the high-brow (or

pseudo-high-brow) that this sort of play will attract. It would bore a low-brow, or even a middle-brow, to tears, so if licensed for a production by the Centaur Theatre I cannot think that the play is likely to be produced elsewhere except by Repertory and similar uncommercial intellectual theatres. To sum up, if the highbrows want to see the play, I really don't see why we should prevent them.

That this stratification of theatre-goers is codified by no less than the Lord Chamberlain's office, with commercial theatre in London seen as represent-ing the apex of theatrical activity, illustrates not just the inevitability of the bitter clashes between the new realist writers of the fifties and sixties and the censor, but also how entrenched and hierarchical the immediate post-war British theatre appeared. Change would be painful for some and liberating for many. Despite his reader's views on *Hinkemann*, the Lord Chamberlain overrode Game's recommendation with a handwritten comment appended to the report that 'This play is … a most unpleasant one and I agree it should be banned. License refused. C'. One wonders from this whether he realised that Game was actually advocating the reluctant awarding of a licence! Encouragement to subversive high-brows had to be resisted.

Subversion threatened the Lord Chamberlain's peace of mind in other areas, too. Between 1945 and 1954, four plays that (mis)portrayed Queen Victoria were refused licences – *The Querulous Queens* (1945), *Birthday Bouquet* (1950), *My Good Brown* (1951) and *Our Ladies Meet* (1952), the latter play drawing the comment that the great queen 'may be represented only in strictly accurate historical plays',[36] begging the question as to who is writing the history. This desire to preserve historical perspectives also extended to the present with an increasing concern for the political in the 1950s. The fallacy that the Lord Chamberlain was only concerned with excising references to penises is revealed by considering two reports in 1953, both for projected performances by the Unity Theatre. His powers were broad, arbitrary and sinister – as becomes most apparent when one examines works that were threatened at birth.

In 1953, the Manchester Committee for Clemency for the Rosenbergs and the Unity Theatre (a notable left-wing theatre group originating in the 1930s) submitted a request for a licence to be granted for a short-notice performance of a political work by Eric Paice entitled *The Rosenbergs*. The play centred on the 1951 trial of the American communists Julius and Ethel Rosenberg for espionage, which had taken place as the cold war intensified. Great controversy surrounded the case, with many people believing that the husband and wife were victims of the political witch-hunts being conducted in the United States at the time. A note attached to the reader's report reveals the implicit concern of the Lord Chamberlain at the increasingly political turn that British theatre was beginning to take. 'Unity theatres are v. left wing', he wrote. 'One wonders if it is right to use the theatre for this sort of personal propaganda especially in a case which is still, really sub-judice'.[37] (After numerous appeals by several Western European countries and three stays of execution the Rosenbergs were finally executed on 9 June 1953.) The play, nevertheless, went ahead as a club production and broke the Holborn-based Unity's record for block bookings for a straight play.[38]

The members of Unity were doubtless not surprised by the Lord Chamberlain's obduracy. A request for a licence for Mona Bland's *Strangers in the Land* the previous year had so offended Lieutenant-Colonel Sir St Vincent Troubridge, the Assistant Comptroller (a descendant of one of Nelson's Admiral's and a veteran of two world wars[39]), that it drew a response that again conveyed a mixture of unwitting comedy and totalitarianism:

> The Unity Theatre organization is the theatrical organ of the Communists and fellow travellers, and this is a play about Malaya which the Cardiff branch proposes to produce ... what I object to is not the Communist doctrine ... but the direct and specific accusations of what I can only call collective libel against the British Army and the British community in Malaya. It is not to my mind tolerable that these should receive a licence for further dissemination from so high an official as the Lord Chamberlain. There is also the question of a possible breach of the peace, for I should imagine ex-Service organisations in Cardiff that include men who have fought in Malaya taking violent action against such defamation.[40]

Again, although banned for public performance, *Strangers in the Land* was presented as a club performance in 1952. Its power to influence, however, had been severely restricted.

The denunciatory tone of Troubridge's comment – provoked by intimations of subversion – was most frequently displayed when the readers were forced to consider works that treated a subject that they initially referred to euphemistically as 'inversion' – homosexuality. Until 1958 there was an absolute ban on homosexuality as a theme for the stage and this appears to have been ruthlessly enforced between 1945 and 1954. Consequently, *Outrageous Fortune* (1945 – 'pervert theme'), *Surface* (1945 – 'pansies'), and *Oscar Wilde* (1945 – 'perverts and perversions') were suppressed in a manner that replicated the brutality of the treatment of homosexuals in law (gay relationships being a criminal offence in Britain until 1967). *Hiatus* (1950) was deemed problematic on account of the sexuality of the husband ('John is an invert'), *Third Person* (1951) contained a 'notorious homo', *Les Oeufs de L'Autruche*, translated as *Ostrich House* (1953), demonstrated nasty foreign practices ('it belongs to its country and will not travel'), *The Trial of Oscar Wilde* (1954) was saturated in 'a general atmosphere of sodomy' and *The Wicked and the Weak* (1954) drew an exasperated 'This will not do at all!', since it included a gay prostitute, dressed in 'stage lace panties'. Beyond the humour of this and the tragedy that stage suppression of homosexual themes mirrored the continual persecution of homosexuals in British society at large, lay the paradox that it was the theatre that offered for many homosexuals a rare possibility of sanctuary and that the London theatre of the late 1940s was dominated by Binkie Beaumont, Terence Rattigan and John Gielgud – whose sexual inclinations were deemed unpalatable by the body that prided itself on being entrusted with maintaining the moral health of the nation's drama.

The Shakespeare Memorial Theatre

An infinitely more beneficial institution was the Shakespeare Memorial Theatre (SMT), whose work, coupled with the rapid growth of regional theatre sustained by grants from the Arts Council, helped refute the notion that British theatrical activity was entirely London based. Destined to become the home of the Royal Shakespeare Company in 1961, Elizabeth Scott's modernist theatre (opened in 1932) was in a somewhat dilapidated state by the end of the war. The reputation of the SMT was at a low ebb, too, and this was something that the governors of the Stratford theatre were keen to address with the appointment of Sir Barry Jackson,who had achieved much as both an administrator and a director at the Birmingham Repertory Theatre before the war. The SMT's chairman, Fordham Flower, sensitive to charges of a narrow provincialism, told the press on the day of Jackson's accession in 1946 that this represented a change of direction, the board now being 'determined that quality in acting and production should take precedence over profits, and to prove that the charge of local complacency is no longer valid'.[41] Consequently, Jackson's first season in charge was a clear break with the past. The 1946 programme saw an entirely new company with the deliberate exclusion of any actors who had previously performed at Stratford. The freshness that this introduced was apparent with the twenty-year-old Peter Brook's production of *Love's Labour's Lost* – 'a masque of youthful affectations'[42] in the view of *The Times* – which launched the young director's career.

Unfortunately, however, for all its accolades this play was a commercial success amongst many failures, with the SMT recording its largest ever loss (£13,385[43]) at the end of Jackson's first season – taking Flower's earlier statement somewhat too literally. Jackson's second season, 1947, evinced solid if unspectacular work, with Jackson being concerned to revamp both the management and technical capabilities of the theatre. Sensing diminishing support for his ventures, however, he decided to submit his resignation at the beginning of 1948. With supreme irony, 1948 saw his labours beginning to bear fruit with a spectacular run of productions, including Paul Scofield and Robert Helpmann alternating as Hamlet, which, according to Sally Beauman, chronicler of the Royal Shakespeare Company, established 'the style that was to dominate Stratford for the next decade, the Tennent formula: the best star actors, exquisite sumptuous costumes, highly elaborate, superbly designed sets, tightly controlled, sure-footed productions'.[44] Indeed, Jackson's successor, Anthony Quayle, invited Binkie Beaumont onto the board of the SMT, valuing the enviable list of contacts that the impresario was able to bring. One consequence of this saw established stars from the Tennent stable rotating with newer talent – John Gielgud, for example, being persuaded to direct *Much Ado About Nothing* (1950) and Peter Brook *Measure for Measure* (1949), with Gielgud as a legendary Angelo. Binkie Beaumont's influence was not merely confined to London.

1946: London

One of H.M. Tennent's most important playwrights provided the company with its first new commercial success of the post-war era. Terence Rattigan's *The Winslow Boy* (1946) was the factually based account of a father's attempt to clear the name of his son who had been wrongfully dismissed from a military academy. It contained many examples of class-based language and a proliferation of 'thanks awfully''s that were later to earn Rattigan the scorn of the Kitchen-Sink playwrights, as well as a stilted and chauvinistic depiction of a 'new woman' (fifty years after she had emerged in literature) – the independent, left-wing daughter Catherine – but it also demonstrated Rattigan's brilliance at creating characters masking emotional vulnerability with public stoicism (as in *Separate Tables* (1954)), as well as the playwright's flair for the bravura role. Sir Robert Morton's curtain line at the end of Act Two when he accepts the brief to defend Ronnie, following a brilliant and brutal cross-examination of the boy in his father's home, still manages to take the breath away and its force was emphasised by the tight direction of the original production (a further Tennent hallmark), a facet confirmed by J.C. Trewin's observations on the differentiation between the characters:

… the play gives to students of acting an uncommon contrast in styles between the firm, quiet realism of Mr Frank Cellier as the Winslow father, whose passion for justice (mingled with pride of family) makes him press the case to the end, and the more theatrical, highly charged manner of Mr Emlyn Williams' as the counsel, who wins the case.[45]

The performance of the inevitable star actor, Emlyn Williams, further embellished the original production, and together with J.B. Priestley's *An Inspector Calls* (1946), opening at the New Theatre on 1 October 1946, with Ralph Richardson creating the part of Inspector Goole, it seemed that a new era of the star actor was beginning.

There were few bigger stars than Laurence Olivier. The Old Vic Company's production of *King Lear*, immediately preceding *An Inspector Calls*, proved a huge popular success, the entire run selling out, and Olivier, who had spent the summer shouting to the cows at his home at Notley to extend his range and breath control,[46] was accorded much admiration. Harold Hobson summarised his achievement in the *Sunday Times*:

Mr Olivier's Lear is very old: he is also strong. There is about him none of that senility which many great actors have affected. … Mr Olivier's Lear is a man who by temperament is capable of being tortured: but he is worth torturing. The cries and lamentations, the curses and the threats that are torn out of his breast are like the crash of thunder and the stab of lightning. They are not the whimpering of a weak old man: they are the groaning and the whimpering of the universe. This is a cosmic grief.[47]

Others, however, whilst greatly impressed by Olivier's depiction of the king, were less enthusiastic about the production as a whole. Ivor Brown was particularly critical of Olivier's directing, feeling that at over four hours the evening was too long, the music sometimes drowned out the words and 'there were some shocking cases of masking by players standing with their backs to the audience and obscuring the faces of others'. Whilst acknowledging that 'Mr Olivier's contribution as an actor is remarkable in detail as in general power', he viewed the event as 'a masterpiece in promise, an assembly of performances – most of them excellent – rather than a production wholly achieved, fast-moving, confident, with all its elements fused'.[48] The difference in emphasis between these two reviews highlights the importance of comparing a range of critical testimonies on any production, as well as developing a sense of an individual critic's Weltanschauung. Hobson, who was to become one of the most important theatre critics of the post-war period (writing for the

Sunday Times from 1947 to 1976) consistently viewed the actor as the most important member of the theatrical triumvirate of actor, director and playwright, whereas Brown was more interested in the technique of the director and the economic pressures on the theatre (such as Entertainment Tax, against which he campaigned). The role of the theatre critic was slowly metamorphosising away from being that of a chronicler of the process to that of a participant within it.

The Foreign Revelation

The success of John Osborne's *Look Back in Anger* in 1956 has been seen by many as the crucial event that determined the re-orientation of British theatre in the late fifties,[49] but there were other less visible milestones on the journey from stilted drawing-room drama to more diverse theatrical genres. The opening up of the London stage after the war to creative contact with New York and Paris, for example, was an event every bit as important for the evolution of twentieth-century English drama as the advent of Osborne, Wesker and the other 'new wave' dramatists. This fresh artistic contact introduced new techniques in acting, with Jean-Louis Barrault and the Comédie Française at the Edinburgh Festival in 1948 illustrating how English actors performed primarily with their voice whilst their French counterparts utilised the entire body. Brecht's stress on the 'Gestus' of a performer, with body movement unlocking textual meaning, was to prove similarly illuminating. New ideas about acting and directing were absorbed by considering the work of Elia Kazan and the 'Method' technique developed by Lee Strasberg. The brash, glittering, technically perfect American musicals, symbolised by Rodgers and Hammerstein's smash hit, *Oklahoma!* (1947), provoked English producers to consider more innovative ideas about stagecraft. Exposure to new types of play by Sartre, Genet, Anouilh and Ionesco on the one hand, and Arthur Miller and Tennessee Williams on the other, provided a creative impulse that could not have been envisaged during the war and contact with new dramatic theories, such as French existentialist drama, and later Brecht's 'Epic Theatre', led a number of playwrights to apply these varied theatrical approaches to their own work. Although it is true to state that there was little new *English* writing between 1945 and 1955, it is disingenuous to conclude from this that the London theatre was a cultural wasteland, particularly given the rapidly growing interest in drama. This was borne out by the foundation of the first university drama department at Bristol in 1946; the increasing desire on the part of actors to receive a formal training at a drama school such as the London Academy of Music and Dramatic Art (LAMDA, founded 1861), the Royal Academy of Dramatic Art (RADA, 1904), the Central School of Speech and Drama (1906) and the Royal Scottish Academy of Music and Drama in Glasgow (RSAMD, 1950); the establishment of learned groups such as The Society for Theatre Research (1948); and the proliferation of new drama periodicals, including *Theatre Notebook* (1946) and *Plays and Players* (1953). In many ways this ten-year period was crucial to the developments of the fifties and sixties which were to make the English stage one of the most vibrant in the world, and it formed an important period of apprenticeship for actors, directors, playwrights and critics alike.

Theatre Criticism 1: Harold Hobson

In the immediate post-war period, an era of newsprint and limited media technology, the principal way of obtaining an informed consideration of the activity of the London stage was to consult the Sunday newspapers, and in particular the *Sunday Times* and the *Observer*. Readers, tired of a war-time diet of morale-boosting light comedy and oft-revived patriotic classics, quickly developed a voracious appetite for information and discussion about drama. By the mid-fifties it was quite common for theatre enthusiasts to buy both publications and compare the views of their respective critics, and there is some irony in the fact that the allegedly ground-breaking Jimmy Porter is engaged in this very middle-class activity at the beginning of *Look Back in Anger*, when, having thrown down the *News of the World*, he turns to Cliff and says:

> JIMMY: Haven't you read the other posh paper yet?
> CLIFF: Which?
> JIMMY: Well, there are only two posh papers on a Sunday – the one you're reading, and this one. Come on, let me have that one, and you take this.
> CLIFF: Oh, all right.
> (*They exchange*).

Proprietors, aware of the growing marketability of newspaper theatre critics, began to take a keen interest in their appointment, the most notable (and idiosyncratic) example of this being that of Lord Kemsley, the owner of the *Sunday Times*. In 1945 the paper's flamboyant theatre critic of twenty-two years' standing, James Agate, had had to escape from a male brothel in his nightshirt. Kemsley, the only newspaper man in London who was unaware of Agate's reputation as an energetic homosexual, was so shocked by this that he had wanted to dismiss him forthwith. W.W. Hadley, the paper's editor, however, had pointed out that this would bring a considerable amount of bad publicity, given Agate's fame, and Kemsley reluctantly agreed. He nevertheless set in motion plans for Agate's eventual replacement as theatre critic, not by Agate's friend Alan Dent, as had been widely predicted, but by the then Assistant Literary Editor, Harold Hobson. Hobson's appointment was sealed with Kemsley's infamous adjuration, 'Hobson's all right. Hobson has a daughter. Let's have Hobson'.[50]

Happily, Hobson's qualifications for the post depended on rather more than his heterosexuality, and he quickly built up a loyal readership, attracted by his mischievous wit, autobiographical style and passionate devotion to the process of theatre-going, which he conveyed with an admirable consistency. This was all the more remarkable, given that at the time of his accession in 1947 new, indigenous writing consisted of little more than bizarre offerings such as William Douglas Home's *Ambassador Extraordinary* (1948), the plot of which centres on a Martian visitor who tries to blackmail the world into submission by the threat of wholesale destruction, and who is only appeased when the Foreign Secretary agrees to sell his daughter to the enraptured alien. Faced with this unstimulating fare, Hobson chose to focus less on the deficiencies of British drama than on the paradigm for inspiring drama offered by the increasingly frequent French companies, plays and productions that London theatre producers invited into the West End. By taking inspiration from the vibrancy of contemporary French drama, he believed that British drama might be able to overcome this enervating period of stagnation. That one of the most powerful theatre critics in London at this time offered French drama his patronage, not only earned him a Légion d'Honneur from the French government in 1960, but played a part in ensuring that French theatre gained a foothold on the post-war London stage, in the same way that Kenneth Tynan's later advocacy of realist theatre helped enhance its popularity. The power of Sunday theatre critics was at its zenith between 1947 and 1962, with movements being bolstered as well as documented by their observations.

The Influence of the French

Eileen Herlie's performance as the Queen in Cocteau's *The Eagle Has Two Heads* (1946) marked the first significant production of a French play in London after the war, and although ornate and rhetorical (J.C. Trewin termed it a 'magniloquent piece of nonsense'[51]), the excitement of international cultural contact so soon after international conflagration guaranteed a successful run.

Further interest in French drama was aroused at the second Edinburgh Festival in 1948, with a performance of Hamlet by the French Laurence Olivier, Jean-Louis Barrault. Audiences were intrigued by the way that the Frenchman employed the whole of his body to express himself, compared to which English actors appeared to be locked in rigor mortis.[52] The restricted nature of English acting was similarly emphasised by the London visit of the Comédie Française the following month, in October. Performing *Le Misanthrope* at the Cambridge Theatre, the whole company, according to Hobson, 'in its light-hearted exploitation of every note and inflection of which the human voice is capable, shows us within how limited a vocal range our English actors work'.[53] Foreign contact was beginning to break down British insularity and highlight technical deficiencies.

French drama in Britain received a significant boost at the end of the following year, when the titular head of the London theatrical establishment, Laurence Olivier, chose to perform Jean Anouilh's existentialist work *Antigone* as the concluding work in his trilogy of plays at the Old Vic in 1949. The production also marked Olivier's final collaboration with this theatre, following what most chose to see as his sacking by the Board of Governors (who had become frustrated by the increasing amount of time that Olivier was devoting to other projects, such as his film version of *Hamlet*). *Antigone* was well-received, with audiences ever keener to experience new approaches, but not all French imports were so welcomed, neither was Hobson in thrall to all things French, as a review of a London performance of *Caligula* by Albert Camus in 1949 demonstrates:

> Caligula throttled his mistress, rammed poison down the throat of an old man who shot round the stage like a terrified mouse, seduced a middle-aged lady before the eyes of her husband and the guests at a dinner party, and still yelled and shrieked for fresh experiences. Caligula yearned, I yawned, the more fortunate among us went to sleep, and a few brave souls left the theatre. The evening went on and on, until at the end of three hours the stage lights were lowered while a band of singularly leisurely conspirators stabbed Caligula to death in the darkness. After this there came a moment of supreme horror, for the lights went up, and Caligula was seen clinging, with bleeding mouth, to a mirror from which the glass had been thoughtfully removed. He then uttered the electrifying threat, 'I'm still alive', and I dare say that not a man in the audience did not turn pale, fearing that there was more to come. The alarm proved groundless, but I doubt if my nerves will ever be the same again.[54]

There have been few reviews that have so accurately conveyed the desperation that envelops an audience when confronted by a long and tedious drama.

1950 was to prove the year of the French play on the London stage, albeit in translation. At the beginning of the new decade the most popular domestic dramatist was Christopher Fry. In January 1950 he was enjoying unparalleled success, with three of his plays running simultaneously in the West End – *Venus Observ'd* (starring Olivier as the Duke of Altair), *The Lady's Not For Burning* (concluding an eight-month run at the Globe) and an early religious work, *The Boy With a Cart* (at the Lyric). The appetite for what he termed his 'sliced prose' (a term that emphasises the linguistic dexterity of his works) seemed unquenchable. A fourth Fry work, appearing in February at the Globe, marked a new departure in that it was not only in prose but was also a translation of Anouilh's *L'Invitation au Château*, renamed *Ring Round the Moon*. The work was significant in that it convinced many that as well as being intellectually stimulating, new French drama could be entertaining in a less uncompromising manner.

The feeling of envious admiration for French drama was deepened by the performances that Jean-Louis Barrault's company gave on their visit to Britain in the autumn of 1951. In 'Visitors',[55] the French theatre's most devoted (and influential) admirer in England wrote of Madeline Renaud's role in Marivaux's *Les Fausses Confidences* that 'I have never seen the dawn of love so beautifully, so delicately portrayed as in her performance of Araminte', yet even this rhapsodic praise was surpassed after Hobson had seen Edwige Feuillère in Claudel's *Partage de Midi* at the St James's Theatre:

> … when in twenty years time or so, one comes to consider the theatre since 1930, this performance of 'Partage de Midi' will be reckoned, along with John Gielgud's 'Richard of Bordeaux', Olivier's 'Richard III', and Ralph Richardson's 'Johnson Over Jordan' as one of the half-dozen greatest, most exciting experiences the stage has given us.[56]

By 1952, however, it was clear even to Hobson that the robustness of imported French drama was highlighting the atavism of indigenous writing. On the return from one of his many trips to Paris in March 1952, Hobson had been struck by the marked differences between the two capitals. The most striking aspect of the London stage was 'its extraordinary detachment' and 'its indifference to the world in which it is living'. This remoteness appeared deliberate and unremitting:

> I came back to a country whose newspapers are mainly filled with tidings of war, insurrection, industrial unrest, political controversy, and

parliamentary misbehaviour; and to a theatre from which it seems to me, in the first shock of re-acquaintance, that all echo of these things is shut off as by sound proof walls.

The list of entertainments to which he had been invited that week – comedians at the Palladium, a 'persuasively restful' production of *Uncle Vanya*, a dramatisation of Jane Austen's *Lady Susan* and a revival of the Stratford *Tempest* – verified this impression. The crux of the article then adumbrates the premise behind much of Kenneth Tynan's impending polemical criticism: 'That the human race is passionate, pathological … and even philosophical is recognised in the West End. … But … that it is also political the contemporary English theatre by implication and neglect absolutely denies'.[57] Hobson goes on to add that while much in contemporary politics is worth ignoring and that French drama, unlike English, possesses the advantage of being able to utilise such searing topics as collaboration, the treatment of broader issues might be rewarding in Britain, too. The theatrical battlelines of the mid-fifties were gradually being drawn.

American Musical Theatre

No powerful advocate was required for the first American import onto the British stage in 1947: Richard Rodgers and Oscar Hammerstein's earliest collaboration, the musical *Oklahoma!* First performed in New Haven, Boston, in 1943 and premièring as a Tennent production in London on 30 April 1947 at Drury Lane, it struck audiences of Great Britain as both mesmerising and revelatory.

Its originality lay in the way that it recast the template of the musical. Instead of beginning with an energetic, well-orchestrated number, the curtain rose to total silence, with not a single dancing girl in sight, and the only figure on stage an old lady sitting in a bonnet, busy with a butter churn. Off-stage a male voice was then heard gently singing a ballad, as opposed to the customary upbeat and exuberant number, and even Curly's opening lyrics seemed idiosyncratic –

There's a bright golden haze on the meadow,
There's a bright golden haze on the meadow.
The corn is high as a elephant's eye,
And it looks like it's climbin' clear up to the sky

– until the opening song developed into the famous paean to life:

Oh, what a beautiful mornin'
Oh, what a beautiful day.
I got a beautiful feelin'
Everything's goin' my way.

Richard Rodgers was later to explain the rationale behind this ground-breaking opening:

> By opening the show with the woman alone onstage and the cowboy beginning his song offstage, we did more than set a mood; we were, in effect, warning the audience 'Watch out! This is a different kind of musical'. Everything in the production was made to conform to the simple open-air spirit of the story; this was essential and certainly a rarity in the musical theatre.[58]

But it was neither this innovation nor the general optimism of this story of conflict between cowmen and farmers in 1907 alone that struck such a chord with London audiences. The warmth and humanity of the book (libretto), the technical precision and exhilarating energy of the dancers (unusually not introduced until the end of Act One),[59] the first on-stage killing in a musical (of the 'baddie', Judd) and the unfamiliar simplicity of the set, costumes and melodies (running counter to the usual Tennent practice), all shone like a beacon on the Drury Lane stage. Oscar Hammerstein's assessment of the global effect of the work had a particular resonance for London in 1947: 'It has no particular message. It imparts a flavour which infects the people who see it. It's gutsy. *Oklahoma!* is youthful, and irresponsible, and not very intellectual, but it has a heartiness of life.'[60] After the restrictions of war and the economic stringencies of peace, the need to be responsible and the obligation to respect one's peers, it is no surprise that *Oklahoma!* was to prove enormously popular. 'Everything is very simple – but of what complex simplicity!', J.C. Trewin exclaimed.[61]

Oklahoma!'s success trailed the way for several more important musicals up to 1954, predominately of American origin but occasionally British. These included *Annie Get Your Gun* (at the Coliseum, 1947), *Bless the Bride* (Adelphi, 1947), *King's Rhapsody* (Palace, 1949), *Carousel*, (Drury Lane, 1950), *Kiss Me, Kate* (Coliseum, 1951), *South Pacific* (Drury Lane, 1950), *Call Me Madam* (Coliseum, 1952), *Porgy and Bess* (Stoll, 1952), *The King and I* (Drury Lane, 1953), *Guys and Dolls* (Coliseum, 1953)and *Pal Joey* (Prince's, 1954). The appeal of the musicals for British audiences was matched only by the appeal of their profitability for theatre producers, as a letter from Lawrence Langner, the Director of the Theatre Guild, to Binkie Beaumont makes clear in 1951:

I thought you would enjoy reading the rare notices that OKLAHOMA! received when it returned to New York. It is now packing them in in an enormous theater, the Broadway, which would correspond to Stoll's Opera House. We have kept the prices the same, and it is going to gross more than it did originally. This shows that you can bring OKLAHOMA! back to London after three years on the road.[62]

Whether a licence to print money or not (adumbrating the West End in the eighties and nineties), the sheer proliferation of the genre on the London stage at this time does refute the notion that this was a glamour-starved period for the London stage. Another American offering, Tennessee Williams' *A Streetcar Named Desire* was to prove similarly sensational, but infinitely more controversial.

A Streetcar Named Desire and Entertainment Tax

Public anticipation for the opening of *A Streetcar Named Desire* at the Aldwych in 1949 had been enormous. The theatre had received over ten thousand postal applications[63] to witness the appearance of Vivien Leigh in a modern American play directed (for the enormous salary of £500 per week[64]) by her husband, Laurence Olivier. Scrupulous efforts were taken to maintain the illusion of a theatrical royal couple, including contractual stipulations as to the size and position of the names on the posters:

> [Vivien Leigh's] name alone shall be starred above the title of the play, and it is further agreed that the name of Mr Bonar Colleano [playing Stanley Kowalski] shall appear at the bottom of all such printing and billing matter, preceded by the word 'with'.[65]

The fights which had broken out amongst members of the eager and impatient first-night queue brought further welcome publicity for this spectacular event. After the opening performance, though, the critical reaction in the press was sharply – and antagonistically – divided. Some critics were attracted to the poignancy of Vivien Leigh as the abused Blanche; *The Times*, for example, spoke of Vivien Leigh's performance being 'impressive ... for its delicately insistent suggestion of a mind with a slowly loosening hold on reason'.[66] They also admired the frankness of the acting demanded by the director, which whilst it was not according to the 'Method' style, nevertheless dispensed with the poise and good breeding more usually associated with British acting, for the sake of emotionally committed performances. Others, however, were outraged by what they chose to see as an indecent, lavatorial work. Anthony Cookman's half-hearted assertion in the *Tatler* that it was 'a vigorous piece of melo-drama',[67] suggests that he was disconcerted by the frank depiction of Blanche's sordid past and demise into madness. J.C. Trewin's description in the *Observer* went further, characterising it as 'a messy little anecdote' and 'intrinsically cheap', although he did admire Vivien Leigh's perform-ance for being 'an astonishing exhibition of technique allied to stamina'.[68] Baroness Ravensdale of the Public Morality Council spluttered that the 'play is thoroughly indecent and we should be ashamed that children and servants are allowed to sit in the theatre and see it',[69] Princess Alice can-celled a visit, stating that it was not the 'kind of entertainment she would enjoy',[70] whilst simple disgust was expressed in the parish notes of the Reverend Colin Cuttell, priest-Vicar of Southwark:

> Is there no statesman in high places who will speak out from other than political and economic motives and tell the United States to keep the sewage? A pathological obsession with sex is a mark of this age, as it has been the mark of any dying civilisation from Babylon to Rome. Perad-venture the Lord Chamberlain (chief licensee of all theatres) is on a journey or sleepeth ...[71]

Unsurprisingly, the playwright Tennessee Williams had tenaciously fought against any cuts to preserve the integrity of his work, even sending a telegram, prior to production, warning of his refusal to bow to any stric-tures from the Lord Chamberlain:

> DEEPLY DISTURBED OVER PROPOSED CUTS IN SCRIPT SINCE ALL MATERIAL NOW CUT HAS PROVEN ESSENTIAL TO CHARACTER DEVELOPMENT AND QUALITY OF PLAY DONT ENJOY SOUNDING CONTRACTUAL BUT NO CUTS OR CHANGES OR ADDITIONS CAN BE MADE WITHOUT MY APPROVAL AS AUTHOR[72]

Any discomfort that the increasingly beleaguered government of Clement Attlee, still reeling from the foreign exchange crisis of 1947, might have felt as a result of such attacks on its alleged moral laxity was exacerbated by the row that developed over the decision of the Arts Council to grant the play tax exemption on the grounds that it was partly cultural and partly educational. To offset the high cost of production (£10,000) the manage-ment, Tennent Productions, had turned itself into a non-profit-making registered charity to avoid incurring entertainment tax (a 'temporary tax', introduced in 1916[73]) – which, at 10 per cent of gross profits, had come to represent over a quarter of the price of a ticket by 1948.[74] This was a familiar practice on the part of theatrical managements, and in particular Tennent's, to take advantage of legislation that was originally designed to encourage straitened managers to stage more productions during the First World War. After the Second World War, the Arts Council had appointed three officials, generally known as the 'Three Blind Mice', to rule on whether the plays claiming exemption could be classed as educational,[75] but this had had little effect on Tennent's profitability: *A Streetcar Named Desire* was Tennent's fortieth such venture.[76] Ivor Brown had frequently condemned this dubious post-war practice in his *Observer* column, commenting two years previously, in a thinly veiled reference to Binkie Beaumont, that 'the distinction between non-profit and profit-making theatre companies has become altogether shadowy when profit makers create "non-profit" subsidiaries with the same offices and largely similar directorates'.[77] The address of both the parent company, H.M. Tennent Ltd and the subsidiary, Tennent Productions Ltd, was the Apollo Theatre, Shaftesbury Avenue.

On this occasion, however, Tennent's action was challenged by Members of Parliament in the House of Commons. When the Financial Secretary, Glenvil Hall, sought to explain that it was perfectly in order for the management to claim exemption on educational grounds, the Conservative Member for Brighton, A. Marlowe, asked whether the Minister was aware 'that this particular play is only educational to those who are ignorant of the facts of life?'.[78] The play was to run at the Aldwych theatre for 333 performances,[79] but following an investigation by a Select Committee of the House of Commons into the practice of managements forming non-profit-distributing subsidiaries in 1950 – convened in the light of the furore surrounding *A Streetcar Named Desire* – the practice of the Arts Council forming associations with commercial managements, to permit the latter to avoid Entertainment tax, ceased,[80] and Tennent's became liable for income tax backdated from 1945. This was a not inconsiderable blow to Binkie Beaumont and the powerful company's first setback.

Necrology or Propaganda?

The proliferation of French and American productions inevitably meant that increased scrutiny was cast upon indigenous dramatic creations in the West End. Even fifty years later, theatre historians vigorously debate whether the new wave of plays following on in the wake of *Look Back in Anger* (1956) at the Royal Court constituted a 'revolution'[81] or merely a movement that derived momentum from attacking what had gone before, thereby thwarting any British playwrighting talent that did not accord with the new fashion. Charles Duff puts this revisionist view succinctly in the introduction to his biography of the Tennent theatre director Frith Banbury:

> My premise is simple: without underrating or denigrating the importance of any writer of the English Stage Company, many of their hypotheses about the state of the West End are wrong; that the standard of individual acting was high, and that its playwrights knew more about the human heart and wrote with greater literacy than many of their successors of the late 1950s and 1960s.[82]

The most accurate assessment is that whilst the years 1952, 1953 and 1954 in the West End were dominated by predictable revivals of classic works and productions of Shakespeare, compelling the critic, Kenneth Tynan, to describe himself in 1954 as 'a necrologist',[83] the memory of this famine, followed by the feast initiated by the London première of *Waiting for Godot* in 1955, has obscured the fact that the period of 1948 to 1951 was one of some diversity. The rest of this chapter will therefore concentrate on two eras: that of 1948–1951, evolution, and that of 1952–1954, stasis. Revolution, if such it was, was to come in 1955.

1948–1951

Tynan's despair of the mid-fifties was nothing new. As early as 1947, his predecessor at the *Observer*, Ivor Brown, was lamenting that dwindling receipts, 'colossal production costs' and high Entertainment Tax were stifling creativity and that the cinema continued to pilfer the finest stage talent; 'The juvenile lead vanished from the playhouse with the speed and certainty of a conjuror's young lady who has been roped and boxed for eternity.'[84]

He also wistfully remarked that the stars of the stage were 'mainly in the grandpa age groups' – but, from today's perspective, what stars they were. Edith Evans as Madame Ranyevskaia in *The Cherry Orchard* (1948), for example, shedding some of her mannerisms and proving that a problematic Cleopatra had not heralded her dotage.[85] The same actress, as Lady Wishforth in *The Way of the World* (1948), giving 'a star-performance in all its authority' (Brown) – even if this did cause the rest of the production to dwindle beside it.[86] Laurence Olivier, in an incredible feat of athleticism, creating a hypnotic Richard III (1949), whose death took Harold Hobson's breath away:

[Olivier] leaves the fighting to Kean, but after Richmond, foot planted on his breast, has spiked him on his sword, he is tremendous. Convulsively freeing himself from his enemy, but still laying on his back, he performs what, with its shooting out of the legs like the darting tongue of the viper, can only be described as a horizontal dance. It is an amazing end to a memorable evening.[87]

Michael Redgrave was Richard II in a production at Stratford (1951) for which the designer, Tanya Moiseiwitsch, had constructed a wooden frame, a central gallery and a projecting fore-stage in an attempt to recreate a Tudor stage. There was also Richard Burton as Hal in *Henry IV* (1951), with a performance which was considered by many to possess originality, deep insight and that longed-for commodity, irreverent youth – witness Hobson again:

> An actor, it cannot be too often said, is not merely an embodiment of other men's ideas. He has a flame of his own to light, and to get it going he sometimes burns the paper his author has written on. Instead of a light-hearted rapscallion Mr Burton offers a young knight keeping a long vigil in the cathedral of his own mind. The knighthood is authentic; the vigil upheld by interior exaltation.[88]

Significantly, what binds these performances together, in addition to their quality, is the nature of the plays – classic works of previous centuries including, in particular, Shakespeare. The dearth of new writing that they were masking was to become increasingly apparent over the next few years.

When speaking of notable performances, it is important to emphasise the appeal of certain music-hall entertainers. By the end of the 1940s music-hall was dying. Its homes at the Holborn Empire, Collins and the Metropolitan had been destroyed in the war, and it was now being stifled by competition from cinema and theatre (and shortly to be finished off by television). This made John Osborne's choice of the decline of music-hall as a metaphor to illustrate the dwindling power of the British Empire in *The Entertainer* (1957) so apt. There were still some performers, however, who were able to retain huge popularity in the ten years after the end of the war, and these included George Formby, famous for witty songs accompanied by his ukulele, Sid Field, a comic actor best known for sketches involving the spiv 'Slasher Green'[89] and Gracie Fields, the 'Lancashire Lass' whose clear, natural voice and perfect pitch were able to sell out the Palladium in October 1950. In the previous year, many felt that they had witnessed her male equivalent at the same venue, when the

'tousled, mercurial, magnetic, triumphant'[90] Danny Kaye crossed the
Atlantic to mesmerise London audiences. Ivor Brown led the adulation:

> He has great variety and certainty of singing voice and a rare gift today
> – he can make a microphone serve him instead of cringing before it as
> his master; he is never 'mike-bound' and static. He can dance with any-
> one and mix sentiment with the burlesque of sentiment as richly as does
> Gracie Fields.[91]

The versatility and *joie de vivre* of these stars enthralled audiences but the
infrequency of their spectacular shows also emphasised the passing of an
era – further evidence of the transitional nature of performance at this
period.

Several new British works appeared between 1948 and 1951, which did
give many cause for optimism that the paucity of innovative indigenous
work was coming to an end. Christopher Fry was particularly hailed in this
respect. Although there had been stirrings of twentieth-century poetic
drama long before Fry's *The Lady's Not For Burning* was produced at the
Arts Theatre in 1948 (including Yeats at the Abbey Theatre, Auden and
Isherwood at the Group Theatre, T.S. Eliot's *Murder in the Cathedral*
(1935), Fry's own *The Boy With a Cart* (1937) and Ronald Duncan's *The
Way to the Tomb* (1945)), what impressed many observers about *The
Lady's Not For Burning* was the medieval fantastication which so differentiated it from other works of the period. For the next three years there was
genuine hope that Fry would create a distinctive theatrical movement, that
of Christian Verse Drama, and become 'the poet dramatist for whom the
stage has been searching so long' (J.C. Trewin).[92] *The Lady's Not For Burning* quickly transferred to the Globe Theatre, with a cast that included
John Gielgud, Pamela Brown and Richard Burton, and it ran for 294
performances.[93] A mere six months later, in January 1950, Olivier took
the lead role of the Duke of Altair in *Venus Observ'd* ('a great occasion' in
Ivor Brown's view);[94] John Gielgud directed Richard Burton and Mary
Jerrold in *The Boy With a Cart* at the Lyric, Hammersmith; and Peter
Brook directed Claire Bloom and Paul Scofield in Fry's translation, *Ring
Round the Moon* – all within two weeks. Small wonder that Ivor Brown
observed that 'Our theatre now is beginning to consist of Large Fry and
Small Fry.'[95]

The flourishing of Fry's work was relatively short-lived, however,
although its eclipsing was due less to any intrinsic failing than a shift in the
theatrical mood towards the gritty realism of Kitchen-Sink drama. The
possibility of its decline in popularity was even raised at the zenith of its
fortunes in February 1950, when the perspicacious Ivor Brown wrote that,

'It is vaguely felt that we need a new style: T.S. Eliot and Christopher Fry have gone off into poetry, which is one way out: the radicals are rightly groping for some way to freshen the sociological play'.[96] This coupling with Eliot has bedeviled Fry ever since. An inferior dramatist to Fry, Eliot sharply divided opinion at the time, with almost as many disliking the 'sex-trouble and cocktail-chatter'[97] of *The Cocktail Party* (Edinburgh Festival 1949, London 1950), as admiring a further attempt to reintroduce verse into English drama. Fifty years on, it is the 'undercurrent of bitterness and war-weary disenchantment'[98] – an aspect of Fry's work seldom noticed on its first appearance – that intrigues as much as the language, whereas Eliot's drama seems formulaic and jejune by comparison.

Although Terence Rattigan created *The Browning Version* in 1948, a brilliant psychological depiction of the academic and personal failure of a deeply disliked schoolmaster in which 'every line seems ... to detonate' (J.C. Trewin),[99] such intelligent works were increasingly perceived as the exceptions that proved the rule that it was the foreign imports that were exciting, innovative and daring. Arthur Miller's much heralded *The Death of a Salesman* (first produced in London in 1950) demonstrated how it was American playwrights who dared to scrutinise contemporary society – as far as political satire was concerned, the London theatre seemed hermetically sealed – and at the beginning of the new decade another tranche of musicals arrived to irk the critics and thrill the public. Whilst J.C. Trewin felt *Carousel* (1950) to be 'sophistication crossed with bland innocence',[100] Ivor Brown loathed the 'sex-hunger' of the sailors in *South Pacific* (1950) 'peeping, from their iron prison, through binoculars at girls undressing on shore'[101] and Harold Hobson reviled *Kiss Me, Kate* (1951) for containing jokes that are 'humiliatingly naive',[102] the public ignored this collective primness and flocked in their thousands to witness these fanfares of colour, light, music and vigour: attributes in short supply in a country still enduring rationing. Up until *Porgy and Bess* (1952) there was a strict embargo on the playing of the tunes from these shows, a marketing ploy that helped stimulate voracious interest in their arrival, and John Elsom reflects the immense appeal of these new musicals somewhat more accurately than the critics who were yearning for a more intellectual renewal, when he writes:

> when I first started to go to the theatre regularly, in the early 1950s, an evening at an American musical was usually one of sheer delight, not unmixed with a sense of guilty awareness that I went to see Shakespeare or Eliot at the Old Vic in a spirit of dutiful respect.[103]

Dutiful respect was to become an increasingly unfashionable commodity in the 1950s.

Institutions 2: the Old Vic and the Concept of the National Theatre

The Old Vic by the early 1950s had experienced an eventful and some-what difficult time in comparison with the heady days of 1944 and the Olivier/Richardson triumphs at the New Theatre. These war-time suc-cesses had led many to believe that the Old Vic would provide the basis for a newly-built national theatre, an idea first conceived in 1848 by Effingham Wilson. Consequently, on a bitterly cold 24 January 1947, its original home, the bomb-damaged theatre in the Waterloo Road, re-opened as the Old Vic Theatre Centre, containing a Theatre School, an experimental stage and the base for a children's theatre company. A dis-tinguished trio of theatre professionals was involved – Michel St Denis, who was in overall charge, Glyn Byam Shaw as director of the Theatre School and George Devine in control of the Children's Theatre – but the initial funding from the Arts Council was precarious, a meagre £9,500 per annum. The Old Vic now had two centres, at the New Theatre in the West End, where Olivier, Richardson and Burrell were to lead the company when not away touring, and in Waterloo Road, where a training centre was to evolve.

By 1949, much of the early optimism about this twin approach had been dissipated. The 'National Theatre' was still a mere concept, even though legislation had been passed in February authorising the allocation of a mil-lion pounds for a building on a South Bank site to be provided by the Lon-don County Council. As it happened, no money was forthcoming. Equally demoralising was the financial loss of £9,000 for the 1947/8 season (almost the entire 1947 grant for the Theatre Centre), whilst Olivier and Richard-son were away filming. The governing body of the company, concerned about the sense of anti-climax that the stars' absences inevitably created, decided not to renew their contracts when they expired in 1949, but this was immediately seen as a clumsy sacking (particularly given that the announcement was made as the company was on a hugely successful tour of Australia) and it brought enormous protest. This public relations disas-ter was compounded by the fact that Olivier's final season at the New Theatre resulted in his legendary *Richard III* (1949) and *The School for Scandal* (1949).

The Old Vic now entered a period of some turmoil, with a decision to cut its West End link at the New, the resultant forced relocation of the Theatre Centre to Dulwich High School for Girls, the resignation in May 1951 of St Denis, Byam Shaw and Devine, and the closure of the Centre in its entirety in 1952. It was not until Michael Benthall's appointment as overall director in 1953 and his five-year plan to produce every Shakespearean work of the First Folio between September 1953 and July 1958, that some stability was created.[104]

The Festival of Britain and 1952–1954

The Festival of Britain which took place in London in 1951 was also designed to convey an impression of stability, being both an affirmation that Britons had emerged from the trials of the immediate post-war period and a showcase for British art and technology. Sponsored by the Labour government and the Labour-controlled London County Council, it gave architects the platform to demonstrate their renewed vigour, be it in the construction of the Festival Hall, the National Film Theatre or the esoteric pleasure gardens at Battersea.[105] As far as the theatre was concerned, however, it provided visible proof that the country contained superlative actors and actresses, but depressingly few new and durable vehicles in which they could perform. The appearance of Edith Evans, Sybil Thorndike and Wendy Hiller together in N.C. Hunter's *Waters of the Moon* was a memorable event, but it was hard for some observers to escape the feeling that this 'planetary cast'[106] turned the dramatist's text into something more substantial than he had actually conceived. Vivien Leigh's performance as Cleopatra alongside her husband, Olivier, as Antony at the St James's Theatre in May moved Ivor Brown 'almost beyond endurance at the close'[107] and John Gielgud's Leontes in *The Winter's Tale*, directed by Peter Brook at Stratford, was a revelation, hailed as 'actual, exciting, believable, pathetic, a man and not the emanation of a fantasy'.[108] Indeed, there now seemed to be no male Shakespearean role that Gielgud could not rescue from critical or academic indifference. But the fact remained that there appeared to be a danger of a 'bardic traffic jam'[109] in the West End, a danger realised in 1953, when Harold Hobson alone reviewed twenty-four different productions of Shakespeare plays in that year, with four separate openings in the first week of July.

Whilst the arrival of American musicals was unabated – *Porgy and Bess* having opened in October 1952 and *Guys and Dolls* in May 1953 – the genre's dynamic example was not having any obvious effect on new British works. N.C. Hunter's follow-up to *Waters of the Moon*, *A Day by the Sea* (1953) was another stellar Tennent production, boasting Sybil Thorndike, Lewis Casson, Ralph Richardson and John Gielgud, but the work itself seemed to be sub-Chekhovian, and unhealthily pandered to the public's appetite for star names – a dangerous trend that imperilled interest in experimental work. Rattigan's *The Deep Blue Sea* (1952) was admired for the tragic power of Peggy Ashcroft's depiction of Hester Collyer, but seemed confused in its construction (perhaps because of a possible gay code that Rattigan was employing in an era of strict censorship, which meant that the two main characters were written as a man and a woman instead of as two homosexuals).[110] *The Living Room* by Graham Greene (1953), another novelist trying his hand at the genre of drama, was accused of employing an increasingly familiar and formulaic treatment of sex and religion (highlighting the demise of Christian Verse Drama), by offering 'theology mixed with sex, corpse mixed with creed [and] theorising about Sin',[111] and even the French play – which, through the translations of Fry, was now regarded by many people as British – began to seem tired and a dead hand on native productions. Harold Hobson continued to eulogise about Jean-Louis Barrault and Edwige Feuillère, but most tastes were shifting. Ivor Brown not only loathed what he termed the 'pusillanimous' nature of Anouilh's philosophy,[112] but began to worry with others about the sheer weight of French drama on the London stage. There were other warning signs for a complacent theatre. The television age had truly begun in 1953 when 56 per cent of the population had watched the coronation of Elizabeth II, and there was a concomitant increase in the number of television licences issued, from 693,000 in the same year to 1,110,439 in 1954.

What is perhaps most noticeable about the London stage between 1952 and 1954 is how completely indifferent it was to contemporary events. The heavy costs of a rearmament programme necessitated by the Korean war; the inflationary pressures that this produced in a still war-weakened country; the continued shortages caused by rationing; the dramatic impact of the welfare state; the two elections of 1951, which resulted in an elderly Churchill regaining power for the Conservatives; the spectre of cold war conflagration; the manufacture of the first British nuclear bomb: all failed to impinge upon the West End stage. There were brief glimmerings of alternative works – a group called Theatre Workshop staged Ewan McColl's *Uranium 235* in 1952, although the play's discussion of the dropping of the atomic bombs on Japan was dismissed as propaganda – but genuinely ground-breaking work was too often deemed perplexing. This was most apparent in Ivor Brown's tentative response to John Whiting's *Marching Song* in April 1954: 'Mr Whiting writes with energy and originality, but what exactly he intends to say, playgoers must decide for themselves'.[113]

The unadventurous nature of the West End mirrored the constrictions of early fifties British society. A contemporaneous description of the then Lord Chamberlain appearing in the *Observer* in 1952, conveys a powerful sense of the period:

Lord Clarendon enjoys shooting and fishing, despite a heavy limp acquired in a childhood accident. He lives as he was brought up to live, surrounded by his treasured Van Dycks, well and happily married, performing his difficult office with charm and skill.[114]

It was this stratification of the theatre through class, the plethora of productions of Shakespeare, the continued dominance of H.M. Tennent's, the obsession with French plays and the avoidance of matters political, which became a source of deep frustration for one man in particular, Kenneth Tynan.

Theatre Criticism 2: Kenneth Tynan

The sheer brilliance of Tynan's observations in late 1954 and 1955 not only provided a revelatory diagnosis of the reasons for the theatre's stasis, but gave a hint of the excitement to come and ushered in a new golden age of theatre criticism. Tynan, who had previously been a dandy at Oxford, a failed actor and a frustrated director before becoming a theatre critic for the *Evening Standard*, succeeded Ivor Brown at the *Observer* in September 1954. He immediately gave notice of his polemical intent:

> I see myself predominantly as a lock. If the key, which is the work of art, fits snugly into my mechanism of bias and preference, I click and rejoice; if not, I am helpless, and can only offer the artist the address of a better locksmith. ... It is a sombre truth that nowadays our intellectuals go to the cinema and shun the theatre. Their assistance is sadly missed; but their defection is my opportunity.[115]

Young (he was twenty-seven on his appointment), attuned to the dissatisfaction of his own generation, fashionably left-of-centre and a lover of American musicals, Tynan was, above all, a stylish, captivating writer. His observations ranged from the refreshingly direct –

> Twenty seven West End theatres are at present offering light comedies and musical shows of which perhaps a dozen are good of their kind. The number of new plays with a claim to serious discussion is three ... One need not be a purist to be ashamed of the discrepancy.[116]

– to the fiercely didactic: 'Night-nurses at the bedside of good drama, we critics keep a holy vigil. Black circles rim our eyes as we pray for the survival of our pet patient, starved and racked, the theatre of passion and ideas.'[117] From the devastatingly witty, such as the famous pastiche of Rattigan's *Separate Tables*.[118]

(The scene is the dining-room of a Kensington hotel, not unlike the Bournemouth hotel in which *Separate Tables*, Terence Rattigan's new double bill, takes place. A Young Perfectionist is dining; beside him, Aunt Edna, whom Mr Rattigan has described as the 'universal and immortal' middle-class playgoer.)

AUNT EDNA: Excuse me, young man, but have you seen Mr Rattigan's latest?

YOUNG PERFECTIONIST: I have indeed.

A.E.: And what is it about?

Y.P.: It is two plays about four people who are driven by loneliness into a state of desperation.

A.E.: (sighing): Is there not enough morbidity in the world …?

Y.P.: One of them is a drunken Left-wing journalist who has been imprisoned for wife-beating. Another is his ex-wife, who takes drugs to palliate the loss of her looks. She revives his masochistic love for her, and by curtain-fall they are gingerly reunited.

A.E.: (quailing): Does Mr Rattigan analyse these creatures?

Y.P.: He does, in great detail.

A.E.: How very unwholesome! Pray go on.[119]

– to the lasceratingly descriptive, most notably his denunciation of the typical West End work, set in the fictional Home County of Loamshire, where

the inhabitants belong to a social class derived from romantic novels and partly from the playwright's vision of the leisured life he will lead after the play is a success – this being the only effort of imagination he is called on to make.[120]

His reviews seemed to provide the excitement so patently missing from the West End itself. He gave hints of important theatrical movements in Europe, such as Brecht's Epic Theatre, and lamented the theatre world's ignorance of their significance – 'We in London hear the distant thunder of the guns: but how shall we judge of the outcome?'.[121] He welcomed the relevance and innovation of Theatre Workshop's *The Good Soldier Schweik* (1954) – 'With half a dozen replacements, Theatre Workshop might take London by storm'[122] – and he lambasted Britain's social, political and cultural insularity, which Kathleen Tynan said he saw as embracing fear of America, fear of the advent of commercial television, fear of criticism, fear of emotional engagement, fear of an open sexuality and a fear enforced by censors of film and theatre, who both discouraged political attacks on the establishment.[123]

Tynan's writing had touched a nerve in many. *Plays and Players*, in its end of year report, 'Credits and Discredits for 1954', had three simple wishes for 1955: 'Better plays, better acting, better productions'.[124] In the four months to the end of 1954, Tynan had offered several prescriptions for 'the theatre of passion and ideas'. The question now remained: who would administer the cure?

Chapter 2

1955–1962

The Arts Theatre

In March 1955, a recent graduate from Cambridge University directed the London première of a work from a country whose dominance of the current West End stage was verging on theatrical imperialism. Eugène Ionesco's *The Lesson* was the twenty-five-year-old Peter Hall's fourth production for a small, off-West End venue in central London, the Arts Theatre Club. The piece was not new – it had been written in 1951 – but it played a crucial role in supporting the introduction of Absurdist drama in Britain, the first of four seminal events that were to occur during 1955 and 1956 and transform English language drama. The three others were the emergence of the English Stage Company in 1956, the encounter with Epic Theatre following the visit to London of Brecht's company, the Berliner Ensemble, in August 1956, and the growth, success and example of Joan Littlewood's Theatre Workshop at the Theatre Royal, Stratford East.

The Lesson

The subject-matter of *The Lesson* is both simple and perplexing. An eighteen-year-old girl arrives at the home of an elderly professor for private tuition. At first, she imposes herself through wilfulness and youthful exuberance, but the balance of power gradually shifts during chaotic lessons on linguistics and mathematics. As the professor delves into ever more complex linguistic theories, the pupil begins to suffer from an agonising toothache which is ignored by her teacher, until, at the zenith of his power, he launches into a disquisition on the meaning of the word 'knife' and then stabs the young woman to death. Panic-stricken, he summons his maid, who rebukes him for the murder and reveals that this is the professor's fortieth victim of the day. As the couple plan to place the body in a coffin, a prospective pupil arrives for another lesson.

It was the very illogicality of the work, its refusal to provide a closure, that contrasted so markedly with the resolution of well-made plays such as Rattigan's, and its use of allusion, implication and vague suggestion inspired some and baffled many. Ionesco's emphasis on the impotence of language as an effective means of communication contained resonances of the ineffectual cold war diplomacy of the early fifties, but it was difficult to observe any clear-cut didactic intent on the part of the playwright (indeed, Ionesco was to state in 1958 that his work offered 'a testimony, not a didactic message'[1]). The attempt to re-orientate a theatre audience away from a desire to detect clear-cut meaning in a play, however, placed the work firmly in the avant-garde, and it was this that London's chief francophile, Harold Hobson, celebrated, on 13 March 1955, in the *Sunday Times* with the appropriately titled review, 'Something New':

> [Some] people are not content with the drive, the tension, the humour, the fear of 'The Lesson' … They are not contented to be excited, transported or even amused. They want to know what the play *means*. What does a sunset mean, or the Victory of Samothrace?

Although the first-night audience at the Arts Theatre Club was not completely won over, this play was an early skirmish in the battle to inculcate new forms of thinking on the part of drama practitioners and audiences alike, a battle that flared up again six months later when one of the most influential works of the post-war period, and a further piece of Absurdist theatre, made its London debut.

Waiting for Godot: August 1955

Waiting for Godot received its English première on 3 August 1955 and was also directed by Peter Hall for an audience of barely 300 at the Arts Theatre Club. Like *The Lesson*, *Waiting for Godot* was – ironically – another translated French import that arrived in London some time after its continental European début in 1953. News of its notoriety had travelled ahead of it, however, and it was already something of a *cause célèbre* in cultural circles.

The rehearsal period for the play had not been propitious, since the Lord Chamberlain had objected to the propriety of the work's language and requested several changes, only to some of which was the playwright prepared to acquiesce. As early as April 1953, shortly after the hundredth Paris performance of the play, Beckett had written to Susan Manning:

Have made a good deal of money with it already (more, in a couple of months, than with all my other writings put together) and hope to make a good bit more. There is talk of New York, but in my opinion it could not play unexpurgated either in England or America, and I refuse to expurgate it.[2]

Beckett was thus insistent that the fall of Estragon's trousers at the end and the exchange between the two tramps on the subject of erections must remain for the London production, so it had been necessary to stage a club performance to ensure that the play received any sort of British airing.[3]

The play opens with an old man, Estragon, sitting on a low mound, repeatedly attempting – and failing – to remove his boot. The effort leaves him exhausted and on the entrance of his companion, Vladimir, he gives up, proclaiming 'Nothing to be done'. This mixture of futility and frustration permeates the whole work and provides the central dramatic trope, namely, the continual eclipsing of the intention to act by the inability to act. It is encapsulated in the well-known exchange:

ESTRAGON: Let's go.
VLADIMIR: We can't.
ESTRAGON: Why not?
VLADIMIR: We're waiting for Godot.
ESTRAGON: (*despairingly*) Ah![4]

The two men are waiting for a message from Godot, whose real identity, or symbolic import, is deliberately left open. Absurdist theatre functions by being implicit rather than explicit, allusive not confirmatory. Visitors arrive, but Godot is not among them; instead Pozzo, a bully with an eloquent turn of phrase, and his slave, Lucky, who appears both oppressed and sinister, stay to exchange banter before Lucky launches into a complex and intractable speech. Shortly after they have left a boy arrives who reveals that he minds the goats, is fed fairly well, sleeps in the loft and is not sure whether he is happy or not. He also explains that Godot beats his brother, but not him, and that he has a message for the two men: 'Mr Godot told me to tell you he won't come this evening but surely tomorrow'. The sense of 'perpetual postponement'[5] is now quite apparent to the audience.

The second act takes place on the following day and the previously bare tree, which with the mound comprises the entire set, has sprouted four or five leaves – refuting on the simplest level the notion that *Waiting for Godot* is a play in which 'nothing happens twice'. Events are broadly repeated, although this time Pozzo is now blind. The boy returns, but he has no recollection of the previous day's visit. His communication is similarly tormenting:

> VLADIMIR: You have a message from Mr Godot.
> BOY: Yes, sir.
> VLADIMIR: He won't come this evening.
> BOY: No, sir.
> VLADIMIR: But he'll come tomorrow.
> BOY: Yes, sir.

Further questioning of the boy elicits the information that his brother is now sick, as well as a description of Godot:

> VLADIMIR: (*softly*). Has he a beard, Mr Godot?
> BOY: Yes, sir.
> VLADIMIR: Fair or ... (*he hesitates*) ... or black?
> BOY: I think it's white, sir.
> (*Silence*).
> VLADIMIR: Christ have mercy on us!

In the first Arts Theatre production, Paul Daneman, the actor playing Vladimir, inadvertently took off his hat at this moment (something he had not done in rehearsal), which Hobson viewed as a sign of reverence, setting off the theory that Godot is actually God – an arguable but enduring interpretation.

On the boy's exit, the two men consider hanging themselves, but they have no rope. Their final exchange reflects the stasis of the whole piece. After more peering into hats, Estragon hints at decisiveness:

> ESTRAGON: Well? Shall we go?
> VLADIMIR: Pull on your trousers.
> ESTRAGON: What?
> VLADIMIR: Pull on your trousers.
> ESTRAGON: You want me to pull off my trousers?
> VLADIMIR: Pull ON your trousers.
> ESTRAGON: (*realizing his trousers are down*). True. (*He pulls up his trousers*).
> VLADIMIR: Well? Shall we go?
> ESTRAGON: Yes, let's go.
> (*They do not move*).

But the play refuses to close, leaving both the tragic and the comic suspended over the ending.

This rejection of closure and the dismissal of a linear progression of plot (embracing a beginning, a middle and an end) set the play apart from almost every work that had been produced on the British stage other than *The Lesson*. Frequently revealing that rational thought is not always possible, it emphasises that action is less important than language or the absence of language (a theme that both Beckett himself and Pinter were later to develop). The inarticulacy of Vladimir and Estragon – often paradoxically conveyed in passages of great lyricism – suggests that the play is an attempt to reflect in form *and* content the complexity of the modern world. The shadow of the Holocaust, the unreliability of religious belief, the lack of certainty in society all hang over the work and lead to the feeling that the only sane reaction to contemporary horrors is a desperate humour, hence the tragi-comic strand. It would be too simplistic and glib to offer either resolution (comedy) or redemption (tragedy), so the characters are all held in a limbo and the final exchange is depressingly irresolute.

This is clearly not to say that *Waiting for Godot* is devoid of dramatic interest, since tension is created through a series of juxtapositions between, for example, violence and humour, fear and safety, a sense of sin and a sense of hope (symbolised by Godot's expected arrival), and passages of poetic lyricism and passages of inarticulation. These supersede the more familiar conflicts of character and plot.

There are constant hints of violence throughout the work – Estragon's being beaten up the night before the play begins, the threat of Pozzo's whip, the running sore on Lucky's neck, Lucky's assault on Estragon by kicking him in the shins, the constant sense of vulnerability that the two men feel –

VLADIMIR: Well? What do we do?
ESTRAGON: Don't let's do anything. It's safer

– and the sinister reference to an earlier holocaust that Estragon alludes to in Act Two:

ESTRAGON: The best thing would be to kill me, like the other.
VLADIMIR: What other? (*Pause*) What other?
ESTRAGON: Like billions of others.

This sense of the violent is contrasted with moments of verbal and visual humour, something which comes over more clearly in performance than on reading the play. The influence of the music hall is evident with the futile struggling with boots, the investigation and sniffing of hats, the falling down of trousers and the interplay between the characters and the audience, such as when Vladimir asks for his seat to be kept while he leaves to urinate. Beckett also glances at future critical reaction when in the men's humorous search for ever more offensive insults to hurl at each other and so pass the time, they begin with the tame 'Curate' and end with the fierce 'Critic'.

Perhaps the most powerful juxtaposition is that of the men's sense of optimism at the possible nirvana of Godot's entrance, contrasted with their own sense of worthlessness. In many ways, they do possess a consciousness of original sin. Vladimir asks in Act One:

> VLADIMIR: Suppose we repented.
> ESTRAGON: Repented what?
> VLADIMIR: Oh. … We wouldn't have to go into details.
> ESTRAGON: Our being born?

Pozzo has a similar belief in the inadequacy of humanity in general:

> Let us not then speak ill of our generation, it is not any unhappier than its predecessors. (*Pause*). Let us not speak well of it either. (*Pause*). Let us not speak of it at all. (*Pause*). It is true that the population has increased.

This descent into linguistic nothingness parallels the poignant longing for some form of resolution – be it nothingness or salvation – that Vladimir and Estragon increasingly exhibit. It is the dominant thematic leitmotif, evident in Vladimir's plaintive 'Will night never come?' and the men's desolate attempt to use up the minutes –

> VLADIMIR: That passed the time
> ESTRAGON: It would have passed in any case.
> VLADIMIR: Yes, but not so rapidly –

as well as in the characters' mutual distress –

> VLADIMIR: You don't know if you're unhappy or not?
> BOY: No, sir.
> VLADIMIR: You're as bad as myself

– and their inability to feel that they have a substantive presence:

> ESTRAGON: We always find something, eh Didi, to give us the impression we exist?

Perhaps Lucky is so named because, in his confusion, he is the only character unaware of the true horror of his situation.

Such an innovative, profound and unexpected work was bound to provoke strong feelings in 1955. Peter Bull, who played the part of Pozzo, later described the reaction of the first-night audience:

> Waves of hostility came whirling over the footlights, and the mass exodus, which was to form such a feature of the piece, started quite soon after the curtain had risen. ... The curtain fell to mild applause, we took a scant three calls and a depression and sense of anti-climax descended on us all. Very few people came round, most of those who did were in a high state of intoxication and made even less sense than the play.[6]

The critical reaction in the daily newspapers was one of blank incomprehension and no little irritation that a talented production team had been wasted on such unpromising material. Some critics barely sought to conceal their loathing. Milton Shulman in the *Evening Standard* claimed that 'the excellent work of the cast cannot obscure many deadly dull and pretentious passages';[7] Stephen Williams in the *Evening News*, picking up on the fact that Beckett had once been the secretary of James Joyce, summarised the work as 'an occasional faint flash of the genius that was James and long invertebrate stretches of tedium that was Joyce';[8] David Lewin in the *Daily Express*, under the evocative title, 'Nothing happens, it's awful (it's life)', wrote that although the play was well acted, 'there are passages when no one could carry the thought along. And I too became weary of waiting for Godot ... who never comes';[9] and W.A. Darlington, who maintained a career-long suspicion of plays without a beginning, a middle and an end, considered in a *Daily Telegraph* article, 'An Evening of Funny Obscurity', that Beckett was the Head Boy of 'a school of dramatists at present whose pupils love obscurity for obscurity's sake'.[10] The opening night of *Waiting for Godot* was a monumental flop as far as the reviews were concerned. There was one Sunday newspaper critic, however, already attuned to the nuances of Absurdist theatre, for whom the arrival of *Waiting for Godot* was most opportune.

Hobson and 'Tomorrow'

The title chosen for Hobson's *Sunday Times* review of *Waiting for Godot*, which appeared on 7 August 1955, four days after the première of the play, was simply 'Tomorrow'. The article, one of Hobson's best known, represented not just the remarkable discovery for London of a remarkable play, but provided Hobson with an opportunity to convince an English public that here at last was an Absurdist play that merited close attention, since it was not boring or baffling, but 'insidiously exciting'. Examining the review over forty years later, it is easy to detect Hobson's excitement that the British theatre was on the verge of seismic upheavals:

> Mr Beckett has, of course, got it all wrong. Humanity worries very little over the Day of Judgement. It is far too busy hire-purchasing television sets, popping into three star restaurants, planting itself vineyards, building helicopters. *But he has got it wrong in a tremendous way*. And this is what matters. There is no need at all for a dramatist to philosophise rightly; he can leave that to the philosophers. But it is essential that if he philosophises wrongly, he should do so with swagger. Mr Beckett has any amount of swagger. A dusty, coarse, irreverent, pessimistic, violent swagger? Possibly. But the genuine thing, the real McCoy.

The lack of contemporary theatrical accoutrements – a lavish, naturalistic set, well-bred, recognisable characters, a linear development of plot and the reassurance of a comprehensible meaning – is the very basis of the appeal of this new type of play for Hobson.

He then sought to secure the play's reputation by stressing its relevance and theatricality, in direct contrast to the claim made by the anonymous critic of *The Times*:

> Vladimir and Estragon have each a kind of universality. They wear their rags with a difference. Vladimir is eternally hopeful; if Godot does not come this evening then he will certainly come tomorrow, or at the very latest the day after. Estragon, much troubled by his boots, is less confident. He thinks the game is not worth playing, and is ready to hang himself. Or so he says. But he does nothing. Like Vladimir he only talks. They both idly spin away the great top of their life in the vain expectation that some master whip will one day give it eternal vitality. Meanwhile their conversation often has the simplicity, in this case the delusive simplicity, of music hall cross-talk, now and again pierced with a shaft that seems for a second or so to touch the edge of truth's garment. It is bewildering. It is exasperating. It is insidiously exciting.

Hobson's conclusion to this review emphasises his desire to create an audience for Absurdist drama. It also manages to trump the memorable claim that the play is 'insidiously exciting' by combining an enthusiastic adjuration to visit the Arts Theatre with a colourful and original lyricism:

Go and see 'Waiting for Godot'. At the worst you will discover a curiosity, a four-leaved clover, a black tulip; at the best, something that will securely lodge in a corner of your mind for as long as you live.

Hobson's sentiments are overstated, but his achievement is that he recognised that in certain circumstances arguments need to be overstated in order to gain an audience. A grateful Beckett read the criticism with emotion and considered it to be courageous and touching.[11]

Whenever devotees of the British theatre think back to the gladiatorial struggle that was waged between Kenneth Tynan of the *Observer* and Harold Hobson of the *Sunday Times* in the second half of the fifties, a struggle that made London theatre seem so vibrant and exciting in an era struggling to emerge from post-war austerity (rationing only ended in 1954), they remember the rarity and significance of these two critical titans agreeing. Sunday 7 August 1955 was one such occasion. Tynan opened his review of *Waiting for Godot* with the sentence, 'A special virtue attaches to plays which remind the drama of how much it can do without and still exist' and the tenor of his review is that the work is not pretentious, as many of the first-night audience had found, but ground-breaking: 'It forced me to re-examine the rules which have hitherto governed the drama; and having done so, to pronounce them not elastic enough. It is validly new, and hence I declare myself, as the Spanish would say, *godoista*'.[12] What differentiated Hobson's attitude from Tynan's, however, was that Hobson recognised the play as the latest example of European Absurdist drama and that he was determined to champion it with a passionate intensity that verged upon magnificent obsession.

The Old Guard Miscalculates

The critical furore that *Waiting for Godot* generated, and, in particular, the contradictory critical notices of equally passionate intensity, ensured that the play was able to transfer to the West End's Criterion Theatre on 12 September 1955, such was the public desire to witness this theatrical curiosity. It still attracted considerable hostility, not least from the most successful playwright of the past ten years, Terence Rattigan. Since 1950, Rattigan had manufactured a number of sticks with which his critics could subsequently beat him once the taste for his understated, emotional works was eclipsed by a desire for social realism. In 1950, he had foolishly argued in the *New Statesman* that the plays of ideas were anachronistic:

From Aeschylus to Tennessee Williams the only theatre that has ever mattered is the theatre of character and narrative. ... I don't think that ideas per se, social, political or moral have a very important place in the theatre. They definitely take third place to character and narrative, anyway.[13]

Forever associated with H.M. Tennent's glamorous productions and exhibiting a public persona of wealth and upper-middle-class ease, this complacent assertion would leave him dangerously exposed.

The foolishness of this pronouncement was greatly exacerbated by Rattigan's creation, in the introduction to the second volume of his *Selected Plays* in 1953, of an infamous relative. Aunt Edna, originally conceived as Aunt Gladys, was the type of theatre-goer whom Rattigan felt it was dangerous to offend. He described her as being a 'nice, respectable, middle-class, middle-aged, maiden lady with time on her hands and the money to help her to pass it', and asserted that 'Aunt Edna, or at least her juvenile counterpart, was inside my creative brain' every time he wrote a play.[14] This disastrous invention not only misrepresented the achievement of plays such as *The Browning Version*, *Separate Tables* and *The Deep Blue Sea* but provided an irresistible target for those who would soon wish to portray Rattigan as the personification of all that was arid, class-bound and enervating between 1945 and 1956. Even as late as 1955, Rattigan was reviving the memory of Aunt Edna, tragically unaware of the cataclysm that was about to befall him. Having seen *Waiting for Godot* at the Criterion in October 1955, Rattigan penned an imaginary conversation between Aunt Edna and her nephew for another *New Statesman* article. 'How could I like the play', she wails,

> seeing that Mr Samuel Beckett plainly hates me so much that he's refused point blank to give me a play at all?. … Even a middlebrow like myself could have told him that a really good play had to be on two levels, an upper one, which I suppose you'd call symbolical, and a lower one, which is based on story and character. By writing on the upper level alone, all Mr Beckett has done is to produce one of these things that thirty years ago we used to call Experimental Theatre – you wouldn't remember that, of course, and that's a movement which led absolutely nowhere.'[15]

Rattigan did not deserve the systematic denigration that befell his work after the sudden change in theatrical taste after 1956, which led to his virtual banishment from the British theatre and his exile abroad as a scriptwriter, but such patronising and flippant observations made the impending personal catastrophe almost inevitable.

The commercial success of the transferred *Waiting for Godot* was, if anything, aided by such carping from the old guard. It was to play to packed houses until May 1956 and although it is customary to describe *Look Back in Anger* as the first dramatic phenomenon to become a media event,[16] this description more accurately belongs to *Waiting for Godot*.

By continuing to engage on its behalf, Hobson played no small part in ensuring that Beckett's play would come to be regarded as a seminal influence on twentieth-century British drama – and cunningly helped reposition himself on the critical spectrum as a champion of the avant-garde and an enthusiast for new writing.[17] That he did this in exciting rivalry with Kenneth Tynan contributed to the growing sense that the British theatre was on the brink of being revitalised. *Waiting for Godot* was the first step on the road to its reorientation.

The English Stage Company

Genesis

A potential force for revitalisation, the Old Vic Theatre School had enjoyed only a brief flicker of activity, yet one of the prime movers behind this aborted project was shortly to initiate one of the most fundamental shifts in post-war British theatre. Following his resignation from the Old Vic in May 1951, George Devine had gone freelance, directing five operas at Sadler's Wells and five plays for the Shakespeare Memorial Theatre between 1951 and 1955. In 1952 he met Tony Richardson, then a young television director, who persuaded Devine to appear in a production of Chekhov's *Curtain Down*.[18] It soon became apparent as their friendship grew that the two men shared a desire to create a programme of intelligent work for a committed public in a way that had been only sporadically possible in the West End up until then because of the conditions of commercial production, or had been accorded limited appeal by being relegated to ghetto status in the theatre clubs. Accordingly, they devised a nine-page memorandum that lamented the lack of an outlet for the 'modern movement in theatre',[19] highlighting yet again that many theatre practitioners were feeling in the early fifties that other art forms were evolving whilst theatre was stagnating. The dynamism of continental cinema was a consistent leitmotif in Tynan's laments, for example, while intriguing things were happening in ballet at Covent Garden and modern literature was seen to be developing in an exciting manner through the work of writers such as Philip Larkin, Kingsley Amis, Donald Davie, John Wain, Robert Conquest, Elizabeth Jennings and D.J. Enright. Although 'The Movement' (a term devised by J.D. Scott in 1954) began to be disavowed by its alleged members in 1957, A. Alvarez's introduction to his 1962 anthology of 'fifties poetry, tellingly entitled 'The New Poetry or Beyond the Gentility Principle',[20] points out how the anti-romantic, witty, sardonic and occasionally satirical tone of Movement poetry quickly set it apart from its immediate poetic predecessors. Whereas T.S. Eliot described himself as 'Anglo-Catholic in religion, royalist in politics and classicist in literature',[21] Alvarez identified the 'predominantly lower-middle class, or Labour, ideal of the Movement'.[22] Long-held values were beginning to be questioned, class assumptions challenged and the cosy political and cultural consensus brought about by increasing affluence subverted.

In addition to a manifesto for modern theatre, Devine and Richardson's memorandum contained a detailed budget, a proposed repertory, a list of twenty-one neglected writers (with only two being British, emphasising the two visionaries' task) and plans for the formation of a small, permanent company, training courses for actors and writers and a suggested first ten productions.

The need for a permanent base was paramount and with this in mind Devine began to negotiate with Alfred Esdaile, a retired music-hall entertainer, who managed the lease for the Royal Court Theatre, located in Sloane Square at the top of the King's Road. Devine wanted a three-year tenancy for the venue, which had seen three brilliant years of activity between 1904 and 1907 when Harley Granville Barker had helped establish the reputation of G.B. Shaw, but negotiations were protracted. A series of developments soon convinced Esdaile that the market value of the theatre could be very high. The Arts Council approved Devine's plan (which lent status rather than money, the Arts Council budget being only £820,000 for the whole country in 1956[23]); Devine convinced Anthony Quayle that the Royal Court could become an innovative, contemporary and non-Shakespearean base for the Shakespeare Memorial Theatre (vital if Stratford were to counter the likely siting of a new national theatre at the Old Vic); and the current production at the theatre, Laurier Lister's revue, *Airs on a Shoestring*, proved to be unexpectedly long-running and profitable. Consequently, in the autumn of 1953, Lister demanded £70,000 for the tenancy – an impossible sum and a 'bitter blow'[24] to Devine.

The whole project might have foundered there, were it not for the fact that a wholly separate group of people had also been attempting to challenge the West End hegemony. The poet and playwright Ronald Duncan had launched the Taw and Torridge Festival in Devon in 1953, together with the composer Benjamin Britten, J.E. Blacksell and Lord Harewood, with the modest aim of enabling some of its productions to tour other arts festivals and perhaps stop off briefly in London. Funding, as ever, was the problem, and Blacksell suggested that a wealthy Manchester businessman, Neville Blond, be approached about becoming the chairman of the newly formed English Stage Company (ESC). Blond, a shrewd negotiator, agreed in November 1954 with the proviso that a permanent London base be sought, and he immediately approached Esdaile and persuaded him to grant the ESC the tenancy of another one of his theatres, the Kingsway.

At this point, the ten-man board required an artistic director, and Oscar Lewenstein, Esdaile's General Manager and a former member of the Unity Theatre movement, recalled Devine's 1953 project. After a meeting between Duncan and Devine, it was agreed in March 1955 to offer the post to Devine at a salary of £1,500 per annum, Devine's only stipulation being that Richardson be made his associate director.

The turnaround in Devine's hopes for the project had been as swift as it was unexpected, and the helter-skelter pace continued. It quickly became apparent that the Kingsway was actually unsuitable, given the cost of repairing the damage to it caused by the Blitz and the difficulty of obtaining planning permission for the work. Ironically, the ESC turned back to the Royal Court, a move facilitated by Esdaile's membership of the board, and Devine was able to hold preliminary auditions in August 1955 for the new company.

The ethos that Devine imbued in the ESC was simple: he believed in the supremacy of the writer and he wanted to re-position London theatre away from the West End's disengagement with important contemporary issues. Looking back, he observed that there was no shortage of issues to agitate and concern the ordinary theatre-goer:

> There had been drastic political and social changes all around us; the new Prosperity State was more than suspect, both political parties looked the same. No man or woman of feeling who was not wearing blinkers could not but feel profoundly disturbed.[25]

It is little surprise, given these sentiments, that he was to find such an active and effective champion in Kenneth Tynan. His beliefs were further reinforced on the tour of Noguchi's *Lear* between September and December 1955, when he visited the Hebbel Theater in Berlin and was able to meet Bertolt Brecht and Helene Weigel. Not only did Devine secure permission to stage *The Good Woman of Setzuan* – one of the earliest performances of a Brechtian play by an English company – but he was able to gauge the extent to which Brecht and the Berliner Ensemble had created a 'people's theatre', observing that 'Brecht's theatre is above all a theatre of its time, of its place, and of its nation. This is its exemplary value'.[26] It would be fallacious to state that subsequent Royal Court practice under Devine was deeply indebted to the Brechtian model (many of Devine's early ideas had been formulated before his contact with Brecht), but in its desire to challenge and disrupt conventional expectations, its need to question the contemporary cultural hegemony and its artistic and technical innovation, the ESC shared Brecht's aspirations.

With the creation of the company and the formulation of its first season, Devine displayed his renowned pragmatism. By opening with a work by a novelist, Angus Wilson's *The Mulberry Bush* (1956), and choosing to deploy the potentially controversial *Look Back in Anger* as the third production (for the rights of which he had paid £325), he was able to reassure the more timid members of his board, whilst remaining true to his own hopes for the company. The twenty-two actors and actresses that he gathered together for the first season were chosen with surprisingly little bias towards the Old Vic Theatre School (only Joan Plowright and Sheila Ballantine had served that apprenticeship) because Richardson felt the style of such graduates to be generally unsuited to realistic theatre.[27] The group was young and vibrant, however, and included Robert Stephens, Kenneth Haigh and Alan Bates, in addition to Plowright and Ballantine. Devine also strove hard to dissolve the age-old barriers between artistic and technical staff – still very much apparent in the hierarchy of an H.M. Tennent production – leading actors into the workshops for parties, when time permitted, or arranging picnics at which company members could mix together.

One further unorthodox (and, of course, prudent) policy was the payment of wages that at their highest (£25 per week) represented barely half the West End average. Although star performers were sometimes brought in, many performers were to speak of the invaluable nature of the Royal Court experience as a compensation for the low financial reward, and it is a testimony to this process that so many performers were repeatedly drawn to the ESC. Comparable circumstances had necessitated a similar policy for Lilian Baylis at the Old Vic before the war, with equally beneficial results.

The gulf between the financial scale of a Royal Court production and a blockbuster West End one is apparent when one examines the recently discovered first-year production costs of the H.M. Tennent musical, Leonard Bernstein's *West Side Story*, which opened on 12 December 1958. Whereas the ESC could spare at most £25 per week for its highest paid actors, in its first year alone *West Side Story* devoured £10,755 for scenery, £5,302 for costumes, £5,881 for hotel accommodation and £8,050 in 'Rehearsal Expenses'.[28] Such lavish expenditure on a musical simply seemed to generate more money, however – the profit for the fourth year of the Drury Lane run of *My Fair Lady* (April 1961 to March 1962) was £138,381. How would the ESC be able to compete?

Contrary to received opinion, the story of the company's first season at the Court is not one of instantaneous commercial and popular success following the première of *Look Back in Anger* on 8 May 1956. The debut work, Angus Wilson's *The Mulberry Bush*, which had already been seen in Bristol, attracted several disappointing notices following its first night on 2 April 1956. Philip Hope-Wallace of the *Manchester Guardian* spoke of 'a rather diffident start' to the project[29] and the *Illustrated London News* echoed many by observing that the play seemed untheatrical and was 'better as a novel'.[30] The effect on the box office was marked and this seemed an inauspicious omen. Although the second work to enter the repertory a week later, Arthur Miller's *The Crucible* was a much finer play and received a more enthusiastic critical response, ticket sales were equally patchy. The play, inspired by the political witch-hunts of Senator McCarthy in the early fifties, had also been seen previously in Bristol (in 1954), and this might partially explain why this production, too, performed to only forty-five per cent capacity. To compound the financial difficulties, Devine had been forced during the rehearsal period to reinstate a character that he had cut – that of Giles Corey – at the instigation of the playwright, who had threatened from New York to have the play withdrawn if his wishes were not followed. Limited funds, expedient casting decisions, simple, inexpensive sets and exciting performances by complete newcomers – the *Sunday Express* was already remarking on Joan Plowright's 'splendid performance' in *The Crucible*[31] – this atmosphere of living on the edge was to permeate the company's first season at the Court.

Look Back in Anger

The third play to enter the repertory was to be directed by Tony Richardson and needed to be a success. In August 1955, Devine had placed an advert in the *Stage* stating that the ESC had been formed with the object of producing new plays, and particularly new plays by new writers. John Osborne, an intermittently employed repertory actor then living on a house-boat tied up near Chiswick, had in June completed the script of a play (variously titled 'Farewell to Anger', 'Angry Man', 'Man in a Rage', 'Bargain from Strength', 'Close the Cage Behind You' and 'My Blood is a Mile High'),[32] which he had so far unsuccessfully tried to place with several agents. Kitty Black, for example, then the principal play reader for the literary agents Curtis Brown and, significantly, a previous reader for Tennent's, prefaced her rejection with the comment that 'I feel like the headmistress of a large school in which I have to tell its most promising pupil that he must think again'.[33] *Look Back in Anger*, however promising, simply did not fit the Tennent formula.

Within days of sending the script in response to the advert, Osborne received a letter from the ESC offering twenty-five pounds to secure an option on the play and suggesting a meeting on the house-boat between Devine and the playwright. Over 750 scripts had been sent to Devine and Richardson, but Osborne's was the only one that intrigued both the directors: '[George] read three pages and then brought it upstairs. "Look at this", he said. "This might be interesting."'[34]

In an era in which it was considered to be slightly daring to use garlic, travel abroad or wear a duffle coat, it was not surprising that many of *Look Back in Anger*'s unorthodoxies, which admittedly can appear tame, jejune and even sexist forty years on, provoked equal measures of admiration and disapproval. The opening curtain rose to an unfamiliar scene of cramped, suburban shabbiness (gone was the uncluttered stage of the first two productions), with Alison Porter performing the most mundane of tasks – the ironing. One contemporary witness, Bernice Coupe, remembered that the first shock of the evening was the depressing nature of the Porters' flat, and she was particularly disconcerted by the sight of the ironing-board to which Alison seemed chained – an object which belonged in the home and certainly not in the theatre.[35]

Another early surprise was the fact that the actors were not articulating in politely strangulated accents, but speaking in a variety of regional tones that had previously been the preserve of maids, bobbies and artisans. A recording of Richard Burton playing the film role of Jimmy Porter still has the power to shock with the violent intensity of the delivery, the un-mellifluous rasp of the accusations and the passionate unpredictability of his frequent outbursts. For many people in the fifties, where a well-formulated diction was proof positive of intelligence, Jimmy Porter's combination of volubility, accent and intellectual prowess was very hard to accept, and this challenge to contemporary assumptions was compounded by the sheer irreverence of many of Jimmy's attacks. Whether the target was J.B. Priestley, likened to Alison's Daddy, 'still casting well-fed glances back to the Edwardian twilight from his comfortable, disenfranchised wilderness',[36] or senseless, upper-class ambition, symbolised by Alison's brother, Nigel, variously described as 'the straight-backed, chinless wonder from Sandhurst' and 'the platitude from Outer Space',[37] it was difficult to perceive which aspect of Jimmy's critique should be construed as the more heterodox: the passionate and implicitly left-wing nature of the attack, or the confident and riveting new idiom in which it was formulated. To many, in particular the young and the university-educated, this depiction of a re-invigorated, eloquent, liberal conscience at work was the revelation they had been waiting for. Frustrated by the mental atrophy that they discerned in British society, they were thrilled by Jimmy Porter's clarion call to rebellion, be it in his exasperation at British docility ('Nobody thinks, nobody cares. No beliefs, no convictions and no enthusiasm'[38]), his dangerously radical toying with taboos –

> I've just about had enough of this 'expense of spirit' lark, as far as women are concerned. Honestly, it's enough to make you become a scoutmaster or something, isn't it? Sometimes I almost envy old Gide and the Greek Chorus boys. Oh, I'm not saying that it mustn't be hell for them a lot of the time. But, at least, they do seem to have a cause[39]

– or in his central complaint, that intelligent people such as himself had no opportunity to contribute to society:

> There aren't any good, brave causes left. If the big bang does come, and we all get killed off, it won't be in aid of the old-fashioned, grand design. It'll just be for the Brave-New-nothing-very-much-thank-you. About as pointless and inglorious as stepping in front of a bus. No, there's nothing left for it, me boy, but to let yourself be butchered by the women.[40]

The hyperbole of Jimmy's last sentence is typical of Osborne's technique: a serious point is pricked by exaggeration, raising the question as to whether there is more to the work than a passionate denunciation of society's failings. This fine linguistic distinction was lost by many in the immediate critical reaction that greeted a play that broke with the timidity of the recent British theatrical past. The journalist Edward Pearce, then a young student, remembers how disappointing the reality of post-war life had proved to be with the onset of fifties affluence and consensus, compared to the excitement of the pre-war causes that he had read about in his text books. Everything had 'settled down into a blancmange-like existence of common sense, tolerance and half-a-grain change' and he, too, longed for a good, brave cause – 'preferably not to die for, but to get paid for' – as well as 'the therapy of conflict'.[41] *Look Back in Anger* was significant because it represented such a break with the past and suggested that the old world was now over. Even Rattigan, in yet another personally disastrous comment, inadvertently recognised this. Confronted by a reporter from the *Daily Express* during the interval of the first night, he claimed that Osborne was saying 'Look, Ma, I'm not Terence Rattigan'.[42] The conventionality of its form merely accentuated the revolutionary nature of its content – the speaking from the heart, the escape from emotional inhibition, the passionate outbursts – and it was the generational conflict that the work seemed to incite that attracted the most interest after the première of the work on 8 May 1956.

The first-night reaction to *Look Back in Anger* contained in the daily newspapers, however, was mixed. Patrick Gibbs in the *Daily Telegraph* claimed that Jimmy Porter was 'a character who should have gone to a psychiatrist rather than have come to a dramatist',[43] whereas John Barber of the *Daily Express* was attracted to the work because the hero was 'like thousands of young Londoners today': the play itself was 'intense, angry, feverish, undisciplined. It is even crazy. But it is young, young, young'.[44] Colin Wilson voiced a common view when he wrote in the *Daily Mail* that Osborne was a good dramatist who had somehow written the wrong play,[45] and even Milton Shulman of the *Evening Standard*, who was unable to share John Barber's enthusiasm, feeling that the work was 'a self-pitying snivel' and a failure because of 'its inability to be coherent about its despair', conceded that 'When he stops being angry – or when he lets us in on what he is being angry about – he may write a very good play'.[46] Good try, better luck next time, seemed to be the general consensus. Reviews such as these, that considered the work to be significant, but not quite complete, were not 'good box-office'.

There is a pertinent irony to 'the desultory talk of being "saved by the Sundays"'[47] which, Osborne relates in the second volume of his autobiography, *Almost A Gentleman*, was passing round the ESC after the appearance of the daily reviews, since the play itself in the opening scene presented the Sunday newspapers as symptoms of the prevailing intellectual paralysis. Osborne recalls that at the time he considered both the *Sunday Times* and the *Observer* to have been equally obsessed with anything French (clearly alluding to Hobson's obsession with Anouilh, Ionesco and Beckett):

> For as long as I could remember the literary and academic classes seemed to have been tyrannized by the French. The 'posh papers' every Sunday blubbered with self-abasement in the face of the bombast of the French language and its absurd posture as the torch-bearer of Logic, which apparently was something to which no one in these islands had access. Certain writers gave the impression that it was downright indelicate to write in English at all, which is why the *Sunday Times* and the *Observer* were peppered with italics until they sometimes looked like linguistic lace curtains.[48]

Given this dim view of the intellectual judgement of the 'posh papers', it seems that to have expected the salvation of so English and contemporary a play from such devotees of the French was a rather desperate exercise in keeping the company's hopes up. Osborne may have been frustrated by these publications' Francophilia, but Jimmy Porter still retained a latent respect for their writing. Although he mocks the pretentious excesses of what are clearly the *Sunday Times* and the *Observer* – 'I've just read three whole columns on the English Novel. Half of it's in French. Do the Sunday newspapers make you feel ignorant?'[49] – both he and Cliff are first seen 'sprawled way out beyond the newspapers which hide the rest of them from sight', and Jimmy evidently recognises the social implications of adhering to the religious ritual of working one's way through the Sunday papers:

> JIMMY: Haven't you read the other posh paper yet?
> CLIFF: Which?
> JIMMY: Well, there are only two posh papers on a Sunday – the one you're reading, and this one.[50]

As successive commentators have pointed out, there is a latent streak of respect for certain English institutions and an element of nostalgia running through this ostensibly revolutionary work. John Osborne himself, for all his deprecation of these two papers, was certainly interested in their views when he made his way to a newsagent in Mortlake the following Sunday and sat reading their verdicts on 'a corporation bench in the bright May early morning sunshine'.[51] He was convinced before he had read them that the previous evening's performance of *Look Back in Anger* was destined to be its last.

'It is the best young play of its decade' (Kenneth Tynan, 'The Voice of the Young', *Observer*, 13 May 1956); '… he is a writer of outstanding promise' (Harold Hobson, 'A New Author', *Sunday Times*, 13 May 1956). Cheerfully brushing aside Jimmy Porter's critique of their publications – Hobson perceptively wrote that the hero possesses 'a sort of admiring hatred' of the 'posh papers' – the two most influential theatre critics were united in their admiration for this third production of the ESC. For Tynan, *Look Back in Anger* was 'a minor miracle' in that it displayed qualities that

> one had despaired of ever seeing on the stage – the drift towards anarchy, the instinctive leftishness, the automatic rejection of 'official' attitudes, the surrealist sense of humour … the casual promiscuity, the sense of lacking a crusade worth fighting for and, underlying all these, the determination that no one who dies shall go unmourned.

It challenged an assumption encapsulated in Somerset Maugham's verdict that state–aided university students were scum (Tynan memorably ends his first paragraph with the warning that *Look Back in Anger* 'is all scum and a mile wide'); it contained a hero who was not passive and acquiescent but 'simply and abundantly alive'; it broke with a sterile theatrical past and bore testimony to 'that rarest of dramatic phenomena, the act of original creation'; it dramatised the dilemma of the eloquent young – 'The Porters of our time deplore the tyranny of 'good taste' and refuse to accept 'emotional' as a term of abuse; they are classless, and they are also leaderless'; and it offered the prospect of a dramatist to lead this alienated class out of the wilderness – 'Mr Osborne is their first spokesman in the London theatre.'

Quite simply, Tynan had discovered the antithesis of the much-loathed Loamshire play, and he overstates his case with a passion and plausibility that are reminiscent of Hobson's delight in discovering *Waiting for Godot*. Tynan's concluding comments are a deliberate challenge to all those who considered themselves to be modern and forward-looking:

> I agree that 'Look Back in Anger' is likely to remain a minority taste. What matters, however, is the size of the minority. I estimate it at roughly 6,733,000, which is the number of people in this country between the ages of twenty and thirty. And this figure will doubtlessly be swelled by refugees from other age-groups who are curious to know precisely what the contemporary young pup is thinking and feeling. I doubt if I could love anyone who did not wish to see 'Look Back in Anger'.

Such startlingly committed writing helped launch the *Look Back in Anger* bandwagon, and managed to conceal the embarrassing whimsy of the play's ending.[52] Tynan, the politically committed critic, felt that he had come across the first post-war, political playwright who had correctly identified the plight of the alienated young. And he was British.

The *Look Back in Anger* phenomenon derived its momentum from many sources. Firstly, there was the almost instantaneous identification by the media of a group of young, committed writers dedicated to challenging the status quo, handily (and somewhat artificially) gathered together under the title of 'Angry Young Men' (a term brilliantly coined by a Royal Court publicist). The public aggressiveness of this group, either energetically berating journalists or denigrating previously unsullied icons, such as when Osborne likened the Royal Family to a gold tooth in a mouthful of decay,[53] helped keep the group in the public eye. Allied to this was the utilisation of other cultural movements by young people as ways of disrupting consensus and challenging notions of respect (with all its class and generational implications). Most important among these movements was rock and roll (with its anthem, Bill Haley's 'Rock Around the Clock', leading to riots in cinemas on its release in May 1955), followed by fashion (with Teddy Boys appropriating the formerly sedate Edwardian jacket as their call-sign and adding drainpipe trousers as a visible statement of independence) and alternative, irreverent comedy (typified by the television shows of Tony Hancock, which explored suburban angst, a topic previously considered too mundane for mirth). Literary culture, too, soon became, in the words of Stephen Lacey, 'imbued with a sense of loss, of disillusion with the immediate past and a loathing of the material priorities of a newly affluent Britain',[54] emotions that *Look Back in Anger* was perceived to have unleashed. There was also now the possibility that a new, untapped audience might decide to turn to drama and a relief that, at last, an indigenous playwright had written something that could start to challenge the notion that only the French could write stimulating works on contemporary dilemmas.

The phenomenon was not instantaneous, however. Tynan's review was tremendous publicity, but it was not until the BBC televised an extract on 16 October 1956, viewed by an estimated five million people, that box-office takings dramatically increased, from £900 to £1,700 per week.[55] On 28 November, the play was televised at peak viewing by ITV, helping to cement its notoriety and giving the widest possible publicity to the work of the ESC, thus marking the beginning of a relationship between television and the stage which would not always be so symbiotic.

Separate Tables and the Lord Chamberlain's Secret Memorandum

Jimmy Porter was the most obvious and memorable manifestation of the new theatrical era of 1956, but there were other, less visible indications that playwrights were beginning to sense a new freedom to present previously unacceptable subject-matter. In 1954, a Terence Rattigan double-bill, *Separate Tables* and *Table Number Seven* had been produced at the St James's Theatre, with the second play attracting attention for its discreet coded meaning. In this piece, the formidable Mrs Railton-Bell, a sanctimonious and judgemental resident of the Beauregard Hotel in Bournemouth (note the symbolic name of the residence), discovers that a fellow resident, Major Pollock, has been convicted of pestering a woman in a local cinema and is masquerading behind bogus military honours. She endeavours to marshal the other residents behind her, with a view to ejecting him from the hotel for his 'offence of a disgusting nature' but, after a climactic confrontation between her daughter Sibyl and the Major, where they discover a mutual apprehensiveness about social contact, sex and the world in general, together with a compassionate demonstration of support from fellow residents, the Major derives the strength to stay.

Emotionally charged, tightly structured and full of the lonely, gentle and empathetic characters that pervade all his plays, this is Rattigan's work at its finest (and often most maligned). The decision of the Major to stay is presented in an understated manner, in keeping with the restraint demanded of the period, but it is also a highly dramatic moment, as is the eventual repudiation of Mrs Railton-Bell. The three-act piece could be read as a satire on the emotional constriction of fifties Britain, for the scarcely plausible nature of the Major's crime (the one fault of the piece) certainly implies that the work is about more than a claustrophobic dining-room for middle-class pensioners. In August 1956, Rattigan made this explicit in a letter to the American producer of *Separate Tables*, Robert Whitehead. He expressed the wish that the Major's actual 'offence' – approaching men in a cinema for companionship and possibly sex – be portrayed honestly in the United States (an impossibility in the United Kingdom, given the Lord Chamberlain's absolute ban on the mention of homosexuality): 'The play as I had originally conceived it concerned the effect on a collection of highly conventional people of the discovery that one of their members was a sexual deviant,' with the main theme being 'obviously homosexuality'.[56]

Whitehead's reply was lukewarm, however, and he conveyed the fear that public opinion, in his view, was not as sufficiently advanced as Rattigan believed. The producer was of the opinion that the subject was already something of a cliché on the Broadway stage, that critics had perceived the code in the work and that the Major might be linked to John Gielgud, who had been arrested for soliciting in 1953: not an inducement to buy tickets if taken altogether. Rattigan's own description of the Major as 'a sexual deviant' reveals a continuing discomfort about his own sexuality, but even in this most taboo of areas there would shortly be movement.

Following an increasing number of works that alluded to same-sex relationships, the Wolfenden report advocating the decriminalisation of homosexuality (1957), greater public discussion of the topic, and even plays that contained openly homosexual characters, such as Geoff in Shelagh Delaney's *A Taste of Honey* (which had actually been written by the eighteen-year-old Delaney as a response to the attitude to homosexuality evident in Rattigan's insipid *Variation on a Theme* of the same year), the Lord Chamberlain issued a memorandum to his readers that attempted to clarify the situation:

I have decided to make a change in the policy of the censorship, and I think it desirable to place on record as clearly as possible the nature of the change so that all concerned may be fully aware of it.

First, the reason behind this change. For some time the subject of homosexuality has been so widely debated, written about and talked about, that it is no longer justifiable to continue the strict exclusion of this subject from the Stage. I do not regret the policy of strict exclusion which has been continued up to now, and I think it has been to the public good. Nevertheless, now that it has become a topic of almost everyday conversation, its exclusion from the Stage can no longer be defended as a reasonable course, even when account is taken of the more effective persuasion which the living Stage can exercise as compared with the written word. I therefore propose to allow plays which make a serious and sincere attempt to deal with the subject. It will follow also that references in other plays will be allowed to the subject which appear necessary to the dialogue or the plot, and which are not salacious or offensive. Licences will continue to be refused for plays which are exploitations of the subject rather than contributions to the problem; and similarly references to the subject which are unnecessary or have merely an exploitation value will be disallowed.[57]

Such attempts to refine the criteria for censorship merely illustrated the unwieldy nature of the mechanism and would further illustrate the indefensibility of the Lord Chamberlain's powers over the theatre in a democratic society.

For Terence Rattigan, though, the change came too late to salvage his career. Savaged for being the symbol of the old order, appearing anaemic when juxtaposed against the vibrancy of the Angry Young Men and crucified by Tynan for his embodiment of upper middle-class values – 'I didn't spot much real acting going on, but then there wasn't much reality there to begin with'[58] – the disaster of *Variation on a Theme* confirmed that his style of theatre had been eclipsed by that of the Royal Court and the Theatre Royal, Stratford East. Embittered and depressed, he escaped into self-imposed exile in Bermuda, leaving his biographer, Geoffrey Wansell, to conjecture that if he had forced the redrafting of Major Pollock's real 'offence' into the 1956 American production of *Table Number Seven*, it 'could have transformed his reputation as a dramatist overnight'.[59]

Theatre Workshop

Genesis

If sex and sexuality were still problematic topics in 1956, socially didactic and politically acerbic productions became increasingly visible and were by no means the exclusive preserve of the English Stage Company.

The enthusiasm which greeted Theatre Workshop's production of Brendan Behan's *The Quare Fellow* at the Theatre Royal, Stratford East on 24 May 1956, barely two weeks after the arrival of *Look Back in Anger*, lent further credence to the view that British theatre was undergoing a meaningful shift. Before examining *The Quare Fellow*, however, it is necessary to consider the genesis of this extraordinary group of theatre practitioners, both to dispel the enduring notion that this was their first production of note,[60] and to investigate their methodology, so at odds with contemporaneous West End practice.

The origins of the company can be traced back to pre-war Salford, a manufacturing and cotton conurbation to the north and west of Manchester, when Ewan MacColl (then known as Jimmie Miller) joined the Clarion Players in 1929 to perform in Upton Sinclair's *Singing Jailbirds*. At this time, the depression of the late 1920s was beginning to cause mass unemployment in Britain, and MacColl quickly felt that if the old subject-matter could be replaced by socially relevant topics and the format of drama could break the tyranny of the proscenium arch, the theatre could aid in the political education of local workers:

> We felt that the heroes of the theatre had to change, that conflict had to be brought back. That the theatre had to reflect what was happening immediately around us, and the problems of a society in the throes of economic crisis, with a third of the working population unemployed.[61]

So, in 1931, an agitprop group was formed and took the name 'The Red Megaphones', with the aim of performing street theatre to groups of striking factory workers and their families, and thereby illustrating the culpability of capitalism for the dire state of poverty that many of their street audience endured. The essence of politically didactic street theatre is flexibility (speed), precision of message (quick-wittedness), simplicity of presentation (obstinacy) and the ability to improvise, and, in many ways, these performance criteria remained the bedrock of the later Theatre Workshop. A further antecedent emerged in 1933 when MacColl became convinced of the need for proper training for the group of performers. Research into the theories of Adolphe Appia, the Swiss theorist and designer, persuaded him that non-naturalistic and symbolic sets, creative lighting designs and a harmony of music and action should all lead to a synthesis of the arts in the ideal theatrical performance.[62]

The arrival of Joan Littlewood in Manchester in 1934, twenty years old, highly talented and alienated by her training at the Royal Academy of Dramatic Art (RADA) (she 'thought the place was a waste of time'[63]), provided MacColl with a new and inspirational collaborator. By this time the group had become the 'Theatre of Action' and issued its own overtly political manifesto:

> The Theatre of Action realises that the very class which plays the chief part in contemporary history – the class upon which the prevention of war and the defeat of reaction solely depends – is debarred from expression in the present day theatre. This theatre will perform, mainly in working-class districts, plays which express the life and struggles of the workers. Politics, in its fullest sense, means the affairs of the people. In this sense, the plays done will be political.[64]

The all-inclusive nature of the intended company (rejecting the hierarchy of a West End theatre with a stage hand on the lowest level and the star performer at the pinnacle) again adumbrates the egalitarian practices of Theatre Workshop at its heyday and provides an alternative model to the hegemony of Binkie Beaumont and similar producers.

For the remainder of the thirties the group of performers experimented with writing, staging, lighting and designing, increasingly moving into indoor venues as news of their activities spread through Manchester and the north. MacColl and Littlewood, who married in 1936, were able to support themselves through radio work for the BBC, and a large-scale production of Hans Schlumberg's anti-war play, *Miracle at Verdun*, produced in the Lesser Free Trade Hall in the same year, testified to Littlewood's organisational capabilities as well as her genius for motivating disparate groups of amateur performers. To capitalise on this production's success, the group continued its inexorable evolution by adopting another new name, Theatre Union, and another new manifesto, which, whilst retaining the ethos of social awareness, crucially reorientated the company away from a specifically political purpose to a more focused theatrical one:

> The theatre must face up to the problems of the time; it cannot ignore the poverty and human suffering which increases every day. It cannot, with sincerity, close its eyes to the disasters of its time. Means Test suicides, wars, fascism and the million sordid accidents reported in the daily press. If the theatre of to-day would reach the heights achieved four thousand years ago in Greece and four hundred years ago in Elizabethan England it must face up to such problems. To those who say that such affairs are not the concern of the theatre or that the theatre should confine itself to treading paths of 'beauty' or 'dignity' we would say 'Read Shakespeare, Marlowe, Webster, Sophocles, Aeschylus, Aristophanes, Calderon, Molière, Lope-de-Vega, Schiller and the rest'.

This list of great playwrights alone testifies to the amount of research and training which the group members had been undergoing in the preceding years, and looks forward to the successful productions of revitalised classics that Theatre Workshop were to enjoy in the mid-fifties. By 1942, the experimentation had to cease altogether, however, given the frequency with which company members were called up for war service, although contact between individuals was sustained.

The final transmutation of the group's name occurred towards the end of the war, when Joan Littlewood sent out letters in March 1945 to various members of the old group, urging their reformulation under the title Theatre Workshop. The name now possesses tremendous resonance for the history of post-war theatre, but its discovery, according to Littlewood, was as spontaneous and collaborative as so much of its later work:

> 'What are we calling our theatre?' asked Howard. 'When it's christened it's born.'
> 'Well, we've had Action and Union.'
> Someone hit the right note. I wrote it across my diary: 'The Workshop'. A theatre, a workshop? Everyone made fun of it, but years after, 'Workshops' sprang up all over the place.[65]

The years immediately following the war comprised more financial destitution, one-night stands around the country and ingenious attempts to marry theatricality to social comment. The 1946 touring production of MacColl's *Uranium 235*, with its interrogation of the morality behind the dropping of the atomic bombs on Japan, was firmly in keeping with Theatre Workshop's rationale as a 'theatre with a powerful social dynamic',[66] as was its desire to treat the process of mounting a theatrical production as a collaborative, work-in-progress exercise, with the script as a fluid creation rather than a fixed entity. The writing of the script called for MacColl to undergo a period of education (a leitmotif running through all Workshop productions), with two company members giving him 'a crash course in Atomic Physics'.[67] The structure of the work needed to be episodic to contain the didactic, pacifist slant:

> You needed to explain the whole history of Atomic Energy. So I did this; in many scenes, in a whole series of styles. Energy as a gang boss in a Hollywood gangster movie, Max Planck and Niels Bohr explaining the quantum theory as a couple of knockabout comics with phoney German accents. Einstein as a comic figure.[68]

Company members were required to play many roles (Howard Goorney

took eight), make numerous costume changes (there were fifty seven characters) and adapt to several, self-reflexive scenes (fifteen altogether). Joan
Littlewood, a multi-talented performer in her own right, established
classes in movement and voice work, and a sense of company loyalty,
forged in adverse financial circumstances, grew up, but it was clear that by
1953, following a succession of bases in Kendal, Manchester and Glasgow
and a number of acclaimed, but financially unrewarding tours overseas,
only a permanent home could sustain the group's continued existence. It
was then that Theatre Workshop was offered the lease of the Theatre
Royal, Stratford East.

Reinterpretation of Classics

The Theatre Royal was located in a deprived part of the East End of
London, not very far from the West End theatres, but a metaphorical million miles away from their lavish milieu and narrow outlook. This was no
disincentive to the company, however, since it positively relished the
prospect of creating a loyal, local working-class audience for its shows.
This aspiration was only partially to be achieved even in its heyday, though,
with the bulk of its audience travelling from outside the borough to discover Theatre Workshop's appeal, and the refusal of West Ham council to
provide it with a grant on its arrival in 1953 pointing ominously to the
funding crises that were continually to beset the company during its most
notable period, 1953 to 1963. Indeed, the disproportion in the Arts Council grants finally awarded to Theatre Workshop and the English Stage
Company during this period is plainly apparent in the table below,[69] and
raises the question as to whether more prescient funding decisions, not
influenced by the Establishment, could have prevented the group's virtual
dissolution in 1963:

Financial Year	Theatre Workshop	ESC
1954/55	£150	
1955/56	£500	
1956/57	£500	
1957/58	£1,000	
1958/59	£1,000	£5,500
1959/60	£1,000	£5,000
1960/61	£2,000	£8,000
1961/62	£2,000	£8,000
1962/63	£3,000	£20,000

In 1953, the 'make do and mend' philosophy of the company was sufficient to sustain it. Whatever practical skills company members possessed
were utilised in renovating the auditorium and stage and most of the company slept in the theatre after the day's manual labour; local traders,
amused and intrigued by these strolling players, donated materials, with
which the theatre was patched up, and food; Gerry Raffles, Joan Littlewood's resourceful and adored partner – and the indispensable general
manager of Theatre Workshop, who probably single-handedly kept the
company afloat through his financial acumen – always seemed to find a
tiny amount of money to avert the almost daily financial disaster; and in
between all this community activity, there was still time for rehearsals conducted by Joan Littlewood:

> And what rehearsals! I have never known anything like them, before or
> since. Our release from the slogging routine of one-night stands – load,
> unload, rig, warm up, perform, de-rig, unload – gave us more time and
> energy for our real work. We still shouldered the labour between us –
> repairing seats, curtains and carpets, cleaning out the boiler-room, cel-
> lars, urinal; hand-printing posters, distributing them, sticking them
> up in the tube station, when we could, and fly-posting all over Strat-
> ford. We made the sets, props, costumes and meals and still found
> time to read and train – and we were lucky if we received three pounds
> a week.[70]

If George Devine's English Stage Company at the Royal Court was a 'writers' theatre', Joan Littlewood's Theatre Workshop at Stratford East on the
other side of town was a practitioners' one. Collaboration was the name of
the game. Rehearsals served as voyages of discovery, where the script
could be adapted, improvised or discarded by accomplished performers
such as Harry H. Corbett, Avis Bunnage, Frances Cuka and Barbara
Windsor under the guidance of Joan Littlewood herself. Designers were
treated as equal partners in the process, with Sean Kenny (later to design
the trend-setting multi-purpose stage machinery in *Oliver!*) and John Bury
(a subsequent head of design at the National Theatre) producing innovative, non-naturalistic sets to take into account the evolutionary nature of
rehearsals. Writers, too, were expected to be malleable, and this has
inevitably led to disputes as to authorship, particularly in the case of
Shelagh Delaney's *A Taste of Honey* (1958): how far, for example, did the
final version reflect the original script as written by the eighteen-year-old
from Salford in 1958? Even in 1994, Joan Littlewood was able to annoy
the writer when she wrote in her autobiography that during the first run 'I
don't think [Shelagh] noticed the difference between her draft and the

company's adaptation'.[71] The primacy of the writer in the theatrical process was not important to Theatre Workshop.

The inevitable comparisons that these two companies on the East and West fringes of London attracted as initiators of the new spirit in British theatre – united by a desire to inculcate new practices and draw inspiration from the contemporaneous, but with distinct theatrical methodologies – added considerably to the sense of excitement of the period, but it is important to note that Theatre Workshop predated the ESC in London by three years. It first came to national prominence with innovative productions of the Elizabethan and Jacobean classics, *Arden of Faversham*, *Volpone* and *Richard II*. Howard Goorney, a member of Theatre Workshop, argues that the 'concentrated period of training, rehearsing and playing' – thirty-six plays were performed in the first two years – made the 1954/55 season and the year 1956 the vintage period at Stratford East.[72]

Theatre Workshop's practice of repertory performances, with a new production every two weeks, utilitarian production values (*Arden of Faversham* and *Volpone* were both costumed for £10[73]) and salaries that the company could afford (£2 per week in 1953/4, rising to £4 in 1955[74]) foreshadows George Devine's project. This offers further confirmation that the reorientation of post-war drama did not begin with a 'big-bang' of 'Anger'.

The Theatre Workshop production of *Richard II* in January 1955 initially attracted the attention of the critics because it offered a neat point of reference for the Old Vic version of the play that was running simultaneously and starred John Neville as the doomed king. Howard Goorney claims that the general consensus was that the Old Vic won on points, but for Harold Hobson there was little doubt which was the more intriguing production:

> There were two new productions of 'Richard II' in London last week, one at the Old Vic, the other given by Theatre Workshop in the draughty and frozen, but picturesque, Royal at Stratford. The object of the Old Vic performance is simple. It is designed to enable a well-graced young actor, John Neville, to get out of the most richly mellifluous part in the English drama all the beauty that he can. The second presentation is a very different affair. Ultimately it turns out to be less successful than the Old Vic's. But of the two, it is the more interesting, controversial and subtle.[75]

Roared on by young female fans (whose enthusiasm Hobson contrasts approvingly with the 'mournful' audience at Stratford-upon-Avon), the 'confident and handsome' Neville acted in the vein of John Gielgud, possessing 'the same self-pitying smile, so sadly bright, the same stretched nerves, the same soaring voice, the same pale commanding look'. His interpretation – accomplished, crafted, unthrilling – was 'the beginning and the end of the performance'. Hobson was eager to contrast this dominating vision, in the manner of the actor-managers of the Edwardian period, with the ensemble playing of the Theatre Workshop production:

> The Stratford performance, on the other hand, is not in the least devised in order to exhibit the graces of the leading actor, Mr Harry Corbett. What Theatre Workshop aims at is an interpretation of the play, not a bravura performance.[76]

Hobson happens to dislike this interpretation and criticises Littlewood for, in his view, building her production around the line 'Hath Bolling-broke/Depos'd thine intellect?' and allowing John Bury to create a set 'excessively grim in scenery and lighting'. But he is fascinated by the depiction of Richard by Corbett, even if he is to wonder whether ultimately he has witnessed the murder, not of a king by his nobles, but of an actor by his director:

> From the start, Mr Corbett's Richard is more than half-mad. His high, treacherous, sing-song voice, his glazed eyes, his up-tilted chin, his fancifully managed hands, his swift, light, stooping, little runs and leaps are all marks of a man who has only a distorted grasp of reality, and is living in an interior world of his own that touches objective existence only with disastrous obliqueness. You may not like this sort of performance; you may say that it would have surprised Shakespeare considerably; what you cannot maintain is that Mr Corbett does not do it magnificently.

Theatre Workshop's ability to impress and infuriate had now reached a wider domain, and this was cemented when the company revived *The Good Soldier Schweik* in March 1956 for its first transfer into a West End theatre, the Duke of York's. This time Hobson was again a somewhat lonely voice, but he was ecstatic:

> It is a pleasure to welcome Theatre Workshop into the West End. Here is a most paradoxical organisation. Operating almost exclusively in the East End of London, reputedly Left wing, and certainly one of the few

companies in this country which forgets the National Anthem [the play-ing of which still preceded West End shows], Theatre Workshop has nevertheless done more to raise the international reputation of Britain on the Continent than any of our most famous or chauvinistic actors or companies.[77]

What the critic particularly admired was the way that the company threw 'out of the window the naturalistic acting which is the staple of the British theatre', but this eulogy alone could not prevent the show closing after a bare three weeks. It was only when Theatre Workshop produced its most important play by a living writer, Brendan Behan's *The Quare Fellow* in that climactic month, May 1956, that the stoical ensemble which had been travelling for over twenty years was finally deemed to have arrived.

Behan and *The Quare Fellow*

The physical condition of the script of *The Quare Fellow* that arrived on Joan Littlewood's desk – a play that had been staged two years earlier in 1954 at the Pike Theatre, Dublin (but rejected by Dublin's Abbey Theatre) – was emblematic of its author's Bacchic personality: 'The typing frequently went careering off the page, there were beer stains and repeti-tions, but you'd hardly read five pages before you recognised a great entertainer'.[78] Having passed Littlewood's first test, she asked Gerry Raffles to invite Behan over to England, only to receive the reply 'Drink-ing with some Toronto Irish. Send us an injection'.[79] A second fare was sent, but similarly guzzled. Littlewood began work anyway.

Set in a prison and covering the twenty-four-hour period prior to the execution of a prisoner, the Quare Fellow (who has been convicted of murdering his brother and is never seen by the audience), the script offered tremendous material for a left-wing company inculcated with a tradition of ensemble playing. Songs, irreverent banter about religion (Behan was a lapsed catholic) and moments of visual humour abound (such as when Dunlavin manages to swig meths unbeknown to the warder massaging his legs) and, crucially, there are no star roles, with many char-acters presented as types, such as Prisoner A and Prisoner B, Warden 1 and Warden 2. This allows the spotlight to be focused on the juxtaposition between the monotony of prison existence and the atmosphere of nervous expectation as the execution approaches, and the tension is exacerbated by the fact that two prisoners are originally due to be hanged, one receiv-ing a pardon less than twenty-four hours before his sentence is due to be carried out. He becomes known as the 'Lifer'.

Littlewood's preparatory work with the company without the presence of the author concentrated on examining the mundaneness of prison life, and Goorney supplies a valuable insight into her working methods:

> Rehearsals were well under way before the cast were given scripts or told what parts they were playing. They had just to set about creating the atmosphere of prison life, marching round and round the flat roof of the Theatre Royal as prisoners on exercise. The day to day routines were improvised, cleaning out cells, the quick smoke, the furtive conversation, trading tobacco and the boredom and meanness of prison life were explored. The improvisations had, of course, been selected by Joan with the script in mind, and when it was finally introduced, the situation and the relationships had been explored. The bulk of the work had been done and the groundwork laid for any cutting and shaping that was necessary.[80]

Behan finally arrived after this initial preparation and approved of Littlewood's revisions. Having watched a run of the first act (without a single Irishman in the cast), the company assembled in the bar, to be regaled with stories of 'quare fellows he'd known and Pierrepoint who'd hanged them, of scows and villains and his own attempts at escape'.[81] The contemporaneity of the work was heightened by its modern idiom and the increasing questioning in Britain in 1956 of the justification for capital punishment. The Hangman of the production (played by Gerry Raffles) was clearly modelled on the famous British executioner, Albert Pierrepoint, and the anti-hanging stance of the work was intensified by matter-of-fact discussions about the practicalities of the execution. This is illustrated when the young clergyman, Crimmin, (who later faints at the execution), is educated about the Hangman's technical proficiency:

CRIMMIN: What does he want the cap for?
WARDER REGAN: He gets the quare fellow's weight from the doctor so as he'll know what drop to give him, but he likes to have a look at him as well, to see what build he is, how thick his neck is, and so on.

Three weeks after the première of *Look Back in Anger*, Kenneth Tynan was able to eulogise about another play that he accurately predicted would not simply belong to his transient column but to 'theatrical history'. Feeling that the production was the best advertisement for Theatre Workshop thus far – 'a model of restraint, integrity and disciplined naturalism' – he particularly admired the didacticism of the play and the tension that was created:

The tension is intolerable, but it is we who feel it, not the people in the play. We are moved precisely in the degree that they are not. With superb dramatic tact, the tragedy is concealed beneath layer after layer of rough comedy.[82]

Behan himself was to contribute directly to the publicity that surrounded this momentous production. Invited to be interviewed on the BBC by Malcolm Muggeridge, after a screening of the meths massaging scene in Act One, he turned up drunk to the studio, abused some young debs and their chaperones in the refreshment area – 'I'd like to fuck you, the lot of you,[83] – and had to be propped up during the interview by the redoubtable Littlewood. Howard Goorney describes this incident, which provoked scores of protests, as 'unfortunate'.[84] His director, perhaps recognising its publicity value, records that the following day every bus or taxi driver who passed them slowed down to shout 'Hi Brendan! You was properly pissed on TV last night. Good on yer!' All of which contributed to the play being 'safely launched'.[85] The era of civilised cocktails in well-made plays was vanishing fast.

Waiting for Godot, Look Back in Anger, A Taste of Honey: a Reassessment

At this juncture, it is necessary to complete the revaluation of the relative importance of the highs of fifties British theatre – *Waiting for Godot, Look Back in Anger* and the hitherto neglected *A Taste of Honey* – with a personal testimony from an audience member. Jack Reading, the Vice-President of the Society for Theatre Research, was at the opening nights of the first two plays and saw the third in its first week. He confirms in a letter to the author the hypothesis that the notoriety of *Look Back in Anger* stemmed as much from hype as achievement:

> *Waiting for Godot* left the members of its audience who sat it out to the end completely *stunned*. We knew we had seen things on the stage that could not be related to anything theatrical previously experienced. It was almost beyond discussion or rational appraisal. It had been an entirely new experience: a play (for want of a better word) that had taken its audience into a new extension of imagination.
>   *Look Back in Anger*, on the other hand, was merely *stimulating*: the set had been accepted as not un-ordinary and not as ground-breaking as some later commentators now suggest; the characters, the story and the plotting were unremarkable; we knew of graduates who had declined to

enter the rat-race of usual employment; the direction was pedestrian and the final curtain of animal talk had been squirmishly embarrassing. What had been different was the vehemence of the delivery of the off-the-top outbursts of Jimmy.

The point I am making is that the claim now made for the play as the water-shed of post-war theatre is something developed *after* the event. It did not seem so at the time. Its importance is a myth which, like all myths, feeds on itself, aided, and very much aided, by that brilliant coinage of Angry Young Man. This has given journalists and writers a caption head-line much in the same way as the later catch of 'Kitchen Sink' had to explain the exploration, dramatically, of every-day working and low life.

Which brings me to the premise that *A Taste of Honey* has been over-looked as an example of a new theatre in advance of its time – and in many ways. The set was just as squalid as that for *Look Back in Anger* but nothing like as conventionally realised. John Bury was using finan-cial restraints to explore a new field of scenic suggestion rather than social realism. The story line was certainly taboo-breaking, revealing a life-style, presumed to exist but seldom touching the lives of most folk in the audience – a mother practically on-the-game, a pimp of a boyfriend, an unschooled neglected daughter, a coloured-boy pick-up (in a scene of intense poignancy), a pregnancy (YES black-white coitus: the ultimate dread), and the homosexual helpmate (this itself a revolu-tion on stage, permissable presumably because his homosexuality was not discussed or practised).

In addition to all these new-at-the-time aspects the staging of the play was equally revolutionary. Littlewood's direction methods resulted in a style, acceptable, workable, but more direct and real than any acting to be seen further to the west in London. I suppose it was like the scenery. It was the first time I had experienced the direct aside trick of actor-audience participation. Both a revelation (was this the way it had been done in the 18th century before the coy hand-to-mouth aside took con-trol?) and a novelty, which was soon to catch on and be repeatedly used since in films (eg *Tom Jones*) and on TV.

A Taste of Honey was being considered and gestated at about the same time as *Look Back in Anger* but reached the stage later, but it has an equal, if not greater, claim to be a break point of the British theatre. Alas, it had no banner-title to wave and, after all, was in the East End poor relation theatre.

In summing up, I would say that *Look Back in Anger* showed a rebel-lion against the acceptance of a squalid life: *A Taste of Honey* showed an acceptance of it. The former was more in tune with the needs of the age and a new drama: the latter was Chekhovian and, perhaps, although modern in approach, dated in intent.[86]

Brecht

Pre-1956 Productions

The theatre of Bertolt Brecht was in tune with the needs of a new drama, too. Brecht had written his first full-length play, *Baal* (1918–22), shortly after the First World War, developed his technique of 'distanciation' – the famous 'Verfremdungseffekt' – during the 1930s, defined his 'Non-Aristotelian' theatre in *Kleines Organum für das Theater* in 1949 and passed on his theatrical methodology to his accomplished theatre company, the Berliner Ensemble, from its formation in the same year. Britain's practical experience of Brecht's dramaturgy, however, had been extremely limited before 1956. An adaptation of *Schweik* by Theatre of Action in 1936 and a performance of *Senora Carrar's Rifles* by the Unity Theatre in 1938 represented the sum total of productions before the Second World War, and a below-par Joan Littlewood – 'colourless, indecisive and often inaudible'[87] in Harold Hobson's view – took the title part of *Mother Courage* in a production at the Devon Festival in Barnstaple in July 1955, which even Kenneth Tynan judged a 'discourtesy to a masterpiece [that] borders on insult.'[88]

Tynan's disappointment at this home-grown effort stemmed not least from his recent embracing of Epic Theatre as one possible model for a reinvigoration of British drama. As early as 1954, Tynan was lamenting the fact that the critical acclaim that was being accorded to the Berliner Ensemble in continental Europe, particularly after the legendary production of *Mother Courage* with Brecht's wife, Helene Weigel, as the indomitable but myopic business woman, was not arousing interest in London's West End. From the moment that *Mother Courage* won the first prize at the Festival Internationale d'Art Dramatique in Paris in July 1954, the Theater am Schiffbauerdamm in East Berlin became a mecca for European theatre practitioners eager to learn about the new phenomenon of Epic Theatre, but Tynan despaired at the inertia and complacency of British producers and felt left on the sidelines: 'We in London hear the distant thunder of the guns: but how shall we judge of the outcome?'[89]

At the beginning of January 1955, Tynan took matters into his own hands and travelled to the Théâtre National Populaire to view the famous performance of *Mother Courage* for himself. The visit did not disappoint. Not only did he witness 'a glorious performance of a contemporary classic' which 'has been acclaimed everywhere in Europe save London',[90] but the critic, who loved rubbing shoulders with the 'stars' (to which the enormous correspondence in his British Library archive testifies), was able to meet the playwright in person. He described Brecht as 'ovally built, and blinking behind iron-rimmed glasses', conversing in 'wry, smiling obliquities, puffing on a damp little cigar',[91] and could now add an admiration for the persona to an admiration for the theory. It is scarcely surprising, then, that the fourth seminal event in 1955 and 1956 for English theatre – the visit of the Berliner Ensemble itself to London in August 1956 and the first proper introduction to Epic Theatre – should find as its most passionate advocate the crusading critic of the *Observer*.

The Berliner Ensemble in London: August 1956

On 5 August 1956, just prior to the London season of the Berliner Ensemble which was to open on 27 August with Weigel's *Mother Courage*, Brecht had pinned the following instruction to the company's notice-board:

> For our London season we need to bear two things in mind. First: we shall be offering most of the audience a pure pantomime, a kind of silent film on the stage for they know no German. … Second: there is in England a long-standing fear that German art (literature, painting, music) must be terribly heavy, slow, laborious and pedestrian.
> So our playing needs to be quick, light, strong. … The audience has to see that here are a number of artists working together as a collective (ensemble) in order to convey stories, ideas, virtuoso feats to the spectator by a common effort.[92]

Unhappily, Brecht himself was not permitted to judge of the success of his exhortations, since he was to die of a heart attack on 14 August, but this stress on the visual was both important and effective, as can be seen by analysing Tynan's notes on his original programme for the first night of *Mother Courage* (recently discovered in his archive) and his *Observer* review, which pays significant attention to props, set and songs.[93] What most thrilled Tynan, though, was the playwright's emphasis – in works that are set in the past – on the problems of contemporary life:

> As Eric Bentley said, 'Brecht does not believe in an inner reality, a higher reality or a deeper reality, but simply in reality.' It is something for which we have lost the taste: raised on a diet of gin and goulash, we call Brecht ingenious when he gives us bread and wine. He wrote morality

plays and directed them as such, and if we of the West End and Broadway find them as tiresome as religion, we are in a shrinking minority. There is a world elsewhere. 'I was bored to death,' said a bright Chelsea girl after *Mother Courage*. 'Bored to life', would have been apter.[94]

This 'world elsewhere' was powerfully conveyed for Tynan by the performance of Brecht's wife, Helene Weigel, as Mother Courage ('her performance is casual and ascetic: we are to observe but not to embrace her') and by the irreverent rendition of the National Anthem before the curtain rose:

> the melody is backed by a trumpet *obligato* so feeble and pompous that it suggests a boy bugler on a rapidly sinking ship. The orchestration is a criticism of the lyrics, and a double flavour results, the ironic flavour which is 'A-effect'.[95]

The German company had been brought to the London stage by Peter Daubeny and this impresario was to continue to play a crucial role in opening up the West End stage to world theatre during the next two decades.

Originally an actor who had trained with Michel St Denis's London Theatre Studio, Daubeny had been forced to give up his acting career and move into management following the loss of an arm during the Second World War. In the fifties he specialised in organising visits from foreign companies, including the Comédie Française and the Compagnie Edwige Feuillère (responsible for the huge success of *La Dame aux Camélias* in 1955); dance companies from as diverse locations as France, Spain, India and Yugoslavia; and more politically problematic visits, given their communist connections, from the Berliner Ensemble (in 1956) and the Moscow Art Theatre (in 1958). In 1961 Daubeny introduced the new wave of American theatre to a London audience, in the form of Jack Gelber's *The Connection*, and the resultant publicity proved both his skill as an impresario and the taste of audiences for international theatre. Consequently, in 1964 Daubeny became the artistic director of the World Theatre Season, which usually ran for two or three months at the Aldwych Theatre each spring and quickly became an established event in the theatre calendar. Benefiting from Daubeny's eclectic tastes, wide foreign contacts and boundless energy, the seasons did much to break down the parochialism of the West End and early highlights included Feydeau's *Un Fil à la patte* (1964), the Moscow Art Theatre productions of Gogol's *Dead Souls*, Chekhov's *The Cherry Orchard* and Pogodin's *Kremlin Chimes* (1964), and productions of O'Casey's *Juno and the Paycock* and *The Plough and the Stars* at the Abbey Theatre, Dublin (1964).

The sheer range and exoticism of Daubeny's choices cannot possibly be conveyed in a concise list of individual performances, but his early achievements (and, by implication, importance) are documented in his autobiography, *My World of Theatre* (1971). The magnitude of his work was such that after his death in 1975 there was nobody able to match his commitment and the World Theatre Seasons ceased.

The ESC's *The Good Woman of Setzuan*: November 1956

Tynan's fascination with Epic Theatre was shared by George Devine, who had been negotiating with Brecht in December 1955 for the rights to stage *The Good Woman of Setzuan* by his soon-to-be-launched English Stage Company. Brecht was eager for an English playwright to travel to East Berlin to work with him on producing an acceptable English text, so five months before *Look Back in Anger* opened, Devine made a remarkable suggestion:

> I think your idea of our sending a playwright to Berlin to work in col-laboration with you is a first class one. I would propose John Osborne, not well known here but whose play *Look Back in Anger* I will do in my first season. … This young chap has the right humour and social feeling and you could mould him as you wished.[96]

In spite of this powerful endorsement, Brecht declined the suggestion in a telephone call to Devine in early January 1956,[97] although Osborne was still to play a role in the production as a member of what he termed the 'stoic peasantry'.[98]

In April 1956, Devine published an article in *Encore*, a magazine that was fast becoming the house journal of those determined to launch British theatre in a new direction, in which he reported on his recent visit to the Berliner Ensemble. There were many reasons for admiration: like Tynan, he viewed the Ensemble as proof of the success of subsidy, an issue that was increasingly to dominate British theatre; the work being produced was modern and relevant, the theatre and art of Brecht arising 'essentially of their time and place'; the approach to performance was one of work-in-progress with the emphasis on personal and collective discovery – 'To watch a Brecht production is to stumble upon the agreeable chaos of an artist's studio, to have the artist turn up a picture and tell you, "This – this is more-or-less finished"'; the philosophy, far from being rigidly political, was eclectic, Devine being surprised that Brecht 'admonished all the young actors to go to see John Gielgud and Peggy Ashcroft who were playing in Berlin at the time in *Much Ado About Nothing*'; and the strong artistic conception and clear political framework were of 'exemplary value', since the Berliner Ensemble

> answers a need and is given the means to answer it because it *is* a need. In the light of this logic, all attempts to *impose* a theatre or an art are basically esoteric. Brecht's art is biased, but all creative work comes out of strong prejudice and is not any the less valuable for it. Brecht's theatre still has a justification towards humanity – any art is bound to which is practised as humbly and as well as this.[99]

It is disingenuous to claim, however, that Devine was to develop the Royal Court along the lines of the Berliner Ensemble. Although he valued the collective endeavour, sense of purpose, shared convictions and desire to explore the non-illusionistic practices of the German company, Devine's vision of creating theatre that was modern and relevant was not predicated on a particular theory of theatre or guided by a codified system of beliefs. In any case the eagerly awaited production at the Royal Court of *The Good Woman of Setzuan* in November 1956, with Peggy Ashcroft as Shen Te, which followed on quickly from the triumph of the Berliner Ensemble at the Palace Theatre, was not an unqualified success. The rehearsal process had been too short to inculcate the cast in the methodology of Epic Theatre, even if it had been fully understood by Devine (the mistranslation of 'Mensch' as 'Woman' seems to indicate a misunderstanding about the representational nature of the work); the shadow of the cold war, and, in particular, the Hungarian Revolution of the same month, were to cloud objective reaction to the work, siting it as a weapon in an ideological and possibly militaristic battle; and some critics, in particular Harold Hobson, in addition to becoming increasingly hostile to the Marxism of Brecht, were disturbed by the appearance of the promising Osborne, fearing that he might be corrupted by such immersion:

> There is an alarming rumour … that John Osborne, who appears in *The Good Woman of Setzuan* (not to much advantage, by the way), is likely to be influenced by Brecht in the new play he is writing to follow up the striking *Look Back in Anger*. … I earnestly hope that this is not so, though Mr Osborne himself does not deny it. Mr Osborne has a decided theatrical talent for representing young people as morbid, cowardly, self-pitying, complaining and weak-willed. It is in this that his genius lies, not in devising techniques to suit the sort of people who

have failed at eleven-plus. It will be a desolating day for his own future and, in a small way, for the future of the English theatre, if anyone persuades him that the case is otherwise.[100]

The play Osborne was writing at the time was *The Entertainer*.

Legacy

In spite of the luke-warm critical notices – the reactionary critic of the *Daily Telegraph*, W.A. Darlington, wrote of 'one of the dullest evenings I have had in the theatre … three hours by the watch (but they felt like six)', with the only consolation being observing Peggy Ashcroft 'impersonating a horrid little Chinese man'[101] – Epic Theatre was from now on to exert a significant influence on British theatre. *The Good Woman of Setzuan*, better translated as *The Good Person of Setzuan*, had demonstrated how in Brechtian theatre the audience was being asked to witness the events of the play, look afresh at the issues being raised and resolve the central dilemma through discussion and reflection after the performance was over.

At the start of the play, three Gods arrive in Setzuan stating that the earth can remain as it is if they can find sufficient good people. After several aborted attempts to secure overnight accommodation for the gods, the waterseller Wang – the play's choric commentator – flees through fear of the repercussions of his failure, but the prostitute, Shen Te, a person who is described as being unable to say no, agrees to provide shelter for the Gods. The next morning, delighted at having found the one good person that they were seeking, the gods prepare to leave, but Shen Te denies that she is virtuous, explains that she has to sell herself to live and then poses the central dilemma of the play for both the gods and the audience – how can she be good, 'when everything is so expensive?'.[102] Embarrassed at being drawn into matters economic, the gods agree to make Shen Te a payment of 1,000 silver dollars for their lodging, but urge her not to publicise this for fear of misinterpretation.

Following this opening interlude, the first scene reveals that Shen Te has used the money to open a tobacco shop with a view to doing as much good as she is able, but the poverty of the district quickly begins to threaten the viability of the business. In addition to distributing rice to the needy, she agrees to put up her relatives, explaining the rationale behind her action by directly addressing the audience in verse:

They are without shelter.
They are without friends.

They need someone.
How could one say no?

This charitable ethos is soon seen to be a liability in such an environment, however. More and more family members arrive having heard of Shen Te's good fortune, Shen Te prefers to give tobacco away free to an Unemployed Man, rather than earn profits through trade, and she eventually concludes (what the audience can clearly witness) that the shop is slowly sinking beneath the waves, such is the weight of the desperate people clinging to it.

Already it is possible to detect elements of 'Verfremdung': the technique of making the familiar seem strange. The direct addresses to the audience; the episodic scenes; the characters as representational types (the Man, the Woman, the Nephew); the passages of dialectic, such as when the Nephew asks Shen Te how she could be sure that the Unemployed Man was not lying about his joblessness, to which she replies 'How do you know he was?'; and the interpolation of songs that comment ironically on the action, are all part of Brecht's fundamental aim of inculcating new ways of thinking on the part of the audience. The stagecraft, too, is intended to disrupt illusion and complacency. The obsession with naturalism and a faithful reproduction of 'real life' in the sets that had so dominated the previous two decades of British theatre were to be avoided at all costs. Verisimilitude was as much an anathema to Brecht as Aristotelian catharsis. The tobacco shop should be signified by a door-frame and a few timbers, props should under no circumstances strive towards naturalism, focusing instead on their representational qualities, and lights need not be carefully hidden behind a proscenium arch, since the audience must always be aware that this is a performance with a didactic purpose that requires intellectual as well as emotional engagement.

The clearest example of 'Verfremdung' and dialectic comes in scene two. Tackled by the Owner of the building for business references (capitalism for Brecht is based on the maintenance of a correct appearance as much as on trade), Shen Te reluctantly buys a little time by taking up an earlier suggestion of the Man that she should invent a fictitious cousin to whom all creditors could be referred. Following a raucous drinking session, during which the shop gets damaged, the cousin, Shui Ta, dramatically turns up and symbolically extinguishes the light that has been wastefully burning all night whilst the drunken family sleeps off its excesses. It is a magnificent coup-de-théâtre and usefully refutes the criticism that Brecht's theory overwhelms his theatricality. Unbeknown to anyone, Shen Te has created this alter-ego to 'rescue' her from her charitable instincts and keep the business solvent.

The rest of the play examines the consequences of this dichotomy. Taking care not to condemn Shui Ta out of hand, since the focus of the work is on the environment that conditions the behaviour of the characters, Brecht illustrates that whilst Shui Ta evicts the family, preserves the business and rapidly expands it, he also lacks a social conscience, manipulates Shen Te's lover, Yang Sun, into becoming the ruthless foreman in his tobacco sweat shop and provides accommodation for the workers that enables them to function in the factory but is little better than a slum.

Shen Te is an equally split personality. She saves a young flyer from suicide, gives him new hope with her pledge to help him fly and is thrilled at the prospect of having his child. But she also recognises that in such a cut-throat world she will have to fight like a tiger to protect her offspring, is unable to avoid being exploited by spongers on account of her generous nature and is blind to the fact that Yang Sun is only prepared to marry her so that he can obtain her money to advance his own career. The internal splits of both Shen Te and Shui Ta mirror the external schism of adopting two personalities.

The play concludes with a trial scene – an excellent forum for the presentation of dialectical argument. Shui Ta's visits have become so frequent and lengthy that people have begun to question what has happened to Shen Te. He is accused of depriving her of her freedom and is thus interrogated by the three gods, pretending to be the three judges. Unable to sustain the split personality any longer, Shui Ta asks for the court to be cleared and makes a 'confession' explaining that the gods' edict to 'both be good and yet to live' had torn her in two like a bolt of lightning. However, far from condemning this protective masquerade, the gods, blind to her dilemma, are so delighted that they have rediscovered their good person alive, that they ignore Shen Te's charge that 'something must be wrong with your world'. They pardon everything as a 'misunderstanding' and, in a telling parody of the Greek practice of the *deus ex machina*, rise up to heaven on a pink cloud. As they ascend, the following last desperate exchange takes place:

SHEN TE: I need my cousin.
FIRST GOD: Not too often!
SHEN TE: At least once a week!
FIRST GOD: Once a month. That's enough!
SHEN TE: Oh, don't go away, illustrious ones! I haven't told you everything. I need you desperately.

But the gods ignore her, their abnegation complete.

The ending is deliberately frustrating, a point made when the actor (usually the one playing Wang) steps out of character, walks to the front of the stage and explains apologetically that the actors, too, are dissatisfied with this conclusion. He then places the burden of finding a solution to the dilemma firmly on the shoulders of the audience:

What should the solution be?
We can't find one, not for any money.
Different people, perhaps? Or a different world?
Perhaps different gods? Or none at all?
We're all shattered, and not just from our exertions.
The only way out of this mess would be if
You were to put yourself on the spot
And help the good person find a good ending.
Go on dear audience, get to it now.
There has to be a better one, there must, there must, there must.

The legacy of Brecht's didactic approach for post-war British theatre, both thematically and in terms of performing and staging, is important, if hard to quantify. That the interrogation of social, political and economic concerns could also be entertaining, clearly created an atmosphere in which subsequent English writers such as John Arden (whose *Serjeant Musgrave's Dance* (1959) is generally acknowledged to have been influenced by the technique of Epic Theatre), Edward Bond, Howard Brenton, David Hare and Timberlake Wertenbaker could flourish, without being depicted as slavish acolytes. Brecht's deliberately confrontational approach was unsettling and initially misunderstood, particularly following the publication of Martin Esslin's *Brecht: a Choice of Evils* in 1959, which conceded that the works were accomplished, in spite of the marxism and theory, and John Willett's *The Theatre of Bertolt Brecht* of the same year, which crucially mistranslated 'Verfremdung' as 'alienation', erroneously implying dryness and hostility, and giving succour to those who depicted the playwright as a threatening political entity.[103] Indeed, the cold war continually shaped the reception of Brecht, allowing some to depict Epic Theatre as fixed and propagandistic, instead of fluid and inviting discussion. However, the fact that Brecht chose to write about political issues at all was seen as refreshing, daring and worthy of emulation by many young writers of the sixties, and his legacy for playwrighting is perhaps best summed up by Michael Patterson when he writes that Epic Theatre offers:

first, a means of portraying dramatic characters not as unchanging and

circumscribed entities but as contradictory, alterable beings, their 'individuality' a function of their social situation; secondly, the resulting
primacy of interest in that social situation rather than in the emotions or
psychology of the individual; thirdly, a willingness to forgo suspense
about the outcome of the plot to focus on the way the plot develops,
inviting a consideration of possible outcomes ('epic' method); fourthly,
an encouragement to write plays that are vigorously theatrical … above
all, rediscovering the 'fun' of the theatrical event.[104]

In addition to stimulating playwrights, Brechtian practice was to tower
over the early years of the National Theatre, whose long period of gestation was finally to come to an end in 1963.

A final observation should come from a long-standing observer, the
Guardian's theatre critic Michael Billington, who wrote in 1988 (on the
one-hundredth anniversary of Brecht's birthday) that:

> Richard Eyre speaks of the 'epiphany' he felt on first seeing the Berliner
> Ensemble at the Old Vic in 1965, and of the way the Brechtian aesthetic
> has shaped his own work. David Hare rightly claims that Brecht radi-
> cally affected classical theatre in the 1960s: he points to Peter Hall's *The
> War of the Roses* at Stratford and the work of William Gaskill and John
> Dexter at Olivier's National Theatre. But, at the time, Brechtian values
> altered every aspect of British theatre: plays such as Osborne's *The
> Entertainer* and *Luther*, and Arden's *The Workhouse Donkey* and Bolt's
> *The Man for all Seasons*, the ascetic purity of Jocelyn Herbert's design
> and even the militant commitment of Tynan's criticism were all heavily
> influenced by Brecht.[105]

The First Wave Consolidates

The Royal Court as Theatre Complex

One of the most notable things about the early years of the English Stage
Company was the sheer eclecticism of its activities – no wonder Tynan was
to write in April 1958 on the second anniversary of its first production that
'Two years ago last Tuesday there was no English Stage Company. What a
dull theatre we must have had! And what on earth did we playgoers find
to argue about?'.[106] The Royal Court building itself became a dynamic
theatre complex, functioning as both a training ground and a performance
space. A writers' group was set up to provide practical support for aspiring
playwrights. Sunday night 'Productions Without Decor' were established,

where new playwrights could gain valuable feedback on their work-in-progress from performances with no costumes or sets (N.F. Simpson, Ann Jellicoe and John Arden were all helped in this way). Young directors, including William Gaskill, Lindsay Anderson, Peter Gill, Anthony Page and John Dexter, received on-the-job experience, and this gave rise to famous collaborations between particular playwrights and directors, such as Dexter and Arnold Wesker on the 'Wesker trilogy'. Similar partnerships emerged between playwrights and designers, with Jocelyn Herbert's designs for Wesker's plays (which synthesised minute detail on stage and gritty working-class themes) giving rise to the 'Kitchen-Sink' brand of naturalism, and lunch-time concerts and poetry recitals (by Stephen Spender, Edith Evans, Sybil Thorndike and Lewis Casson, amongst others[107]) similarly added to the vibrancy of the space.

What can be sometimes overlooked by the historian's focus on the ESC's achievement in supporting new writing, however, is the fact that the productions in the early years of the company featured some of the finest actors of the period. Many were young and included Alan Howard, Steven Berkoff, Glenda Jackson, Jeremy Brett, Rita Tushingham, Frank Finlay, Richard Briers, Robert Stephens and Joan Plowright, but established West End stars, intrigued by the activities of this non-West End operation, were attracted too, and this led, in April 1957, to one of the most unforgettable acting performances of post-war British theatre: in a notable collaboration between a representative of the new and a scion of the old.

The Entertainer

Laurence Olivier had initially loathed John Osborne's *Look Back in Anger* viewing it as a 'travesty on England'[108] but a second visit to the play in July 1956 with Arthur Miller altered his perspective. Surprised by Miller's enthusiasm, Olivier posed the following question to Osborne after the performance: 'Do you suppose you could write something for me?'.[109]. The result was *The Entertainer*.

At this point Olivier's career was in a state of flux. In spite of outstanding Shakespearean performances, including a remarkable Macbeth in 1955, and the lead role in a gruesome production by Peter Brook of *Titus Andronicus* in the same year, which reminded many of the horrors of the concentration camps and reawakened a discussion about the 'modernity' of Shakespeare, Olivier was clearly conscious that he was in danger of becoming an anachronism. Looking back thirty years later he was to observe that

I had reached a stage in my life that I was getting profoundly sick of –

not just tired – sick. Consequently the public were, likely enough, beginning to agree with me. My rhythm of work had become a bit deadly: a classical or semi-classical film; a play or two at Stratford, or a nine-month run in the West End. ... I was going mad, desperately searching for something suddenly fresh and thrillingly exciting. What I felt to be my image was boring me to death. I really felt that death might be quite exciting, compared with the amorphous, purgatorial *nothing* that was my existence.[110]

That Olivier, the most versatile actor of the post-war period, should reinvent himself by playing the role of the washed-up music-hall comedian, Archie Rice, the protagonist in a play that simultaneously links the passing of the age of the music-hall to the transient grip of Britain's hold on its empire, is supremely fitting. It was also one of the most adroit and significant career moves that an actor has ever made, since it not only relaunched his career at the same time as he met his future wife, Joan Plowright, but it possessed a remarkable symbolic value for the theatre. Given the status of Olivier, the West End could no longer resist the new drama as something peripheral or irritating. It also left him well positioned to be considered for the post of director of the future National Theatre.

Focusing on three generations of the Rice family, *The Entertainer* exhibits many of the thematic concerns of the 'new wave'. Written in thirteen numbers, with an overture and two intermissions, the structure of the play (possibly influenced by Epic Theatre) replicates that of a music-hall production, but the weariness and cynicism of the Rice family, ossifying in a small flat in a coastal resort, is meant to signify both the dying nature of this form of entertainment (which is something to be lamented) and the depersonalised nature of a country that is finding it difficult to come to terms with its reduced importance on the world stage. The Suez crisis of November 1956 – when Prime Minister Eden's attempts to prevent the Egyptian leader, Colonel Nassar, from nationalising the Suez canal (a vital link to Britain's diminishing empire) had ended in humiliating military failure – is very much in the background. Archie's son, Mick, has been captured whilst fighting abroad and, after false hope has been raised, is reported as having been killed; his daughter, Jean, has been on a march in Trafalgar Square protesting about nuclear weapons, but although she rejects the middle-class comfort offered by her conventional solicitor boyfriend, she cannot embrace the political activism that is sweeping the young with enthusiasm. Archie's second wife, Phoebe, is similarly governed by inertia – humiliated by Archie's philandering, she cannot leave him, and has to seek refuge in alcohol; and Archie's father, Billy, is one of

Osborne's familiar characters who personifies a lost age (he was actually a highly respected music-hall performer in his own right) and induces ambivalent feelings of nostalgia and pity.

The enervating stasis of the family, the emotional confusion of its members and, above all, the desperate stoical cheerfulness of Archie – cracking risqué jokes, seeming to relish his perennial evasion of the tax man but revealingly described as being 'dead behind the eyes'[111] – act as a powerful metaphor for a country that on the one hand is benefiting from increasing affluence but on the other has alienated so many of its inhabitants through class barriers, a collective sense of disenfranchisement and an unacknowledged international impotence. Archie's speech to Jean at the end of the first half is one of the few moments of genuine emotion on his part and it encapsulates the overarching theme of illusory security sought behind emotional deception:

> ARCHIE: Well, Mick wouldn't want us to cut the celebration short. We'll drink to Mick, and let's hope to God he manages. Nick and the income tax man. With you it's Prime Ministers, with me it's dogs. Nuns, clergymen and dogs. Did I ever tell you the greatest compliment I had paid to me – the greatest compliment I always treasure? I was walking along the front somewhere – I think it was here actually – one day, o, it must be twenty-five years ago, I was quite a young man. Well, I was there walking along the front, to meet what I think we used to call a piece of crackling. Or perhaps it was a bit of fluff. No that was earlier. Anyway, I know I enjoyed it afterwards. But the point is I was walking along the front, all on my own, minding my own business, (*pause*) and two nuns came towards me – (*pause*) two nuns –
> (*He trails off, looking very tired and old. He looks across at Jean and pushes the bottle at her*)
> Talk to me.[112]

The critics did not know whether to marvel most at a truly great performance by Olivier, at the achievement of Osborne in writing a second smash hit play within twelve months of *Look Back in Anger*, or at the entrepreneurship of George Devine in premièring this play at the Royal Court a few days after Beckett's revelatory *Fin de Partie* had been produced at the same venue. This embarrassment of riches after such a period of famine perhaps best symbolises the incredible transformation that the Royal Court brought to the London theatre. Tynan was in no doubt that whilst Tony Richardson's direction was lax, the supporting cast underutilised and even the didacticism too ambitious ('Mr Osborne has planned a gigantic social mural and carried it out in a colour range too narrow for the job'), the playwright had created 'one of the great acting parts of our age'. His admiration for Olivier's performance of 'miracles' was untrammelled, and he was deeply affected by the ending: 'The crown, perhaps, of this great performance is Archie's jocular, venomous farewell to the audience: "Let me know where you're working tomorrow night – and I'll come and see *you*."'[113] Harold Hobson agreed with his rival (a rare event) that something special had occurred:

> [its] theatrical effect is enormous. Splendid as Sir Laurence is when showing us Archie on the stage, he is even finer when he gets home to his squalid drunken family. There are ten minutes, from the moment when he begins telling his daughter, with a defiant, ashamed admiration, of a negress singing a spiritual in some low nightclub, to his breakdown on hearing of his son's death, when he touches the extreme limits of pathos. You will not see more magnificent acting than this anywhere in the world.[114]

The new wave had burst the dam.

The Royal Court: 1957–1962

The table below sets out the principal productions staged at the Royal Court during the years 1957 to 1962.

1957	Wycherley, *The Country Wife*
	Beckett, *Fin de Partie, Acte Sans Paroles*
	Osborne, *The Entertainer*
	Ionesco, *The Chairs*
	Sartre, *Nekrassov*
	Faulkner, *Requiem for a Nun*
1958	Osborne and Creighton, *Epitaph for George Dillon*
	Jellicoe, *The Sport of My Mad Mother*
	Ionesco, *The Chairs, The Lesson*
	Wesker, *Chicken Soup With Barley*
	Arden, *Live Like Pigs*
	Beckett, *Endgame, Krapp's Last Tape*
	John, *Moon on a Rainbow Shawl*
1959	Hall, *The Long and the Short and the Tall*
	Williams, *Orpheus Descending*
	Wesker, *Roots*
	Coward, *Look After Lulu*
	Wesker, *The Kitchen*

	Arden, *Serjeant Musgrave's Dance*
	Ibsen, *Romersholm*
	Simpson, *One Way Pendulum*
1960	Pinter, *The Dumb Waiter*, *The Room*
	Ionesco, *Rhinoceros*
	Wesker, *Chicken Soup with Barley; Roots; I'm Talking About Jerusalem*
	Chekhov, *Platonov*
	Delaney, *The Lion in Love*
1961	Ionesco, *Jacques*
	Sartre, *Altona*
	Genet, *The Blacks*
	Wesker, *The Kitchen*
	Osborne, *Luther*
	Albee, *The American Dream*, *The Death of Bessie Smith*
1962	Shakespeare, *A Midsummer Night's Dream*
	Jellicoe, *The Knack*
	Wesker, *Chips With Everything*
	Osborne, *Plays for England*
	Devised pieces: *Brecht on Brecht*
	Beckett, *Happy Days*

Some interesting points emerge when one takes this overview, aside from the magnificent choice of new writing on offer. Firstly, although works of social realism (the plays of the so-called 'Angry' movement) are well represented, they do not dominate. One particular form of play, that which emerged from the tradition of French Absurdism, featured frequently in the Royal Court programme. Roger Blin's visiting productions of Beckett's *Fin de Partie* and *Acte Sans Paroles* in 1957, were succeeded the following month by Ionesco's *The Chairs* (in which Devine himself played the Old Man), double-bills of *The Chairs* and *The Lesson* and Beckett's *Endgame* and *Krapp's Last Tape* (1958), Ionesco's *Rhinoceros* (1960), with Olivier who was famously directed by Orson Welles, Ionesco's *Jacques* (1961) and Beckett's *Happy Days* (1962). New English writing with absurdism as a theme received encouragement, too, most notably with the staging of N.F. Simpson's *One Way Pendulum* (1959) and Pinter's two short works, *The Room* and *The Dumb Waiter* (1960).

Secondly, the company demonstrated its versatility by re-staging old classics, such as Wycherley's *The Country Wife* (1956), Shakespeare's *A Midsummer Night's Dream* (1962) and Chekhov's *Platonov* (1960). The latter production again illustrated the fascination that the Royal Court held for some performers more associated with the West End. Rex

Harrison, earning a fraction of what he had been paid in his previous role as Professor Higgins in the musical *My Fair Lady* on Broadway and in Drury Lane, freely confessed, prior to his performance as Platonov, to being 'fascinated by the new school of playwrights – the Weskers and the Pinters and so forth – and also progressive new theatre companies like the Royal Court'.[115] Even Noel Coward, for many of the new wave the very personification of post-war dramatic decrepitude, ventured into Sloane Square with a new play, *Look After Lulu* (1959), and boasted Vivien Leigh and Antony Quayle as his two leads, but it was not a happy union. The headline in the *Daily Mail* – 'It's a tepid run round the beds'[116] – signalled that tastes had decisively changed.

It should be remembered, however, that the West End did not collapse as a result of the Royal Court's and Theatre Workshop's success. Far from it. Although transfers of ESC and Theatre Workshop productions to the West End, film adaptations of *Look Back in Anger*, *The Entertainer* and *A Taste of Honey*, the publication from 1956 onwards of *Encore* and the establishment of television programmes such as ABC's *Armchair Theatre* and the BBC's *The Wednesday Play* and *Play for Today* further stimulated interest in the issues of working-class realism that many Royal Court productions were raising, there was still a considerable appetite for well-produced, lavishly presented light-entertainment. Binkie Beaumont, the master purveyor of brilliant musicals, continued to earn profits for H.M. Tennent that exceeded those of the ESC by a hundred-fold. For the financial year 1961/2, *My Fair Lady* made the astronomical profit of £138,381[117] and his shows retained the social cachet that many in the new movement so despised. After the first night of *West Side Story* (1958), for which there had been an overwhelming demand for tickets, the American Ambassador to London wrote to Beaumont stating that

> All six of us enjoyed *West Side Story* to the utmost in our respective ways. Leaving our seats, I heard one lady say to another, 'I was watching the P.M. [Harold Macmillan] and the tears were running down his face'. I can't vouch for that, but I can that we all had a glorious time.[118]

The Belgrade Theatre, TIE and Arnold Wesker

One of the great successes of this period for the Royal Court was the trilogy of plays by Arnold Wesker – *Chicken Soup with Barley* (1958), *Roots* (1959) and *I'm Talking About Jerusalem* (1960) – charting the experience of the Kahns, a Jewish family in the East End of London, beginning in 1936 with the threat of the blackshirts of Oswald Mosley and culminating in 1956 with the Soviet invasion of Hungary. As with *The Entertainer*, the family is seen as a microcosm of a larger world and their disillusion stands as a metaphor for the disappointments of the post-war generation. The earliest play of the trilogy, *Chicken Soup with Barley*, was premièred at the first new theatre to be built in England since the Oxford Playhouse in 1938, having been placed there by George Devine as a pilot project, and this matching of new building and new writing provides a further symbol of the renaissance of British theatre in the mid-fifties.

Built in Coventry in 1958 as part of the architectural and social regeneration of the bombed city, the Belgrade Theatre was the first building to result from clause 132 of the Local Government Act of 1948. This had enabled local authorities to levy a tax of up to sixpence in the pound to be used for the provision of entertainment, and was seen as both a further cementing of the principle of state subsidy for the arts and the creation of a rival to the dominant commercial theatre. Since the Belgrade had been erected by a local authority and was to be managed by a trust appointed by them, its remit was to create a social centre as well as a performing space, and thus its design incorporated a restaurant, a coffee-bar, a large foyer with bookstalls that could serve as an exhibition space, six shops, twenty-one bedsits (some of which were reserved for the resident company) and a space in which a Theatre-in-Education scheme could be based. This last proviso was significant in that it illustrated how the link between drama and schools would become increasingly important for theatres from this moment on.

Although 'Theatre-in-Education' (TIE) can trace its roots back to the pioneering work of Peter Slade (Pear Tree Players, 1945), Tom Clarke (Compass Players 1944–52), Caryl Jenner (England Children's Theatre, 1948), Brian Way (Theatre Centre, 1954) and Joan Littlewood, who variously employed improvisation, direct participation and teaching skills in their productions for young people, the establishment of a pilot educational project at the Belgrade in 1965 was a seminal event. A group of 'actor-teachers' was recruited to take drama into local schools and utilise drama-teaching methods and performance skills in the overall educational programme. Straight performances, devising, reminiscence, the theatrical depiction of local history and the investigation of youth issues were but some aspects of early TIE projects, and their success attracted Arts Council funding over the next five years, with similar groups being formed at theatres in Leeds, Nottingham, Bolton, Glasgow and Edinburgh. The Inner London Education Authority with its Cockpit team also became a key supporter of TIE (before the authority's abolition in 1987), but government indifference in the eighties and nineties, coupled with the general squeeze on theatre budgets, has greatly imperilled this important work. This is deeply regrettable since the symbiotic relationship between drama and education through TIE is a valuable one for both fields. As Anthony Jackson observes,

> The material presented is always the product of much careful research and discussion with teachers and education advisers, and schools are fully involved in 'follow-up' work. But at the same time, the efficacy and power to stimulate of good TIE ultimately lie in its considerable measure of independence from the educational system.[119]

One can only hope that the premium placed on this type of work by the Arts Council inquiry into Young People's Theatre in 1965, when it recommended 'life-saving' grant aid for five companies involved in TIE, is echoed by current funding bodies as the new millennium begins.

The Belgrade complex as a whole represented the beginning of a vital decentralisation of theatrical output from London that would, it was hoped, encourage a two-way traffic between the capital and the regions, of both writing and productions. The venue itself could seat 911 people in its stalls and circle and possessed a flexible stage, whose proscenium arch was handsomely finished in timber donated by the city of Belgrade as a gift towards Coventry's post-war reconstruction. The theatre's name was chosen in recognition of this generosity and the Belgrade proudly opened on 27 March 1958. Its first nine months of operations, however, were to foreshadow some of the challenges that the subsidised sector would face over the next forty years. Whilst its very construction heralded an exciting new age for post-war theatre, this age was to be constantly haunted by questions of funding. The theatre alone had cost an enormous £203,000 to build, with the shops and bedsits adding a further £55,000 to the bill – a huge sum of money for a cash-starved local authority. (This sum was still being paid off in the eighties.) In addition to this amount, the first nine months of operations created a deficit of £10,523, after an opening season which included *Half in Earnest*, a musical version of Wilde's *The Importance of Being Earnest*, and Wesker's new play *Chips With Everything*. This programming model – of new writing playing alongside more commercially safe forms of theatrical entertainment – has been followed by the subsidised theatres ever since, as has, less happily, the financial balancing act in the face of precarious funding both from local authorities and the Arts Council.

Two main forms of theatre have subsequently enjoyed local authority and/or Arts Council support. The first is generally known as touring or receiving theatre: these theatres tend be able to accommodate both opera and ballet, and include the Alexandra and Hippodrome in Birmingham, the Empire in Liverpool, the Palace Theatre in Manchester, the Grand in Leeds and the Theatres Royal at Lincoln, Newcastle, Norwich and Nottingham. The second form is repertory or producing theatre: these theatres receive some proportion of their funding from the local authority, but are managed by an independent trust to maintain artistic independence. They are able to create their own productions and include the West Yorkshire Playhouse, Leeds, the Manchester Royal Exchange, the Octagon, Bolton, the Crucible, Sheffield and the Victoria, Stoke-on-Trent.[120] In 1999 the largest producing theatre in England was the Royal Shakespeare Theatre, Stratford, with a capacity of 1,508 and the smallest was the Stephen Joseph Theatre, Scarborough which could seat 406.

Chicken Soup with Barley returned to the Royal Court in July 1958. The transfer of shows between London and non-London venues, and especially between the subsidised and commercial sectors would not always prove so healthily symbiotic, however. Theatre Workshop was to become the classic victim of the commercial success that transfers can bring. Both Behan's *The Quare Fellow* and his follow-up success, *The Hostage* (1958), were transferred from Stratford East to the West End, as were Shelagh Delaney's *A Taste of Honey* (1958), Frank Norman and Lionel Bart's *Fings Ain't Wot They Used T'Be* (1959) and Stephen Lewis's *Sparrers Can't Sing* (1960). Whilst these transfers brought national prominence to the company, they inadvertently threatened the ethos upon which it was based. Aside from the sheer energy involved in supervising productions in two places, Joan Littlewood became demoralised by the appropriation of her work by commercial producers (after all, Workshop productions came ready-made with no rehearsal costs), the luring away of Theatre Workshop actors, such as Harry H. Corbett, from the company (which could not dream of matching the material rewards of West End employment) and the association with commercial practices that militated against everything Theatre Workshop believed in. Consequently, Joan Littlewood left Theatre Workshop in 1960 to pursue other work, leaving the devoted Gerry Raffles to run the company for the next three years.

Harold Pinter

Harold Hobson and *The Birthday Party*

Harold Pinter is arguably the most significant British playwright to have emerged from the fifties. With *Ashes to Ashes*, premièred in the West End in 1996, he is certainly the most enduring, but it is instructive to consider that without the support of a young commercial theatre producer, Michael Codron – one of the new breed of West End producers who would help eclipse the dominance of Binkie Beaumont – Pinter's career might never have taken off. A product of neither the Royal Court nor the Theatre

Royal, Stratford East, Pinter's dramaturgy incorporates aspects of both working-class realism and absurdism, and the fact that this synthesis was to create such interest after the West End première of *The Caretaker* (1960) acts as the strongest confirmation that the new drama evident over the past five years, which broadened the subject-matter and destroyed the hegemony of the well-made play, was here to stay.

Pinter's uniqueness, however, was not something that preoccupied the reviewers of the daily newspapers following the opening of his first London production, *The Birthday Party*, at H.M. Tennent's try-out venue, the Lyric, Hammersmith, in May 1958. W.A. Darlington expressed disgust at being 'condemned to sit through plays like this',[121] and there was such vituperation in the immediate critical response that it is hard to escape the conclusion that some critics, dismayed that their strictures against Beckett and Osborne had had no effect in diminishing public interest, were striving to ensure that this playwright, who conflated elements of both, should be buried without trace.

By the Thursday of the first week of *The Birthday Party*'s run, the decision had already been taken to close the production, in the light of the damage to the box office that the dismal notices had wrought. Nevertheless, Harold Hobson decided to attend the Thursday matinée and his visit was single-handedly to prevent Pinter's career from being stifled at birth. Sitting with fifteen other people in an auditorium with a capacity for 800, he watched somewhat self-consciously as the first act ended with feeble applause from the audience. Worse was to follow. As the curtain at the end of the second act descended, following the particularly tense scene when Goldberg and McCann edge with their fingers converging towards Stanley, one of the players was heard claiming that 'This is the most awful drivel I have ever appeared in'. Hobson was indignant:

> The words rang round the echoing theatre, and we – the whole sixteen of us – shrank back in our seats appalled. I have no doubt … that it was merely embarrassment that caused the incident, but at the time I thought that I personally had never known such an act of betrayal in the history of the theatre. I am glad to say that at the end of the play, if we did not precisely cheer … we did at least make as thunderous a noise of approval as sixteen people can.[122]

Although Hobson was to be mocked for frequently reminding his readers over the next decade of his famous review of *The Birthday Party* in the *Sunday Times* the following weekend, it did represent a remarkable discovery of a playwright by a single critic in the face of unanimous disapproval by his colleagues. Hobson's opening paragraph stressed how much was at stake:

> One of the actors in Harold Pinter's *The Birthday Party* at the Lyric, Hammersmith, announces in the programme that he read history at Oxford, and took his degree with Fourth Class Honours. Now I am well aware that Mr Pinter's play received extremely bad notices last Tuesday morning. At the moment I write these lines it is uncertain whether the play will still be in the bill by the time they appear, though it is probable it will soon be elsewhere. Deliberately, I am willing to stake whatever reputation I have as a judge of plays by saying that 'The Birthday Party' is not a Fourth, not even a Second, but a First; and that Mr Pinter, on the evidence of this work, possesses the most original, disturbing, and arresting talent in theatrical London.[123]

Hobson's encomium was unable to save the first run of *The Birthday Party*, but it is probable that without this passionate endorsement Michael Codron would not have risked staging Pinter's next work, *The Caretaker*, in June 1960 in the West End, the production which cemented Pinter's reputation as a writer of menace, comedy and linguistic dexterity. On the face of it, it seems strange that Pinter never became a Royal Court writer, in the manner of Osborne, Arden and Wesker, but this, too, may have had something to do with Hobson, as William Gaskill relates:

> I had shown George [Devine] both [*The Room* and *The Dumb Waiter*] after they were first done in Bristol, but Harold Hobson in his notice in the *Sunday Times* had said that they should be done at the Court and George hated to be told what to do by a critic.[124]

As always, a critic's patronage was to prove a double-edged sword, although a double-bill of Pinter's *The Room* and *The Dumb Waiter* did finally reach the Royal Court in March 1960.

The Pinteresque: *The Room*, *The Birthday Party* and *The Caretaker*

Although Martin Esslin was correct to observe in his 1961 book about the movement that Harold Pinter 'followed in the footsteps of the pioneers of the Theatre of the Absurd',[125] one should be careful in simply claiming that Pinter is the British heir to Beckett and Ionesco. Whilst Pinter's plays share these playwrights' fascination with language, inarticulation, modes of communication and the malleability of discourse, early works, such as *The Room* (1957), *The Birthday Party* (1958) and *The Caretaker* (1960), possess their own distinctiveness. They also embrace more mundane concerns, emerge specifically from the context of the late fifties, with its insecurities about historical mass destruction (the Second World War, the Holocaust) and potential nuclear conflagration, and exhibit a theatricality (be it in their use of words as weapons, humour to increase tension or pauses that are both eloquent and fraught) that is unique to their creator.

Each of these plays is fascinated with the trivia of everyday routine yet manages to generate dramatic tension from habitual activities, in settings that would have appealed to the writers of working-class realism. Rose, for example, at the beginning of *The Room*, is preparing a breakfast of bacon and eggs for Bert and inadvertently highlights the source of potential threat through her initial banal chatter:

> That's right. You eat that. You'll need it. You can feel it in here. Still, the room keeps warm. It's better than the basement, anyway. (*She butters the bread*). I don't know how they live down there. It's asking for trouble. Go on. Eat it up. It'll do you good.[126]

Meg, the landlady of the boarding-house that only has one lodger, is also preoccupied with preparing breakfast at the start of *The Birthday Party*, but her exchange of pleasantries with Stanley contains similarly nuanced suggestions (revealing Pinter's precise deployment of language) – this time about the nature of her relationship with her guest:

> MEG: Was it nice?
> STANLEY: What?
> MEG: The fried bread.
> STANLEY: Succulent.
> MEG: You shouldn't say that word.
> STANLEY: What word?
> MEG: That word you said.
> STANLEY: What, succulent–?
> MEG: Don't say it!
> STANLEY: What's the matter with it?
> MEG: You shouldn't say that word to a married woman.[127]

Davies in *The Caretaker* is similarly fixated on finding a pair of shoes that fit him properly, so that he can make the journey (which he will never begin) to Sidcup to find his papers.

Davies' obsession with proof-of-identity (possession of his papers will confer an existence on him, it seems) is another theme that binds these plays and can be traced to the context from which they have emerged. All products of a period of history barely two decades after the Holocaust, when the cold war of the superpowers was perceived by many in the west to be exerting a dehumanising and depersonalising effect (witness the growth of the Campaign for Nuclear Disarmament (CND) in Britain in the late fifties), these three plays deliberately leave questions about the pre-play history of the characters unanswered. Pinter is not being perverse when we are given two explanations about Stanley's past as a musician, a deliberately vague suggestion about Goldberg's origins in *The Birthday Party* or frustratingly little evidence about Aston's mental condition in *The Caretaker*. He is simply stating that there are occasions in life when it is impossible to be precise about cause and effect, that our existence can be chaotic and unresolvable and that omniscient knowledge is merely a fallacy. The individual confronts an increasingly difficult task in defining him- or herself in the face of potential holocausts, and in this refusal to be concerned about a character's history before the play begins (a position he has rigidly maintained in interviews about his drama) Pinter was being supremely innovative in bucking the theatrical trend of the thirties and forties which insisted on leaving no loose ends for the audience to fail to tie up. That the characters themselves desire to learn about their background – symbolised by Davies' rootlessness and Rose's touching of Riley's eyes – merely heightens the carefully constructed frustration of the drama by focusing on the paradox by which humans desire to learn but are frequently and depressingly unable to do so.

Additional simultaneously contemporaneous and universal themes are the depiction of palpable and imperceptible threats (Why have Goldberg and McCann arrived? Who lives in the basement below Bert and Rose?), which may possess echoes of the Holocaust (the symbolism of the gas stove in Aston's room has often been questioned); the threat and realisation of violence (the destruction of the drum in *The Birthday Party*, the attack on Riley); and, most noticeably, the struggle for territory. As the name of the earliest play, *The Room*, suggests, sites of conflict are clearly defined and an atmosphere of claustrophobia pervades these works. The boarding-house is both a safe haven and a prison for Stanley, Davies is constantly locked up in Aston's den and Rose is disconcerted by the intrusion into her space of Mr and Mrs Sands and, in particular, Riley. (Characters are obsessed with the delineation and then protection of their own space. Intruders are unwelcome and invariably frightening presences.) This is certainly how Hobson viewed *The Birthday Party* in 'The Screw Turns Again':

Mr Pinter has got hold of a primary fact of existence. We live on the

verge of disaster. One sunny afternoon, whilst Peter May is making a
century at Lords against Middlesex, and the shadows are creeping along
the grass, and the old men are dozing in the Long Room, a hydrogen
bomb may explode. That is one sort of threat. But Mr Pinter's is of a
subtler sort. It breathes in the air. It cannot be seen, but it enters the
room every time the door is opened. (There is something in your past –
it does not matter what – which will) catch up with you. Though you go
to the uttermost parts of the earth, and hide yourself in the most
obscure lodgings in the least popular of towns, one day there is the possibility that two men will appear. They will be looking for you, and you
cannot get away. And someone will be looking for *them*, too. There is
terror everywhere. Meanwhile, it is best to make jokes (Mr Pinter's
jokes are very good), and to play blind man's buff, and to bang on a toy
drum, anything to forget the slow approach of doom. 'The Birthday
Party' is a Grand Guignol of the susceptibilities.[128]

For Hobson, the work was supremely theatrical and this is perhaps the
most important facet of Pinter's dramaturgy. Trained at the Royal
Academy of Dramatic Art and the Central School of Speech and Drama,
Pinter spent a number of years gaining acting experience in provincial
repertory, developing into an accomplished actor. The British public was
reminded of his brilliance as a performer in the 1997 television adaptation
of Hugh Whitemore's *Breaking the Code*, where he played the role of a
sinister head of the secret agency, MI5. Pinter's practical experience is
evident in his intuitive and precise sense of what will work on stage, a
factor most evident in his sense of timing. Peter Hall, who after directing
the première of *The Homecoming* in 1963 was to be responsible for a
further eleven new Pinter productions, explains this precision in relation
to the much discussed 'Pinter pause':

Pinter marks his text with three different notations. The longest break
is marked *silence*: the character comes out of it in a different state to
when he or she began it; the next is marked *pause*, which is a crisis point,
filled with the unsaid; and the shortest is marked with three dots, which
is a plain hesitation. ... The words are weapons that the characters use
to discomfort or destroy each other; and, in defence, to conceal feelings. Pinter is always a cockney, albeit sometimes a very well-bred one.
The essence of his work is 'taking the piss': deriding an antagonist while
treating him with extreme friendliness and charm. Ideally, the person
whose piss is being taken should be entirely unaware of the fact. London taxi drivers are experts at the technique.[129]

This highly theatrical combination of the linguistic and the social, the humorous and the threatening, and the struggle for power and the struggle for territory has given rise to another key phrase of post-war drama, the 'Pinteresque'. However amorphous the term may now have become, its existence emphasises the uniqueness of Pinter's dramaturgy, whatever its roots in absurdist theatre.

Into the Sixties

Battles to be Fought

Although by the end of the fifties the face of British theatre had been irrevocably changed by the blood transfusion of new writing, many battles remained to be fought. The Lord Chamberlain still kept a vigilant and restrictive eye on the stage, as a letter from the reader N.W. Gwatkin to Gerry Raffles, regarding Theatre Workshop's production of *The Hostage*, proves:

> A complaint has been received in connection with that rhyme over which we had some trouble – about the Gallic Pawnbroker. The Lord Chamberlain would be glad if you can think of some verse which will not be misconstrued as the obvious rhymes with 'falls' and 'runt' can be, and indeed, have been.[130]

The creation of the National Youth Theatre (NYT) by Michael Croft in 1956, together with Caryl Jenner's earlier Unicorn Theatre Company (1947) and Brian Way's Theatre Centre (1953), had begun to disseminate the notion of a theatre for young people. Founded initially to allow Croft's pupils at Alleyn's School to receive professional direction in Shakespeare plays, the NYT expanded during the sixties to produce London summer seasons that showcased important work, notably Peter Terson's play about life on the football terraces, *Zigger Zagger* (1967), and many famous performers gained experience with the company, including Helen Mirren and Derek Jacobi. But much work would be needed before over 150 Youth Theatres could exist by 1969 and the true importance of Theatre-in-Education be recognised;[131] and the birth of *the* National Theatre, after over a hundred years of thwarted aspiration, still remained a contentious matter. Its establishment was the top priority now for many in the profession, particularly Kenneth Tynan, who in his 'Decade in Retrospect: 1959' revealed that

> My hope for the sixties is the same as my hope for the fifties – that

before they are out I shall see the construction of the National Theatre. Or, rather, two National Theatres, equal in size and technical facilities. One of them would focus its attention on old plays, the other on new ones. The talent is demonstrably there. All it needs is financial succour, official status and a permanent address.[132]

There is no little irony in the fact that the creation of the second national theatre to which Tynan was referring would precede the emergence of the first.

The Royal Shakespeare Company

The metamorphosis of the Shakespeare Memorial Theatre into the Royal Shakespeare Company, and with it the creation of one of the most notable theatre companies in the world, was due largely to the vision of Peter Hall. Since directing *Waiting for Godot* in 1955, Hall's stock had continued to rise with productions of Anouilh's *The Waltz of the Toreadors* (1956), *Love's Labour's Lost* (1956), *Cymbeline* (1957), Tennessee Williams' *Cat on a Hot Tin Roof* (1958) (a club performance to avoid the heavy hand of the Lord Chamberlain) and, in particular, an innovative *Twelfth Night* at Stratford-upon-Avon (1958), where Hall had directed Geraldine McEwan to play the part of Olivia not as the customary strait-laced matron, but as a vain, light-hearted but ultimately heartbreaking young girl.[133] This interpretation was considered heretical by some and revolutionary by others and public interest in him was heightened by comparisons with the even more precocious Peter Brook, who since directing the famous *Love's Labour's Lost* in 1945 had been responsible for notable productions of Anouilh's *Ring Round the Moon* (1950), Fry's *The Dark is Light Enough* (1954) and the devastating *Titus Andronicus* with Laurence Olivier as the tragic roman general (1955). Hobson expressed for many in 1957 the fascination of watching 'the difference in the approach of the brilliant director [Brook], who has faith in his author, and of the director, perhaps equally brilliant, who in this instance [*Cymbeline*, 1957] has faith only in himself',[134] and with Brook, Hall, Devine, Dexter, Anderson, Gaskill and Littlewood all responsible for innovative productions, British directing seemed to be undergoing a renaissance to parallel that of British playwrighting.

Following his production of *Twelfth Night*, Hall was invited by the board of the Shakespeare Memorial Theatre to be its new Director from 1960 in succession to Glen Byam Shaw, but Hall had a raft of stipulations to which he wanted the chairman, Fordham Flower, to acquiesce. Hall's plan was as heterodoxical as his direction. Firstly, it involved the creation of an ensemble of actors, directors, composers, writers and designers who would be employed on three-year contracts to develop a company ethos and maximise creativity; secondly, he wanted the company to consist of performers who were 'not only trained in Shakespeare and the speaking of verse but also in modern drama',[135] and for this it would be necessary to find a second home in London to permit transfers between the two venues; thirdly, the operation should exploit the name of its patron, the Queen, and be renamed the Royal Shakespeare Company. Aside from the artistic rationale behind this plan, Hall was very conscious of the imminent creation of the National Theatre and felt that if Stratford was to avoid being eclipsed by this new operation it had to expand quickly and create its own distinctive identity.

Fordham Flower was convinced by Hall's arguments and permission was given to put the company's accumulated reserves of £140,000 towards the acquisition of the London base.[136] The search for this new venue was less smooth, however, than the business of persuading the chairman of its necessity. Binkie Beaumont was a member of the board of the Shakespeare Memorial Theatre and was vehemently opposed to these expansionist plans. Having seen an incremental reduction in his power through the curtailment of entertainment tax and the increasing popularity of the type of plays associated with the Royal Court, he feared that the creation of a London outpost for the RSC, with performers committed to long-term contracts, would tempt actors and actresses away from his H.M. Tennent stable. Consequently, he made things difficult for Hall, refusing to release any of the theatres that he controlled and persuading Prince Littler, the head of the giant Stoll Moss Theatres empire to be equally unhelpful. Prince, though, had a brother, Emile, who also controlled a group of theatres, and whom he vehemently disliked. Playing on this fraternal rivalry, the machiavellian Hall managed to persuade Emile to allow the RSC to occupy one of his theatres, the Aldwych, and the final piece of the jigsaw was slotted in. A three-year lease was taken out from 1960 and a company of young and highly promising actors (many from the Royal Court and Stratford East) was recruited, including Dorothy Tutin, Ian Holm, Ian Richardson, Patrick Wymark, Eric Porter, Dinsdale Landen, Frances Cuka, Derek Godfrey, Jack MacGowran and Peggy Ashcroft.

The prospects for the new decade looked to be very exciting indeed.

Chapter 3

1963–1968

Whose History?: The ESC, 'A Mixed Bag of Actors'

The recent trend of casting a less hagiographic eye on the activities of the English Stage Company in the fifties is exemplified in the autobiography of the actor Robert Stephens, *Knight Errant* (1995). Stephens' career straddles all the notable theatrical movements of the last forty years. Responsible for a much admired interpretation of *King Lear* in an RSC production of 1993, Stephens was an original member of the ESC in 1956 before becoming part of the earliest National Theatre company in 1963, staying at the Old Vic until 1970. For Stephens, the importance of the Royal Court in theatre historiography needs readdressing:

> We look back now and say what a glorious new era of British theatre that was, and so on, but only the Osborne play [*Look Back in Anger*] was that. The rest of it was pretty dreadful and not exciting at all. I dare say I felt this mainly because I wasn't playing anything worth playing. But the whole attitude to everything was flaccid. And it was all personified in the crass and bogus opportunism of Tony Richardson, the director of the Osborne play, and George Devine's right-hand man. He wasn't a good director, but he was a good operator and wheeler dealer.
>
> He manipulated people to suit himself. Nor was George Devine a great director by any means, and he certainly wasn't a very good actor. So the whole first year was crummy, I thought.

Continuing in this unorthodox (and contentious) vein, Stephens then turns to the influence of Brecht on ESC practice:

> There was a certain amount of ideological, uninformed, left-wing non-sense talked at the court about Brecht, but it never cut very deep. *The*

Good Woman of Setzuan in the first season was a particularly dreadful production by George Devine. You always got a long lecture before rehearsals about alienation and Brecht, but once you started you never heard another word about it. You just went on and did it in the same way as you did everything else. We had all this ghastly Chinesey music.

Peggy Ashcroft as Shen Te had a song to sing about the need for a big blanket to cover the people of the city. She was wearing a half mask and a moustache, and old Teo Otto, who had done the music for the Berliner Ensemble, bellowed from the back of the stalls: 'No, no, no, no; this is Ashcroft, not Shen Te'. She was terribly upset because she didn't know – none of us did – how to do alienation acting. There is, of course, no such thing.

Stephens seems to be suggesting that from his perspective (albeit in an underemployed capacity), the real achievement of the ESC was symbolic, in that it showed how the chains of previous practice might be thrown off. His memoirs also provide a salutary reminder that personalities, disputes and collaborations are as integral to the process of drama as movements, institutions and innovations. An actor's existence is characterised by transience, uncertainty and the hope of a good role, and not by an over-arching sense of the historical or prescience about imminent theatrical breakthroughs. Each night's performance will be an act of original creation, and his recollection of events will inevitably be coloured by his own personal feeling of well-being. Stephens' lack of a fulfilling part at this early stage of the ESC's existence left him dissatisfied, as he candidly admits, but his acknowledgement of the absence of excitement at being part of an allegedly revolutionary phenomenon, also provides a useful reminder of the essential fluidity of all historiography: 'As an actor you certainly didn't feel you were part of the changing face of British theatre, though it certainly did change with *Look Back in Anger*. We were a mixed bag of actors, not a company really.'[1] This description of the ESC as a 'mixed bag of actors', accurate yet surprising, emphasises that historical accounts are never finite, but always open-ended – as the ongoing debate about the role of the Royal Court proves.[2]

If Stephens is equivocal about the importance of the ESC, he is certain in his conviction that the theatre of the sixties owed its greatest debt to the man he understudied at the Royal Court in the part of Archie Rice: Laurence Olivier. Stung perhaps by equally revisionist accounts of Olivier's life, Stephens comments:

It is worth stating that the National Theatre, and the theatre of this nation, owes everything to Larry. It saddens me deeply to see him derided and vilified in books and television programmes by people who know nothing and are not worthy of tying his shoe laces. He was a giant, a perfectionist, a man of fantastic loyalty and abiding courage, who worked himself to a standstill for the theatre and at almost negligible material gain to himself. In that sense, he was a true public servant, and that idea of public service in the arts has become rarer as, over the years, the arts themselves have become short-changed and betrayed by mediocrities in politics and journalism.[3]

This true public servant would remain at the heart of subsidised theatre for the next ten years.

A National Theatre at Last

Genesis

The National Theatre Company gave its very first performance at the Old Vic on 22 October 1963, but it had taken over a century of procrastination before Peter O'Toole took to the stage in an uncut *Hamlet* directed by Laurence Olivier. Although David Garrick had called for the creation of such an institution in the eighteenth century, the idea did not receive general support until 1848, when Effingham Wilson, 'the Radical Bookseller of the Royal Exchange', proposed in a couple of pamphlets that a publicly owned 'house for Shakespeare' be established where the works of the 'world's greatest moral teacher' would be constantly performed.[4] Little was done to advance this suggestion, though, until the publication in 1907 of *The National Theatre: A Scheme and Estimates* co-authored by the critic William Archer and the director and playwright Harley Granville Barker. This blueprint included detailed plans for the embryonic institution. The company was to number 66 (44 men and 22 women), seats would be priced from between 1 shilling and 7/6d and the total start-up costs would amount to a third of a million pounds.[5] Such was the interest that the Shakespeare Memorial National Theatre Committee (SMNTC) was formed in 1908 and a private member's bill to establish a national theatre passed with a small majority in 1913. A site was then purchased in Bloomsbury and it looked as if the opening date of 23 April 1916, the tercentenary of Shakespeare's death, might prove feasible, but the First World War dealt a severe blow to the project's prospects and all plans were shelved.

During the inter-war years, the plan was inhibited by the open hostility of the supporters of Lilian Baylis's Old Vic (who saw their own theatre as the prototype national institution), the economic depression and the inability to raise private funds. Although Granville Barker issued a new edition of the proposals in 1930, in which he advocated having two theatres under the same roof, the original site in Bloomsbury was sold. The campaign did not cease, however, and by 1937 the SMNTC was able to purchase a new site opposite the Victoria and Albert Museum.

Again war intervened, but this time the outbreak of hostilities was to prove anything but detrimental to the campaign. The advent of state support for the arts through the Council for the Encouragement of Music and the Arts (CEMA) opened up the prospect of state support for the project. Equally encouraging was the reconciliation between the Old Vic and the SMNTC which led to the creation of a de facto National Theatre at the Old Vic in 1944, the memorable Olivier/Richardson collaborations and the passing of a parliamentary bill committing a million pounds to the project in 1949. At this point, a second financial crisis delayed allocation of the money, and although Queen Elizabeth, the Queen Mother, laid a third foundation stone in 1951 (this time on the South Bank), interminable, possibly fatal delay once again threatened. Indeed, as the specific location of the new building frequently changed during the fifties, the Queen Mother was reported to have suggested that the foundation stone should be put on castors.[6]

The final financial crisis of this gestation period occurred in 1961, when the Chancellor of the Exchequer, Selwyn Lloyd, declared that no public funds could, after all, be devoted to the scheme. It seemed as if the state's historic hostility to the arts, and, in particular, the theatre, was to be perpetuated, but paradoxically this rebuff initiated a concerted campaign on the part of the Arts Council, and the Labour-run London County Council (partially to antagonise the Conservative government) offered to fund part of the construction and to provide the South Bank site rent-free. A National Theatre Board was then established, but the crucial impetus for the project came from Olivier's decision to subscribe to the cause. A movie star, established classical performer and supporter of the New Wave – having played Archie Rice and married Joan Plowright – his enthusiasm and commitment led him to be appointed as the Director of the National Theatre on 9 August 1962, with a view to assembling a company at Chichester, where he was currently Director of the Festival Theatre. The original idea was to base the company temporarily at the Old Vic until the new building on the South Bank was completed. Few could have envisaged at the time that this would not occur until 1976.

Rationale

Effingham Wilson's original notion of a repository for Shakespearean performances was no longer appropriate, given the success of the Royal Shakespeare Company, and many people questioned how the infant National Theatre would be able to establish its own identity. Vociferous critics of the idea, such as Harold Hobson, feared that a National Theatre would mount revivals of the classics at the expense of new drama, dissuade actors from experimentation, thwart the revival of drama in the provinces and act as a museum for 'culture-starved package tourists'.[7] One of Olivier's first acts, however, was surprising and innovative and went a long way towards solving this dilemma: he recruited Kenneth Tynan, the *Observer*'s theatre critic, to be the new concern's dramaturg, with responsibility for shaping the repertoire, proselytising on behalf of the NT and acting as an eloquent if provocative spokesman. Although Tynan was one of Olivier's most devoted admirers, he wielded great and occasionally destructive influence and had as recently as 15 July 1962 attacked the actor in the *Observer* in an 'Open Letter to an Open Stager', suggesting that Olivier was unlikely to be able to run the Chichester company and function as the star actor at the same time: 'Tomorrow *Uncle Vanya* opens. Within a fortnight you will have directed three plays and appeared in two leading parts. It is too much.' Ironically, the 1962 Chichester production of *Uncle Vanya* was considered to be the best production of Chekhov in England to date.

Shortly after Olivier's appointment as Director of the NT was announced, Tynan, with characteristic bravado, suggested himself as dramaturg. Resisting his initial desire to gain retribution – 'How shall we slaughter the little bastard?'[8] he asked Joan Plowright – Olivier agreed with his new wife that it would be more politic to accept, thereby removing a potentially dangerous denigrator of the project and gaining a valuable and loyal ally. Tynan was to remain at Olivier's side until the end his tenure. Olivier's reply illustrates that he, too, could play the Machiavel: 'it will probably not surprise you to know that I think your suggestion is an admirable one, a most welcome one and one that I'd thought of myself already … *God – any*thing to get you off that *Observer!*'[9]

In addition to Tynan, Olivier recruited two practitioners clearly associated with the new wave: William Gaskill, an admirer of Brecht's Epic Theatre, who had directed the plays of N.F. Simpson and Osborne's *Epitaph for George Dillon* at the Royal Court, and John Dexter, who had been closely associated with the plays of Arnold Wesker. Indeed, the first company demonstrated strong links with the ESC, in that Colin Blakely, Robert Stephens, Frank Finlay and Joan Plowright appeared in the first season and Albert Finney was to join for the second. It would be fallacious to claim, though, that the new NT was a Royal Court Mark 2, since Maggie Smith, then making a name for herself in light comedies in the West

End, Michael Gambon, Derek Jacobi, Michael Redgrave and Max Adrian were all encouraged to join as well, which was no mean feat, given the paltry salaries on offer. The basic wage was a mere £14 per week with an additional £1 per performance, Tynan received £46 per week for ten years and even Olivier only received £120 a week as the full-time Director.[10] As Robert Stephens has already indicated, what the NT did share with the ESC was a spirit of adventure that meant that actors were prepared to work for wages infinitely lower than they might command in the West End.

Tynan's aspiration for the National was to stage the best of world drama and consequently of the ninety-eight productions performed at the Old Vic between 1963 and 1973, forty-seven of them had their origin outside Britain, be it in the nationality of the playwright or the director.[11] By broadening the NT's remit away from the glorification of Shakespeare, the new company was able to avoid the charge of duplicating the work of the RSC and soon began to attract favourable reviews. Indeed, over the ten years of Tynan and Olivier's partnership, the first phase (1963–8) was arguably the most successful, since the second (1969–73) was overshadowed by Olivier's illnesses, Tynan's obsession with staging Rolf Hochhuth's revisionist view of Churchill, *Soldiers*, and in-house political wranglings which saw Tynan subjected to control by committee, and the clumsy replacement of Olivier by Peter Hall.

Olivier's Reign Phase 1: 1963–1968

The first production of the new National Theatre was celebrated more for what it symbolised – the end of over a century of thwarted hopes and tenacious campaigning – than for what it achieved. Olivier's decision to cast Peter O'Toole, who had achieved stardom through the film *Lawrence of Arabia*, in the title role of *Hamlet*, worried both Gaskill and Dexter, who were concerned that this might set an undesirable precedent of employing star actors. During rehearsal, Olivier, who was directing the play, clearly feared the worst – 'No one's going to like it – they never do'[12] – and after three weeks of the run he gloomily observed that it was the worst production of anything that he had ever seen.[13] Such despondency was misplaced, however. Although O'Toole struggled, his reputation as a film star was good box-office, with tickets changing hands on the streets for the inflated sum of £60, and the reviews were respectful if lukewarm in their enthusiasm. Committed to further film contracts, O'Toole was never going to become a member of the company and, as it was, the play only ran for twenty-seven performances.

It was the third and fourth productions of the first season – *Uncle Vanya* and *The Recruiting Officer* – that established the National as an institution of some promise. *Uncle Vanya* had already been premièred at the Chichester Festival, but its revival at the Old Vic, with Olivier as Astrov, Michael Redgrave as Vanya and Joan Plowright as Sonya, was widely viewed as an equally spectacular achievement. Harold Hobson was sufficiently moved to write of it being 'the supreme achievement of the contemporary English stage'[14] and Robert Cushman commented retrospectively that

> *Uncle Vanya* was simply the best English Chekhov – maybe the best classic production and certainly the greatest feast of acting – ever. Michael Redgrave's Vanya was an incomparable tragi-comic creation, a portrait of failure that made the spectator ache with recognition.[15]

The poignancy of the event is heightened in hindsight by the knowledge that the shaking that occasionally gripped Redgrave, and which many interpreted as a sign of alcoholism, actually marked the onset of Parkinson's Disease.

The appeal of *The Recruiting Officer* was based on its blend not just of established talent, but of promising newcomers and directorial insight. William Gaskill wrote in 1988 that from the beginning of the National 'the example of the Berliner Ensemble towered over us',[16] and his programme notes confirm his aim as director to inculcate a desire on the part of the audience to question the political basis for events as well as to engage emotionally with characters – fundamental elements of Epic Theatre:

> *The Recruiting Officer* is based on Farquhar's first-hand experience while recruiting in Shrewsbury. Within the conventional framework of a Restoration comedy, he set down his own detailed observation of the effect of a recruiting campaign on a small country town. There are no longer recruiting campaigns, conscription has been abolished, and war is now in the hands of scientists and politicians. What is the particular compulsion for us today of the image of a group of soldiers arriving in a country town? I think what we recognise from our own experience is the systematic deception of the ignorant to a pointless end by the use of heroic images of the past, a past no longer relevant. We may laugh at the recruits but we recognise our own plight.[17]

The influence of Brecht on the production was clear to all – Harold Hobson disapprovingly noting that 'It is inconceivable that *The Recruiting Officer* should not be a popular success. But I have one doubt about the National Theatre. Brecht looms over it'.[18] Most observers, however, were enthralled by the freshness of the approach, the comic genius of Olivier as

Brazen (in spite of having found Gaskill's improvisational exercises in rehearsal terrifying[19]) and the spirited, willful performance of Maggie Smith as Silvia, a great success for the young actress.

The rest of the National's first season continued to demonstrate the influence of practitioners from the innovative new organisations that had developed in the mid-fifties. The designer Sean Kenny, from Joan Littlewood's Theatre Workshop, had already designed *Uncle Vanya*, Jocelyn Herbert of the Royal Court created the scenery and costumes for *Othello* and George Devine himself was invited to direct Beckett's *Play* in April 1964. The run-up to this production illustrated the slightly ill-defined role of Kenneth Tynan, his ability to antagonise, and the incredible loyalty Olivier was to show to him over the next ten years.

On 31 March 1964, Tynan wrote to Devine objecting to the way that the work had been changed in rehearsal following a visit from Beckett himself:

> … before Sam B. arrived at rehearsals, 'Play' was recognisably the work we all liked and were eager to do. The delivery of the lines was (rightly) puppet-like and mechanical, but not wholly dehumanised and stripped of all emphasis and inflections. On the strength of last weekend, it seems that Beckett's advice on the production has changed all that – the lines are chanted in breakneck monotone with no inflections, and I'm not alone in fearing that many of them will simply be inaudible. … The point is that we are not putting on 'Play' to satisfy Beckett alone. It may not matter to him that lines are lost in laughs; or that essential bits of exposition are blurred; but it surely matters to us. As we know, Beckett has never sat through any of his plays in the presence of an audience: but we have to live with that audience night after night!

Tynan was clearly anxious about the vulnerable nature of the embryonic National:

> I wouldn't dream of writing in this way if it were just a question of difference of opinion between us: you're the director and it's your production. But rather more than that is at stake. 'Play' is the second new play the National Theatre has done. The first, 'Andorra', wasn't an unqualified success. … If it fails to get over the maximum impact, it may jeopardise our future plans for experiment and put a weapon into the hands of those people (already quite numerous) who think the National Theatre, like the Proms, should stick to the popular classics and not cater for minority tastes. It may even provoke the more conservative members of the N.T. Board to start interfering in the choice of plays – which would be disastrous![20]

Devine, however, inevitably saw this intervention as unwarranted and intrusive. Many theatre professionals viewed Tynan as a failed, frustrated actor/director and could not conceive why Olivier valued him so greatly, although it is interesting to note the counterview of one insider, Robert Stephens:

> Ken only came in three afternoons a week, but he was at every board and repertory meeting and really was Larry's right hand. There may have been a lot of bullshit with Ken, but none of it was to do with hier-archy or status among the actors. He was a real breath of fresh air, and terribly amusing and stimulating. Although Larry may have appointed him for the wrong reasons, and no one liked him very much, or even trusted him at all, he certainly made his mark and exerted an enormous influence, mostly, I think, for the good.[21]

Devine certainly did not see it that way. On 9 April 1964, he replied in an indignant, aggrieved letter:

> I have purposely not answered your letter until now as I did not want to get involved during the last week of production. ... The presence of Beckett was of great help to me, and to the actors. Your snide comment about him I will ignore. If you don't agree with the interpretation I can't help it. I assume you read the stage directions: 'voices toneless except where indicated. Rapid movement throughout.' It was always my inten-tion to try and achieve this, as it is, in my opinion, the only way to perform the play as written. Any other interpretation is a distortion. ... As for more than my production being at stake, I find your suggestion that a visiting director should be menaced with conservative members of the National Theatre Board quite preposterous. The simple truth appears to be that you got into a panic about 'Play', in case it did not 'come off'. I'm afraid you'll have to have a bit more guts if you really want to do experimental works,which nine times out of ten, only come off to a 'minority' to begin with. ... I am sorry that this incident occurred. My whole experience at work was excellent up to the last week, when your 'phone call and letter were most disturbing and unhelpful.[22]

Called upon to arbitrate, Olivier appreciated both Devine's outrage at a heavy-handed and unjustifiable attempt to interfere in his artistic deci-sions and Tynan's understandable concern for the health of the National Theatre. Replying to Devine on 12 April 1964 (in a letter dictated in his car on the way to a dress-rehearsal in Cardiff), Olivier acknowledged Tynan's fault, but begged understanding:

You of all people in the world, and probably only you, know and appreciate the job that is mine and however furious incidents and mistakes make me, and justifiably so, that if I had really hoped to have a smooth-running, perfect machine in six months, I would by now have shot myself.

My house is going to take a bit of time to get into even reasonable order and my tree, to change my metaphor, has to be pruned with care and not in heat, when such painful operations are necessary.

You, dear love, have been justifiably angry and I am very sorry about it. Please believe me that I have been just as angry with everybody in the whole organisation from time to time, but I am not going chopping off heads right left and centre until I have decided that what is in them is not worth keeping, or that others are going to give me more.[23]

Such hedging was to characterise Olivier's reign at the National and now seems less bumbling and more pragmatic than it did at the time. Through such smoothing of ruffled feathers, Olivier ensured that the National was successfully born.

Olivier's diplomatic administrative tasks were but one aspect of his function as Director, however. He was very much *the* star actor of the company, its leader and flagship, and nowhere was this more apparent than in his performance of Othello, in the production that opened three weeks after *Play* on 21 April 1964. Olivier's approach to the role illustrates how for him acting was a talent that was innate and instinctive. He discovered the character he was playing by focusing on an external feature and working from the outside in, rather than employing the Stansilavskian technique of identifying an inner emotion and working from the inside out, hence his later discomfort with Lee Strasberg's 'Method' approach to acting. Having cast the young Frank Finlay as Iago, thereby minimising the very real risk of Iago overshadowing Othello, Olivier embarked upon an intensive period of physical training in the gym (he had arranged for one to be installed for the actors at the Old Vic), reduced the lower register of his voice by an octave (another early act had been to appoint Kate Fleming as the National's voice coach) and decided that he would play the moor as a Negro and would thus need to transform his colour. Much effort was needed to achieve this metamorphosis: he shaved the hair from his chest, arms and legs; applied the black liquid Max Factor number 2,880 to his entire body, followed by a second coat of light brown and a third to give a mahogany sheen; had his skin polished by his dresser to make it shine; painted his nails with pale blue varnish and then coated his mouth with gentian violet. Such fastidious preparations took three hours to perform and a further two hours were required to return him to his normal appearance.[24] This was notwithstanding the four hours of performance!

For many, the physical appearance, combined with the magnetism of Olivier, was simply breathtaking. Ronald Bryden in the *New Statesman* described Othello's last speech as being

> spoken kneeling on the bed, [Desdemona's] body clutched upright to him as a shield for the dagger he turns on himself. As he slumped beside her on the sheets, the current stopped. … We had seen history, and it was over.[25]

Franco Zeffirelli went further, believing that Olivier's performance was 'an anthology of everything that has been discovered about acting in the last three centuries. It's grand and majestic, but it's also modern and realistic. I would call it a lesson for us all'.[26]

Not everybody was as bowled over, though. Many were disconcerted by Olivier's blacking-up (something that would be unacceptable in today's multi-racial Britain) – Tony Richardson, for instance, spoke of the 'degrading image of a NEGRO in capital letters'.[27] Olivier was also criticised for selfishness, since his performance so overshadowed the role of Iago played by Frank Finlay.[28] Despite such objections, the production was an enormous box-office success, with 3 performances a week in the first season, and 2 in the second, helping to ensure that 96 per cent of the National's seats were sold during 1964/5. A film version in 1965 was followed by a tour to Moscow – still an inaccessible, hostile place to the West – and the National was at last perceived as giving the RSC, fresh from its phenomenal production of *The Wars of the Roses*, a run for its money.

Othello was kept in the repertory for over two years. One down side to this great success, however, was the emergence of Olivier's stage fright, a problem first evident during a performance of *The Master Builder* and a severe hindrance whilst playing the Moor. On one night Olivier was forced to whisper to Frank Finlay, 'Don't leave the stage, move downstage where I can see you – or I'll run – and whatever you do, don't look me in the eyes',[29] and these panic attacks were to haunt him intermittently until his retirement from the stage.

The National's first season ended in June 1964 and Tynan wrote down his reflections on its first year in a memorandum of October 1964.[30] Identifying the problems involved in building a company in an environment where commercial theatre could offer much higher salaries, he argued that the company needed 'actors who passionately believe in the repertory idea, who feel evangelical and idealistic about it', thereby articulating the constant tension that would exist from now on between state subsidised enterprises or non-commercial ventures and the monolithic West End groups. Such tensions would soon lead to the demise of Theatre Workshop.

What Tynan did not remark upon was the need now for the National to produce a new work by a British writer to counter the charge that the enterprise would inevitably become a museum for the tried and trusted. Such a work arrived in the second season with Peter Shaffer's *The Royal Hunt of the Sun* (1964).

After the success of Shaffer's *Five Finger Exercise* in 1958, Binkie Beaumont had been offered the first option on *The Royal Hunt of the Sun*, which focused on the attempt to conquer Peru for Spain by the conquistador, Francisco Pizarro, and his encounter with the Inca King, Atahuallpa. Whilst staying at Beaumont's weekend retreat, Knotts Fosse, Shaffer overheard John Perry, Beaumont's partner, describe the play in the following way:

> You wouldn't believe it, Binkie, but it's set in the Andes mountains in South America and there's this Spanish army marching over them, and there's a big battle scene and they find this Inca king and all his Indians and there are blood sacrifices, and torture and mutilation and there's dozens of scene changes and a cast of hundreds. ...[31]

A horrified Beaumont, fearful of both the cost and any intimation of bad taste, rejected the script for H.M. Tennent, allegedly citing the difficulties implicit in the stage-direction, 'The soldiers now climb the Andes',[32] but he did pass it on to the National Theatre, of which he was now one of Tynan's 'conservative board members'. Whilst the National might be unable to match the salaries on offer in the West End, it sought to outstrip the commercial sector in artistic ambition and *The Royal Hunt of the Sun* was to prove the perfect vehicle for this. John Dexter saw in the script the opportunity to demonstrate the National's versatility and its willingness to be experimental, and his decision to convey the panoramic nature of the work through a combination of *tableaux vivants*, the vivid, exotic costumes of Michael Annals, the haunting music of Marc Wilkinson inspired by Peruvian bird noises,[33] and sequences of movement devised by the French mime artist, Claude Chagrin, helped create a magical visual and emotional spectacle that some chose to describe as 'total theatre'. Bernard Levin of the *Daily Mail*, one of the new brand of acerbic sixties theatre critics challenging the supremacy of Hobson and W.A. Darlington, was particularly struck by the aural and visual elements of the production – 'A second visit to Mr Shaffer's astonishing play confirms all my first impressions and provokes many more. And they all add up to the finest new play I have ever seen'[34] – whereas Herbert Kretzmer of the *Daily Express* spoke for those who felt the work touched upon fundamental issues:

> Woven deep into the glittering almost musical comedy fabric of the National Theatre extravaganza is the personal relationship between General Francisco Pizzaro and Atahuallpa, Sovereign Inca of Peru. In these two men is posed the eternal problem of conqueror and victim, Christianity and paganism, the new order and the barbaric simplicity of the old. No solution is offered, only pessimism and grief and pain at man's incapacity to live with his brother.[35]

Less immediate reaction, however, has tended to argue that the production obscured the deficiencies of the script, which means that revivals are problematic. Ronald Hayman belongs to this school of thought, writing in 1979 that it

> is ultimately the texture of Shaffer's writing that lets the play down. It would have required verse, or prose poetry … to control the resonances emerging out of the wide-ranging references. Shaffer's prose is workmanlike but at best undistinguished and at worst portentous.[36]

Robert Stephens, too, contends that 'it was a good play only in the sense that it was a great gift to the actors' and director's resources of invention and imagination'.[37]

What was not contended, however, was the general view that the casting of Robert Stephens as the sun god, Atahuallpa, who offers at the end of the work to die and be reborn overnight to prove his divinity, was particularly inspired. Influenced by the 'animal vitality and remarkable technical virtuosity'[38] of Olivier's Othello, Stephens also shaved his head and buffed his skin, employed a balletic dancing movement and developed a particular form of high-pitched articulation that placed great emphasis on consonants – all to convey a sense of the god's 'otherness'. Such was the charisma of his character that when, having been garotted and surrounded by his followers awaiting his resurrection, the beam of morning light failed to stir him, the dismay on the part of the audience was palpable.[39] Stephens' performance added to the growing belief that the actors, directors and designers at the National were coalescing into an accomplished and innovative collective.

By 1968, four strands of work could be detected in the National's repertoire: polished and searching revivals of classics (*Uncle Vanya* (1963), *The Recruiting Officer* (1963), *Hay Fever* (1964)), ambitious experimental work

(*The Royal Hunt of the Sun* (1964), John Arden's *Armstrong's Last Goodnight* (1965)), productions that were influenced by continental European or world theatre practice and examples of significant new writing. Included in this third category were a *Much Ado About Nothing* directed by Franco Zeffirelli (1965); a *Mother Courage* (1965) that attempted to ape the methodology of the Berliner Ensemble; Feydeau's *A Flea in Her Ear*, which was the success of 1966 and compelled Herbert Kretzmer to observe that played 'by a company as expert as that of Britain's National Theatre, the result is a delight and an amazement';[40] Strindberg's *The Dance of Death* (1967), in which Olivier gave a show-stopping performance as the Captain (an achievement which, in Robert Stephens' view, was the finest of his entire National career[41]); and a translation of Seneca's *Oedipus* (1968) that marked both Peter Brook and John Gielgud's first (and in Brook's case, last) appearance at the National.

New writing continued to flourish at the Old Vic as well. Shaffer followed up *The Royal Hunt of the Sun* with *Black Comedy* (1966), which explores the idea of having the stage fully lit while the action is supposedly taking place in darkness. It was a comic tour-de-force, surpassed only by the first work of a young Czech-born playwright, Tom Stoppard, which had first been produced on the Fringe of the Edinburgh Festival in 1966. Following an enthusiastic review of the barely seen *Rosencrantz and Guidenstern* by the *Observer*'s critic, Ronald Bryden, Tynan requested the script and recommended it for production. Seldom has a new play received such a rapturous reception. Combining elements of the absurd (Hamlet's two friends spend their time debating why they have been summoned to Elsinore in the manner of Vladimir and Estragon), demonstrating Stoppard's hallmark, linguistic wit and wry irony, and ingeniously appropriating *the* drama text, *Hamlet, Rosencrantz and Guildenstern are Dead* (1967) seemed to signal a change of direction for new writing. It was comedy that defied labelling, but effortlessly synthesised intellectual debate and humorous observations. The National received nearly as many plaudits as Stoppard for a gamble that had paid off.

By 1968, the increasingly confident institution was succeeding in both showcasing the best of world drama and providing an opportunity for indigenous talent – be it in performing, directing or writing – to demonstrate its energy. The only difficulty stemmed from its very success, in that more people wished to visit their productions than the Old Vic could comfortably house. Although the company began to tour from 1964 and took over the Queen's Theatre for the 1966/7 season, the need to move to purpose-built premises was already becoming pressing. The shadow of the move to the South Bank was to hang over the whole company during the next phase of the National's existence, 1969–74.

The Royal Shakespeare Company

Hall's Reign (1963–1967)

One of the reasons why London came to be seen as the capital of world theatre in the sixties was the existence not just of one, but of two world-class, state subsidised companies: yet the parallel existence of the two companies was the subject of some doubt during the early years of the decade. Although the Royal Shakespeare Company (as it was called from March 1961) established its London base at the Aldwych in December 1960, its opening season was unspectacular, and the monumental disaster of Zeffirelli's *Othello* (1961) with John Gielgud as the Moor (his beard fell off, his body make-up blended into the dark set, the enormous pillars swayed when leant against, and Ian Bannen as Iago had great difficulties with his lines – 'a famous catastrophe'[42] in Peter Hall's view) was only partly effaced by the appearance of a new, young talent, Vanessa Redgrave, as Rosalind in *As You Like It* (1961). The uncertainty of the season's productions was equalled by continued confusion about the company's relationship with the looming National Theatre. A year earlier, Laurence Olivier had informed Peter Hall that he was going to make a stab at the National Theatre and invited him to be his number two, but in a response that typifies Hall's independence of spirit, he politely declined the offer and stated that he was going to establish his own theatre – as 'number one'.[43]

It was the belief of Oliver Lyttelton, Lord Chandos, the chairman of the Joint Council for the National Theatre, that a tripod arrangement should be created binding together the Old Vic, Stratford and the new venture,[44] and initially Hall supported this notion. However, when the Chancellor of the Exchequer, Selwyn Lloyd, announced in March 1961 – to general astonishment – that the government would not support a new National Theatre and would award £400,000 to the Old Vic, regional theatre and Stratford, Hall rejoiced. Stratford's euphoria was shortlived, though. Three months later, after much political lobbying (Lord Chandos even pointing out that the decision insulted the Queen Mother, who had laid one of many foundation stones[45]), Selwyn Lloyd relented. With a grant and the London County Council's offer of £1 million, the scheme was resurrected.

Stratford's attitude now changed entirely, since it feared that what was being planned was less a partnership than a takeover. Fordham Flower, the chairman of the RSC board, was deeply suspicious of Olivier's intentions, believing that he wanted to lessen the RSC's competitive edge, reduce its attraction for actors, have Peter Hall working with him rather than against him (a prescient notion, given Olivier's recruitment of Tynan), exploit Stratford's technical expertise and managerial practices and 'get his mitts on Stratford revenues'.[46] Relations between Hall and Olivier distinctly cooled in early 1962, with Olivier making explicit his sense of insecurity in a letter:

> The trouble as I see it (and have from the beginning of your schemes) is that you have really set out to be the Nat[ional] Th[eatre] yourself, or if you prefer it, for Stratford to develop a position for itself as heir to the throne, or else to make such a throne unnecessary. If this is *not* so (as I know you genuinely want a Nat[ional] Th[eatre]) *it looks like it* (to observers I mean, not to me).[47]

Stratford withdrew from the Joint Council, and hence from the tripod plan, in January 1962.

Fortunately, the 1962 season was much more auspicious for the RSC. David Rudkin's *Afore Night Come* (in which a tramp was ritually murdered on a rubbish dump) ensured that the company maintained a high public profile (part of Hall's propaganda tactics in his battle with the National Theatre); Vanessa Redgrave continued to intrigue, this time as Katherina in *The Taming of the Shrew*; Harold Pinter co-directed a short play with Hall, *The Collection*, that boded well for future collaboration; and Peter Brook directed a much admired *King Lear*, with Paul Scofield as the king, Alec McCowen as the fool and Diana Rigg as Cordelia, which for the first time aimed to persuade the audience that Goneril and Regan had genuine grounds for dissatisfaction. Now that the National had begun its own operation at the Old Vic, the RSC seemed better prepared to face the new competition and its robustness was proved in the following year when the RSC mounted the mammoth enterprise that was to guarantee its existence.

The Wars of the Roses (1963)

Since being an undergraduate at Cambridge, Hall had been fascinated by the rarely performed three parts of *Henry VI* and *Richard III* and for the 1963 season he planned in collaboration with John Barton and the designer, John Bury (recently recruited from Theatre Workshop), a project based on these four works. It was to be named *The Wars of the Roses*. Adopting a policy that he was later to recant – 'I blush at our frenzy of adaptation in the light of the present fashion for authenticity',[48] he wrote in 1993 – Hall agreed that the plays needed to be compressed and Barton therefore prepared a script that reduced the three parts of *Henry VI* into two, renaming the second part *Edward IV* and concluding with *Richard III*. After constant revisions, 12,350 lines had been reduced to 7,450, of which 1,444 had been devised by Barton.[49] Hall sought to justify this creation of sections of pastiche by citing the guiding principle behind the whole project – the desire to stress the relevance of Shakespeare's work to a modern-day audience. Reassured by the proof copy of Jan Kott's soon-to-be influential *Shakespeare Our Contemporary*, which ventured that the depiction of the political process in the Henry trilogy adumbrated the abuse of power in twentieth-century communist states, Hall argued that

> At any given moment ... there is only one way of expressing the intentions of that play. And those intentions must be expressed in con- temporary terms. At any given moment it may mean that there is a slight refocusing of the dramatist's intentions.[50]

The hubris of this belief was emblematic of the self-confidence of the younger generation of this period. 'It was the very stuff of the Sixties', in Hall's view.[51]

This emphasis on the contemporary, with the memory of the Cuban missile crisis of October 1962 very much in people's minds; the stellar cast, including Peggy Ashcroft, Ian Holm and Janet Suzman; and John Bury's monumental, tactile set of tarnished copper plates and a main floor of expanded steel, that echoed as actors walked across it (to ensure 'that the inhuman tramp of authority was heard throughout the theatre'[52]), made an enormous impression on audiences. Shakespeare appeared rein- vigorated, theatre once again seemed relevant and at the cutting edge of modern day thought, and Hall's fierce battle for the independence of the RSC was viewed as necessary and complete. He had created an unortho- dox company of the sixties that functioned by asking questions instead of expecting answers.[53] Bernard Levin in the *Daily Mail* encapsulated the mood of awe by writing of 'a production of epic, majestic grandeur, a landmark and beacon in the post-war English theatre, a triumphant vindi- cation of Mr Hall's policy, as well as his power, as a producer.[54] The whole process was repeated in 1964, together with the complete cycle of history plays, to celebrate the 400th anniversary of Shakespeare's birth.

Peter Brook: *Marat/Sade* (1964) and *US* (1966)

The RSC's policy of aiming to infuse contemporary and experimental works with the discipline and techniques absorbed through immersion in

Jacobean texts (and vice versa) led to an initiative in 1964 that further confirmed the vitality of English theatre at this time – Peter Brook's 'Theatre
of Cruelty' season.

Brook was strongly influenced by European theatre practice and he
ensured that the RSC was continually introduced to innovative continental
ideas. His production of *King Lear* with Paul Scofield was inspired in part
by Jan Kott's stress on the timelessness of Shakespeare, and, fascinated by
the emphasis of Antonin Artaud on violent images and elements of ritual
over the importance of words, he requested that he be granted a dozen
actors to prepare an experimental programme that explored improvisation,
physicality, mime and vocal techniques. Initially, the work of this sub-group
was premièred at the theatre space attached to the London Academy of
Music and Dramatic Art (LAMDA), a club theatre that escaped the stric-
tures of the Lord Chamberlain, but the group entered the main repertory
in August 1964 when *The Persecution and Murder of Marat as Performed by
the Inmates of the Asylum of Charenton under the Direction of the Marquis de
Sade* (quickly known by the shortened *The Marat/Sade*) was performed at
the Aldwych. The production, adapted from Peter Weiss's original by
Adrian Mitchell, seemed, as did the later *The Royal Hunt of the Sun*, to be
an ambitious attempt at that elusive concept, 'total theatre'. Although a
simple reading of the text cannot do justice to the spectacular effect that
Brook's group created, a brief summary of the action suggests why the production was considered both discordant and visually arresting.

The fifty-year-old Marat is sitting in his bath tub, since he is

> disfigured by a skin disease
> And only water cooling every limb
> prevents his fever from consuming him (Herald)[55]

After a mime depicting 'the piercing and bursting of the fat belly' of a
priest, Marat explains why, four years after the revolution, he continues to
attack the church with gusto and condones the continuing executions. De
Sade, who is directing the play of the assassination of Marat within the asylum (where the inmates function as both observers and participants in the
action), then engages Marat in debate, dismisses patriotism, rejects compassion as 'the property of the privileged classes' and masochistically has
himself whipped by Charlotte Corday, the eventual murderer (memorably
played by Glenda Jackson). Towards the end of Act One, different historical characters (including Voltaire) join the action to lambast Marat.

In the shorter second act, Marat (again from his tub) addresses the
National Assembly, and with echoes of the didacticism of Epic Theatre,
accuses it of betraying the nation:

The people can't pay the inflated price of bread
Our soldiers march in rags
The counter revolution has started a new civil war
and what are we doing
The farms we confiscated from the churches
have so far produced nothing
to feed the dispossessed
and years have passed since I proposed these farms
should be divided into allotments.

It has already been decreed by history, however, that Marat is to be murdered by Charlotte Corday when she makes her third visit to his quarters. Thus, after de Sade has instructed the singers to reveal to Marat 'how the world will go after his death' over the next fifteen years, he enjoins Charlotte to perform a stylised assassination. At the climax of the play the increasingly agitated inmates begin to take over the asylum, and de Sade's pleasure at this is matched only by the horror of Coulmier, the director of the asylum, and Jacques Roux, the radical socialist and former priest. Roux's final words, addressed to both the inmates and the audience, represent a classic Brechtian challenge to reflect on what has happened:

When will you learn to see
When will you learn to see
When will you ever understand.

The work concludes with de Sade standing on his chair laughing triumphantly and Coulmier, having incited the nurses to suppress the 'mad marchlike dance' of the uncontrollable patients with extreme violence, finally giving, in desperation, the order to close the curtain.

In his introduction to the published edition of 1964, Brook explained how he believed that verse alone no longer contained the capacity to move audiences, how the 'Verfremdung' of Epic Theatre is able to place an action 'at a distance so that it can be judged objectively and so that it can be seen in relation to the world'; and, crucially, how contrary to received opinion, Epic Theatre is entirely compatible with Artaud's conception of theatre as an 'immediate and violent subjective experience'. Again, this ground-breaking shift from the oral to the visual and the subjective – Brook brought to London the Polish director Jan Grotowski to help investigate what happens to the psyche of the performer beyond the threshold of pain[56] – alienated many critics, but greatly intrigued the public. Brook himself delighted in the hostility of the press:

One of the London critics attacked the play on the ground that it was a fashionable mixture of all the best theatrical ingredients around – Brechtian – didactic – absurdist – Theatre of Cruelty. He said this to disparage but I repeat this as praise.[57]

The eclecticism of Brook and the RSC was further demonstrated by his 1966 production of *US* which, with searing satire, was fiercely critical of American involvement in Vietnam, slightly before this cause was taken up across the world. Less successful artistically than *The Marat/Sade* – audiences found the final descent by the cast into the audience with brown paper bags over their heads particularly embarrassing – the work was nevertheless significant in that it highlighted both the RSC's continuing ability to experiment and disconcert, as well as the increasingly anachronistic role of the Lord Chamberlain. Alarmed that the play might endanger the 'special relationship' between the two allies and that it would put the president of the RSC – the former Prime Minister, Anthony Eden – in a compromising position, Lord Cobbold attempted through quiet persuasion to have the venture dropped. Unabashed, the RSC governors refused to accede to his wishes, backed the project and quietly brought forward Eden's retirement, demonstrating the pragmatism of the chairman, Fordham Flower, whose support of Hall throughout his reign was as unswerving as it was vital. Typically, Brook put the incident to artistic use, reminding the actors that 'if this crisis had taken place in Vietnam, some of us would be dead by now'.[58]

Highs and Lows: Harold Pinter, Emile Littler and 'Dirty Plays'

(The experimentation of the RSC in the mid-sixties was not irksome to the Lord Chamberlain alone. Interviewed by the *Evening News* on 24 August 1964, the impresario Emile Littler, possibly still smarting from Hall's refusal of his earlier offer of the Cambridge Theatre as a London base, argued that works such as *The Marat/Sade* and *Afore Night Come* were unsuitable for public subsidy and besmirched the image of the Queen, who was the company's patron. 'They are dirty plays', he claimed. 'They do not belong, or should not, to the Royal Shakespeare Company.')The row deepened when Peter Cadbury, the chairman of the ticket agency, Keith Prowse and Co., claimed that the RSC was in danger of killing the profitability of theatre as a commercial enterprise, thereby broadening the attack to question the very premise of subsidy. Ironically, the RSC's doughtiest defender was Harold Hobson, now viewed as a rather idiosyncratic critic who believed in the necessity of the Lord Chamberlain's role. A week after Littler's interview, he wrote that

The assumption that plays such as the Royal Shakespeare Company puts into its repertory are in general immensely less acceptable to the public than entertainment plays is false. If the theatres are being emptied, it is the so-called entertainment plays that are emptying them.[59]

That someone who had 'almost died of fright'[60] at *The Marat/Sade* was prepared to write this, confirmed that the RSC could still call upon powerful supporters.

The enterprise of the Theatre of Cruelty season played a part in persuading Harold Pinter to let the RSC have his next full-length play, *The Homecoming*. This was a great *coup* for the company, because Pinter had previously been the only new writer of note whose work had not been premièred in the subsidised sector. Opening in June 1965, it marked not just the beginning of Hall and Pinter's remarkable collaboration (Hall was to direct Pinter's eleven subsequent premières), but reinforced Hall's belief that 'the textual discipline of the classics could and should be applied to modern drama'[61] – the house style of Hall's reign. This invigorating juxtaposition of the Renaissance with the modern was further validated by David Warner's performance as Hamlet in the same season. Twenty-four years old, gangling, classless and gently subversive, Warner gave a performance which eschewed the grandiose and monarchical, thereby disappointing those who wished for a more traditional interpretation of the role. Yet whilst the reviews were mixed – only Ronald Bryden in the *New Statesman* was keenly enthusiastic and even a not unsympathetic Hobson described Warner's outward appearance as that of a 'rather gloomy farm labourer'[62] – audiences, intrigued by Warner's heterodoxical approach, rushed to see the show and it ran for over 150 performances. Looking back, Hall felt that the production 'completely expressed the spirit of the young of that period, gentle and dangerous'.[63]

The five turbulent years of establishing a London base, creating an identity independent of the National Theatre, defining a vision for the company and directing many varied productions, all took a toll on Hall's health. The death of Fordham Flower in 1966, his much loved and highly supportive chairman of the board of governors, was a huge blow and this, coupled with the enormity of planning the move to the Barbican (which was not to materialise until 1982), a tangled personal life and a disastrous *Macbeth* in 1967, persuaded Hall to leave the RSC in 1968 and develop his growing interest in directing opera. Although he was later to state that his departure had been a mistake, he was not about to embark upon a period of quiet retirement. It is one of the supreme ironies of post-war British theatre that in the following decade Peter Hall would take over the running of the other flagship company of the subsidised sector, the National Theatre, at its new home on the South Bank. Hall's successor was another director, Trevor Nunn, who, together with Terry Hands, would continue to nurture the RSC as a world-class company over the next twenty-five years, before Nunn, too, would complete a remarkable circle by becoming the Director of the NT in 1997.

Joe Orton: Disdaining Authority

Agents: Peggy Ramsay

By the early sixties it was becoming apparent that the first generation of realist writers such as Osborne, Wesker and Arden, were being followed by a new generation of playwrights, equally keen to take advantage of the changed theatrical climate, but possessing an even more diverse approach to dramaturgy. This grouping, never self-consciously a band even though the phenomenon was later termed 'the second wave' by John Russell Taylor, included Rhys Adrian, Alan Ayckbourn, Peter Barnes, Caryl Churchill, David Cregan, Stanley Eveling, Donald Howarth, Henry Livings, Frank Marcus, John McGrath, David Mercer, Peter Nichols, Joe Orton, Alan Plater, David Rudkin, James Saunders, Peter Terson, Hugh Whitemore and Charles Wood. Remarkably, all those named above were represented by one agent, Peggy Ramsay, and her influence on the evolution of new writing at this time provides further evidence of the increasingly eclectic nature of the British theatrical process. To the theatrical triumvirate of actor, director and playwright, one now needs to add critic, censor, impresario, director of subsidised institution and agent as significant factors in the development of British drama, not to mention new spaces for performing, non-theatre productions and evolving techniques for acting which would emerge throughout the sixties.

Peggy Ramsay had established her agency (Margaret Ramsay Ltd) in 1953 and although the early years were concerned with establishing a client list, she swiftly laid down the principles that were to make her the pre-eminent theatrical agent of the sixties, seventies and eighties. Firstly, she adhered to the common practice of not tying her clients to contracts to her firm, arguing that this could stifle creativity. Secondly, she endeavoured to be enthusiastic about scripts that she liked without being sycophantic and thirdly, she always spoke her mind, even if that caused temporary pain. Her biographer, Colin Chambers, observes that

Peggy believed that as an agent she should not act as a mere hireling who was afraid to speak out; she had a duty to tell her client the truth as she saw it. 'Once an author has become successful and famous', she wrote to [Robert] Bolt, 'it becomes more difficult to speak the truth, and this is why people like Rattigan become bloodless, because, in time people fear to give them anything but lip service for self-preservation's sake.[64]

Thus, she actively prevented Ann Jellicoe from taking a television contract:

> When I was offered a television adaptation of *Catch 22* Peggy was dead against it. She said it would be interrupted every five minutes by ads and she made me feel ashamed because I wanted to earn some money for once, and yet she was right.[65]

When Alan Plater approached her in 1961 at the start of his career to sell two of his plays, she reminded him that she set great store by her writers' work and that she dealt with art not commerce: 'I don't sell plays! My writers write plays and other people want to buy them';[66] and Alan Ayckbourn, prior to his first West End success with *Relatively Speaking* in 1967, was given some prescient advice in one of her famously analytical letters:

> I hope you aren't disappointed or disconcerted in my interest in your 'development' of characters – I know you can do all the rest as only you can. ... What I really want so much is for you to be fully estimated. A really successful author is often underestimated critically – the prizes tend to go to the boys who write characters and can't write a plot if it killed them.[67]

From such exchanges was born the legend of this forthright, formidable yet generously supportive figure.

Edna Welthorpe, *Entertaining Mr Sloane* (1964) and *Loot* (1966)

One of Peggy Ramsay's most notable discoveries of the 1960s was Joe Orton, whose anarchic, satirical and irreverent comedies, together with his tragically curtailed life, seem very redolent of the period. Overwhelmed by her client list, Ramsay had declared that she would read no more new scripts in December 1963, but, aware of her interest in radio, her secretary helped bend this rule when Orton dropped off a script at her Goodwin Court office a month later, politely stating that he had just had a piece accepted by BBC radio.[68] The script was *Entertaining Mr Sloane*, in which an attractive, bisexual nineteen-year-old comes to lodge at the house of the middle-aged Kath, her brother Ed and their father, Kemp. Sloane submits to Kath's advances and she becomes pregnant, but Ed is equally interested in Sloane. Kemp recognises Sloane as the killer of his former boss and once he threatens to unmask him, Sloane kills him as well. The group dynamics then change, with Sloane now in the thrall of the son and the daughter, and they hatch their famous agreement:

ED: You've had him six months; I'll have him the next six. I'm not robbing you of him permanently.
KATH: Aren't you?
ED: No question of it. (*Pause*) As long as you're prepared to accept the idea of partnership.
KATH: For how long?
ED: As long as the agreement lasts.
KATH: How long is that?
ED: By the half-year.
KATH: That's too long, dear. I get so lonely.
ED: I've got no objections if he visits you from time to time. Briefly. We could put it in the contract. Fair enough?[69]

Needless to say, the unconventionality of this arrangement, the implication, three years before gay sex was legalised for consenting adults over the age of twenty-one, that homosexual desire was on a par with heterosexual desire and the clipped, unadorned sparseness of the dialogue inevitably fascinated some and disturbed others. Orton himself, with a mixture of mischief and a shrewd eye for publicity, helped fan the controversy, by writing to the *Daily Telegraph* under the noms-de-plumes of Peter Pinnell and Edna Welthorpe:

In finding so much to praise in 'Entertaining Mr Sloane', which seems to be nothing more than a highly sensationalised, lurid, crude and over-dramatised picture of life at its lowest, surely your dramatic critic has taken leave of his senses.

The effect this nauseating work had on me was to make me want to fill my lungs with some fresh, wholesome Leicester Square air. A distinguished critic, if I quote him correctly, felt the sensation of snakes swarming around his ankles while watching it.

Yours sincerely,
Peter Pinnell.

Edna Welthorpe soon joined the bandwagon:

> Sir – As a playgoer of forty years standing, may I say that I heartily agree
> with Peter Pinnell in his condemnation of *Entertaining Mr Sloane.*
>   I myself was nauseated by this endless parade of mental and physical
> perversion. And to be told that such a disgusting piece of filth now
> passes for humour!
>   Today's young playwrights take it upon themselves to flaunt their
> contempt for ordinary decent people. I hope that the ordinary decent
> people of this country will shortly strike back!
>   Yours sincerely,
>   Edna Welthorpe (Mrs).[70]

With *Entertaining Mr Sloane*'s notoriety a partial factor, the enlightened
producer Michael Codron (who had been responsible for the West End
success of Pinter's *The Caretaker*) had now proved that new writing could
be commercially successful outside the RSC, Royal Court and National
Theatre, but it was perhaps this very commercial success that persuaded
Emile Littler and Peter Cadbury to include the work amongst their list of
'dirty plays'. From their perspective, worse was to come, when, after an
unhappy touring production in 1965 (which had featured Kenneth
Williams), Orton had produced in September 1966 at the Jeanetta
Cochrane Theatre the masterpiece that was to cement his reputation,
Loot.

Although in structure a rather conventional work – two acts, one
interior suburban setting, a small cast – *Loot* can be seen as being both a
reflection of the changing social mores of mid-sixties Britain and a further
investigation of anarchic, farcical satire that has its roots in Wilde and
Shaw, but its uniqueness is derived from Orton's clinical, mischievous wit.
Two young lovers, Hal and Dennis, have robbed a bank and are forced to
stash the money in the coffin of Hal's mother, who has recently been murdered by her nurse, Fay. Fay is now planning to do the same to McLeavy,
Hal's elderly father, and similarly inherit his wealth. The brilliant creation
Truscott, a spoof on Sherlock Holmes, arrives, posing as an employee of
the Water Board, and there then begins a long and hilarious series of misunderstandings, ludicrous efforts to prevent discovery of the money and
much horseplay with the body that culminates in everyone agreeing to
hush up the robbery and take a share of the loot, apart from McLeavy, the
only upstanding member of the whole group. Truscott has McLeavy
arrested, hints at having him murdered in prison and promises to contact
the others with news of his fate by the evening. The moral is clear: he who
is blind to the endemic corruption around him and is complicitous in

maintaining the status quo (McLeavy's blind trust in authority is constantly reiterated) deserves to suffer the greatest punishment.

The dramatic force of *Loot* comes from its irreverent attitude towards religion, principally catholicism, its scathing attack on those who revere authority, its wry observation of the British obsession with keeping up appearances and, in particular, its quiet celebration of the normality of homosexual relationships – *the* innovation of this 1966 work.

Catholicism and religious reverence (a theme of Orton's *Funeral Games* (1968) as well) are targeted from the very beginning. With the coffin of his wife in front of him, Fay urges McLeavy to think about taking a new wife:

> FAY: Realize your potential. Marry at once.
> MCLEAVY: St Kilda's would be in uproar.
> FAY: The fraternity of the Little Sisters is on my side. Mother Agnes-Mary feels you're a challenge. She's treating it as a specifically Catholic problem.
> MCLEAVY: She treats washing her feet as a Catholic problem.
> FAY: She has every right to do so.
> MCLEAVY: Don't Protestants have feet then?
> FAY: The Holy Father hasn't given a ruling on the subject and so, as far as I'm concerned, they haven't. Really, I sometimes wonder whether living with that woman hasn't made a free thinker of you.[71]

The absurdity of McLeavy's blind devotion to dogma, which Fay attempts to exploit to secure her eighth husband/victim, is exceeded only by his unshakeable (and tragi-comic) belief in the incorruptibility of those in authority. Whilst speculating as to the identity of the bank robbers he articulates a theme that is to become a leitmotif for him, thereby embodying the discredited views that the young of the sixties would associate with the war generation:

> MCLEAVY: What clothes would they wear, d'you suppose? Dust is easily identified. They'd surely not work in the nude? God have mercy on them if they did. Even to avoid the hangman I'd not put up with precautions of that nature.
> FAY: They'd wear old clothes. Burn them after.
> MCLEAVY: If you could get a glance between their toes you'd find the evidence. But to order a man to remove his clothes isn't within the powers of the police. More's the pity, I say. I'd like to see them given wider powers. They're hamstrung by red tape. They're a fine body of men. Doing their job under impossible conditions.
> HAL: The police are a lot of idle buffoons, Dad. As you well know.

MCLEAVY: If you ever possess their kindness, courtesy and devotion to duty, I'll lift my hat to you.

The idiocy of this, the outdated nature of the qualities that McLeavy cites (devotion to duty was anathema to the sixties generation) and, above all, the danger of this complacency, are illustrated in a quintessential passage of Ortonesque linguistic humour at the end of Act One. We have already seen Truscott resolutely maintaining that he works for the Water Board and he now provides further evidence of his amusing buffoonery and sinister amorality:

DENNIS: Can't we stand away from the window? I don't want anybody to see me talking to a policeman.
TRUSCOTT: I'm not a policeman.
DENNIS: Aren't you?
TRUSCOTT: No. I'm from the Metropolitan Water Board.
DENNIS: You're the law! You gave me a kicking down the station.
TRUSCOTT: I don't remember doing so.
DENNIS: Well, it's all in a day's work to you, isn't it?
TRUSCOTT: What were you doing down the station?
DENNIS: I was on sus.
TRUSCOTT: What were you suspected of?
DENNIS: The bank job.
TRUSCOTT: And you complain you were beaten?
DENNIS: Yes.
TRUSCOTT: Did you tell anyone?
DENNIS: Yes.
TRUSCOTT: Who?
DENNIS: The officer in charge.
TRUSCOTT: What did he say?
DENNIS: Nothing.
TRUSCOTT: Why not?
DENNIS: He was out of breath with kicking.
TRUSCOTT: I hope you're prepared to substantiate these accusations, lad. What evidence have you?
DENNIS: My bruises.
TRUSCOTT: What is the official version of those?
DENNIS: Resisting arrest.
TRUSCOTT: I can see nothing unreasonable in that. You want to watch yourself. Making unfounded allegations. You'll find yourself in serious trouble.

It is inevitable that by the end of the work McLeavy's incredible faith in authority figures should result in his ultimate nemesis. Even at the point of his unfair arrest, he clings to empty and meaningless phrases:

MCLEAVY: What am I charged with?
TRUSCOTT: That needn't concern you for the moment. We'll fill in the details later.
MCLEAVY: You can't do this. I've always been a law-abiding citizen. The police are for the protection of ordinary people.
TRUSCOTT: I don't know where you pick up these slogans, sir. You must read them on hoardings.

McLeavy's fate is comic, brutal and prophetic in the light of the miscarriages of justice of the eighties and nineties.

Diaries, Death and Iconography

The confidence of Orton's denunciation of a corrupt establishment and his disdainful attitude to authority struck a chord in mid-sixties Britain. His celebration of gay relationships as a normal alternative lifestyle that happily offended those obsessed with maintaining their social standing (a favourite Orton theme) also appeared refreshingly heterodoxical. At the end of *Loot*, even Hal and Dennis appear to acquiesce to Fay's demand to obey the dictates of social decorum –

HAL: You can kip here, baby. Plenty of room now. Bring your bags over tonight.
FAY: (*sharply*) When Dennis and I are married we'd have to move out.
HAL: Why?
FAY: People would talk. We must keep up appearances.

The irony of a serial killer feeling the need to keep up appearances is obvious, but the remarkable aspect of Hal and Dennis's same-sex relationship, and a sign of the shifting tectonic plates of drama at this time, is the very unremarkability of it for the other characters. Truscott often inadvertently testifies to this, whether in the course of an interrogation –

TRUSCOTT: What were you doing on Saturday night?
HAL (*at last*): I was in bed.
TRUSCOTT: Can you confirm that, miss?
FAY: Certainly not.
TRUSCOTT (*to Hal*): What were you doing in bed?

HAL: Sleeping.

TRUSCOTT: Do you seriously expect me to believe that? A man of your age behaving like a child? What was your mate doing on Saturday night?

HAL: He was in bed as well.

TRUSCOTT: You'll tell me next he was sleeping.

HAL: I expect he was.

TRUSCOTT (*to Fay*): What a coincidence, miss. Don't you agree? Two young men who know each other very well, spend their nights in separate beds. Asleep. It sounds highly unlikely to me.

– or in the witty aphorism, so enjoyed by Orton:

TRUSCOTT (*to Dennis*): I want a word with you. The rest of you outside!

HAL: Can I stay with him? He's the nervous type.

TRUSCOTT: I'm nervous as well. I'll be company for him.

FAY: It'd be better if I was present. He's more relaxed in the company of women.

TRUSCOTT: He'll have to come to terms with his psychological peculiarity. Out you go!

With its emphasis on the unremarkability of the unconventional, *Loot* provided the clearest signal yet that the first wave of fifties drama had metamorphosed into a second wave bred of the sixties.

Orton's life was tragically ended on 9 August 1967, when his partner, Kenneth Halliwell, beat his brains out with a hammer before commiting suicide. His diaries for 1966 and 1967, which his agent Peggy Ramsay had urged him to keep, were published posthumously in 1986, and, given their graphic account of Orton's promiscuity, contributed to an iconography that erroneously suggests that Orton's plays are dominated by celebrations of a hedonistic gay lifestyle. Whilst Orton's final play, *What the Butler Saw* (1967), emphasises the fluidity of sexuality, both works, written within the constraints of censorship, incorporate gay relationships as acceptable without ever letting them entirely dominate the works. Whilst it is best to read the diaries as an account, in Peggy Ramsay's words, of 'how two people are destroyed – one by success and one by failure',[72] one should view Orton's plays as unique dramas that emerge from and then transcend their context, in that they celebrate subversive approaches to authority, sexuality and religion – themes embraced by dramatists from the ancient Greeks onwards. No wonder *Loot* and *What the Butler Saw* continue to enjoy successful revivals well into the nineties.

Staging Change: New Forms for Drama

The second production of *Loot*, which opened in September 1966, earned Orton the prestigious *Evening Standard* Best Play award, ran for 342 performances and banked the large sum of £9,720 for the playwright from the sale of the film rights. West End theatre shows were still the pre-eminent fora for making money, with the waning fortunes of the old impresarios – Binkie Beaumont's empire suffered the ignominy of four plays only lasting one month in May 1964[73] – being compensated for by the arrival of newer ones, such as Michael White and Michael Codron, who were more in tune with the changing tastes of sixties audiences. Not everyone was able to adapt neatly to either the subsidised or the commercial sector, however. At a time when practitioners were interested in exploring new forms, venues and organisations for drama, the gradual alienation of Joan Littlewood from Theatre Workshop – an example of Peter Hall's belief that 'the British never subsidise people: they subsidise institutions. They suspect the artist'[74] – provided a salutary reminder of the tension that existed between the two sectors.

Theatre Workshop: *Oh, What a Lovely War!* (March 1963)

Between 1959 and 1961, the homogeneity of Theatre Workshop's company was threatened by a combination of quite inadequate state funding and (paradoxically) a stream of successful transfers of shows from Stratford East into the West End. *A Taste of Honey*, *The Hostage*, *Make Me an Offer*, *Fings Ain't What They Used T'Be* and *Sparrers Can't Sing* all gained Theatre Workshop greater public recognition and further praise with their showcasing at the Wyndham's, Criterion, New, Garrick and Wyndham's theatres respectively, but the removal of a large body of actors from the company's base threatened the ethos of exploratory, collaborative, practically-based theatre, that depended on a close-knit community of practitioners. Understandably, performers such as Harry H. Corbett had already left the company to earn better salaries elsewhere, and this trend accelerated. To counter this, in 1959 the company abolished the system of paying equal salaries for the transferred shows, but this was merely the destruction of 'a principle of some importance' in Goorney's view,[75] and a sign of things to come.

The need to renovate the Theatre Royal in October 1959, the indifference of the Arts Council to the company's needs for survival (their grant for 1961 was £1,000 against total running costs of £16,500), the perennial challenge of encouraging sufficient numbers of local people to attend the shows and the sheer effort of touring abroad to the Paris Festival (to international acclaim), preparing transfers and discovering new work soon became too much for Joan Littlewood. In July 1961, disgusted by the critical reception accorded James Goldman's *They Might Be Giants*, she left for Nigeria, travelling for therapy with her beloved Gerry Raffles and intending to 'find Wole Soyinka and film his most beautiful play *The Lion and the Jewel*'.[76] She gave one last interview in which she explained her frustration: 'For the past few years I have had dozens of West End managers breathing down my neck. … I cannot accept any more a situation where I am unable to work with a company freely'.[77]

Two years later Littlewood did return to Theatre Workshop for the Stratford East season that Gerry Raffles was coordinating. Initially uninterested in the idea of resuming drama, she was soon drawn to the concept of a show based around the First World War, having listened to some tapes of Bud Flanagan introducing soldiers' songs from the conflict.[78] As with previous Theatre Workshop productions there is much debate as to who was the prime mover behind *Oh, What a Lovely War!* – Charles Chilton, Littlewood herself (as she claims), or even Gerry Raffles – but what is indisputable is that the eventual production, with its intersplicing of songs and newsclips, characters as a group of clowns called 'The Merry Roosters' in a pierrot show and celebration of the stoicism of the combatants in the face of appalling conditions, was hugely praised for its rejection of realism, documentary approach and its emphasis on education through entertainment. Harold Hobson summed up the prevailing mood when he wrote that the 'piece is stamped with originality, with entertainment and pathos, with the true life of the theatre'.[79] A West End transfer and American tour were inevitable, but the ending was changed for the Wyndham's production, with the cynical speech spoken by Victor Spinetti that lamented the fact that wars were still proceeding, being followed, not by a downbeat and thought-provoking 'Goodnight', but by a reprise of the earlier songs. The management, apparently, was nervous of too depressing a finale.[80]

New Spaces: Real and Imagined

The Fun Palace and Centre 42

To avoid such compromises Littlewood increasingly withdrew from the theatre to concentrate on her idea for 'a university of the streets', an ambitious scheme to build an arts complex in the East End of London where people could practise and enjoy activities revolving around science, the plastic arts, music, drama and 'the pleasures of the future'. The complex became known as the Fun Palace and was intended to enable 'self-participatory education and entertainment'.[81] In many ways it was an extension of Theatre Workshop's rationale, but the idea foundered on the inability to obtain planning permission for a suitable site. One of the notions behind the concept, however, the desire to break away from the limitations of drama within fixed locations, such as theatres, fore-shadowed the more portable forms of drama that would mushroom after 1968. Arnold Wesker, too, had been attracted by the idea of revolutionis-ing the purpose of theatre-going. Following a resolution passed by the Trades Union Congress in 1960 that called for greater union involvement in cultural activities, he helped create Centre 42, which had at its hub a series of arts festivals. The group quickly drew the support of Bernard Kops, Alun Owen, Shelagh Delaney, John McGrath and Doris Lessing, and with Wesker as artistic director a festival was held at Wellingborough in 1961, five more in 1962, and a London base, the Roundhouse, was secured in Camden Town. The project suffered the usual difficulties of funding, however, and was eventually disbanded in 1970, but during its limited life it pointed to a diversified future for participative, politically committed theatre that reached beyond large, static institutions.

New Homes for Drama: The Victoria Theatre, Stoke and The Octagon Theatre, Bolton

New buildings were nevertheless needed for an increasingly confident industry, particularly in the regions. Under the stewardship of the coun-try's first Minister for the Arts, Jenny Lee, the principle of public funding took deeper root and between the mid-sixties and the mid-seventies the year-on-year increase in grant aid for drama led to the building or con-verting of more than 100 new venues.[82] In 1962, Stephen Joseph, aided by Peter Cheeseman, helped establish an important new venue, the Victoria Theatre, Stoke. Although born in England, Joseph, the son of Hermione Gingold, had read for a drama degree at the University of Iowa. On his return to England in 1955, he embarked upon what was to become a life-long passion: the staging of plays 'in the round'. The company he created with the express intention of mounting such productions was init-ially based at Scarborough in the summer, before touring around England with a portable theatre, and then arriving at the disused cinema in Stoke, from which the new venue would arise.

Although similar (but not identical) to one of the earliest forms of theatre building (one only has to think of Shakespeare's Globe), 'theatre in the round' had been eclipsed in the twentieth century by the proscenium arch theatre. The foundation of the Victoria Theatre, how-ever, together with the configuration of the Chichester Festival Theatre, illustrated how important stage space was to performance. Once obvious challenges had been surmounted, such as the positioning of the lights to avoid the audience being blinded, sensible blocking to allow an acceptable sight of face and adaptable sets to permit unimpeded vision, audiences and professionals alike quickly became intrigued by the flexibility that such venues offered. Theatre architects were encouraged to break the tyranny of the proscenium arch and in 1967 the Octagon Theatre, Bolton, became the first new theatre to be built in the North-West since the war and the first in the country to incorporate a purpose-built adaptable space. The architectonics of the venue were carefully calculated. The auditorium is an elongated octagon within a hexagon, although only one block of seats is permanent. This allows regular reconfigurations of the performance space, but a sense of intimacy is always maintained, since at any one time the maximum distance from the stage is nine rows.[83] By the end of the 1990s, two more important theatres-in-the-round existed: the Manchester Royal Exchange and the Stephen Joseph Theatre, Scarborough – one man's original vision appropriately memorialised in a title. The proliferation of spaces for drama now began to mirror the diversity of productions, scripts and performances.

Happenings

In many respects, modern theatres-in-the-round seek to replicate the effect of an unplanned, unpredictable gathering of audience members, surrounding the action from all sides and delineating the stage space. The Elizabethan Globe possessed, after all, a pit, in which it was possible to mingle, engage in conversation and presumably become involved through vocal observations, and it is ironic that 1963 saw one of the first examples of a form of drama that was to trace its roots back to spontaneous public gatherings and which was to have a rapid flourishing at the end of the decade – the 'Happening'. The unorthodox American-born theatre director, Charles Marowitz, who was to work with Peter Brook on his Theatre of Cruelty season, found the Open Space Fringe Theatre in 1968 and produce several 'collage' productions of Shakespeare (including *Hamlet* (1966), *Othello* (1972) and *Measure for Measure* (1975), provided an early example of this American phenomenon at the Fringe of the 1963 Edinburgh Festival, and a Happening produced by Michael White and 'coordinated' by Jean-Jacques Lebel in a hall in the Vauxhall Bridge Road, London, well illustrates the chaotic, exciting and bizarre quality of the 'genre'. White described the evening:

The event started with painted girl happeners parcelling the audience in long rolls of white news print. Immersed in this sea of paper, the onlookers were then sprinkled with detergent powder while Carolee went about spraying cheap perfume everywhere. Most of them were clutching a deformed boot or shoe, given to them as they entered. ... Some of the luckier ones were also given a joint to put them in the right frame of mind. ... Various tableaux unfolded before the entranced audience. A girl had a picture of the Pope projected on her bottom. More girls were painted, slapped about with wet fish and strings of sausages, parcelled up in polythene bags. Two schoolgirls flogged a policeman. It was sensational, I suppose. But many of the performances were very evocative and effective. ... It was wonderful to see an audience totally perplexed, not knowing whether they were watching complete junk or a work of genius.

The most remarkable performance of this Festival of Free Expression, though, was, as was so often the case with Happenings, the least expected. The caretaker of the hall, enraged that a tap had been left running in the dressing room, suddenly stormed in:

Actually, Norman's wife entered first. She grabbed me by the hair and screamed. She was going to get the police. It was disgraceful. Then her husband, described by the *Express* as a 44-year-old ex-Army regular, entertained us with his views. Since he was also standing alongside me most people took it for part of the show. Peter Brook went up to him and said: 'I think you're the best thing in the entire evening, a most interesting performance.' So the evening ended in a kind of ecstasy, everyone thrilled that the police came and we were thrown out.[84]

The Method Scorned: Lee Strasberg's *The Three Sisters* (1965)

Equally controversial, and much more scathingly received, was another American visitation, the Actors' Studio Theater production of Chekhov's *The Three Sisters* in 1965. Lee Strasberg and Elia Kazan had founded the Actors' Studio in Manhattan in 1947 to function as a theatre workshop for Strasberg's teaching of the Method approach to acting. Emerging from (although not directly mimicking) the work of Stanislavski, Method acting sought to enable the actor to feel and exhibit true emotion during his performance, constructing a role from within and always retaining some emotional power in reserve, to prevent over-blown, orotund and unnecessarily rhetorical performances. Audiences, particularly film audiences, were often struck by the intensity of early Method devotees, such as

Marlon Brando as Stanley in Elia Kazan's 1951 film version of *A Streetcar Named Desire*, where actors smouldered with passion or were tortured by anguish, without ever quite going over the edge. The simple slogan 'Reveal. Express. Suppress' was often cited at the Actors' Studio as a guiding mantra.

To experience an empathetic reaction with the character being played, the performer was encouraged to identify at a particular moment in the script the emotion that the character was feeling, delve into his own emotional history to identify a period when he might have experienced a similar feeling (a process referred to as 'affective memory') and then utilise this connection in performance. Extensive research into roles was also encouraged: if an actor were to play a surgeon, for example, he was advised to witness an operation. Dustin Hoffman's meticulous preparations for his role in the film *The Marathon Man*, losing a large amount of weight beforehand, is an illustration of the lengths to which Method actors will go to ensure a 'realistic' performance.

By the mid-sixties, Strasberg had become a legend. The roll-call of actors who had attended the twice-weekly sessions between 11am and 1pm on a Tuesday and a Friday, when Strasberg would ask his students to perform excerpts on the stage of the converted Greek Orthodox church and then clinically dissect what he had seen, counselling improvements in the Method manner, was breathtaking. Marlon Brando, James Dean, Paul Newman, Geraldine Page, Shelley Winters and Marilyn Monroe had all flocked to the studio to benefit from Strasberg's teaching, but not everybody was a worshipper at the shrine. Strasberg's virtual humiliation of some performers was perceived by many as being dictatorial and coercive; his connection with Monroe, whom he had coached intensively and placed under the supervision of his wife, Paula, during the filming of movies such as *The Misfits*, attracted the charge of exploitation – the last thing this tragic icon required was to penetrate her deeply unhappy childhood experiences to create the emotional foundation to be a tragic actress (Strasberg once conceived the idea that she should play Lady Macbeth); and in Britain, this mode of acting, which directly challenged the vocal, ornate, well-mannered and polished personas of so many British performers, was treated with great suspicion. A good example of the collision of these two traditions can be seen in the restrained, undemonstrative performance of Laurence Olivier in *The Prince and the Showgirl* (1957), and the effervescent, complex and intriguing display of acting by Marilyn Monroe. Olivier's dislike of Method acting was an open secret. Preferring to construct a role from the outside rather than from within, he took as his inspiration not a rediscovered and intense experience from his past, but a piece of costume or an aspect of his make-up. His prejudices were to be confirmed by the Actors' Studio Theater's visit in 1965.

One paradox of Strasberg's project is that although he initially founded his Studio as a response to his years of isolation in Hollywood and frequently spoke of his antipathy to the values that it represented (even trying to persuade his early devotees to reject lucrative film contracts), it is in the realm of film acting that his practice has had the most noticeable effect. It was not until March 1963 that he created a company to showcase his theories for the theatre (perhaps fearing the scrutiny that this would engender) and not until 1965 that he dared to take the company to the most exciting theatrical city of the time: London. Strasberg was invited by the impresario Peter Daubeny, who ran the World Theatre season at the Aldwych from 1964 to 1973, and he strove hard to ensure that a star cast of Actors' Studio members was gathered together, but in spite of the presence of actors of the calibre of George C. Scott, it was apparent that the company was under-rehearsed and chaotically directed. The first night of *The Three Sisters* was a disaster. The delivery was ponderous, lines were missed and the whole production ran almost sixty minutes over time. Whilst there were a few elements of note (Kim Stanley's Masha was considered to be an innovative interpretation), the critics fell over themselves to repel the interloper. 'I could barely restrain myself from screaming aloud with the pain of my throbbing nerves', observed an outraged Bernard Levin in the *Daily Mail*. Penelope Gilliatt in the *Observer* went further when she claimed that 'The admirable World Theatre Season's last dismal task has been to mount the suicide of the Actors' Studio'[85] and the commentators were virtually united in declaring Strasberg to be a fraud and the Method a travesty. The myopia of this, stemming from the combination of a poor production and a collective chauvinism, would be repented only when more plausible Method performances were viewed in London. The Actors' Studio Theater, however, had given its last performance.

Female Playwrights

Whilst the decade up to 1968 saw the creation of both large metropolitan state companies and spontaneous theatre collectives, exciting developments in theatre design and companies eager to break away from a reverence for the proscenium arch, vibrant European practice and less successful American examples, one much needed change for British theatre seemed painfully slow in coming. The Angry Young Man movement had, in its very slogan, been gender-specific – women's concerns were generally subsumed in men's – Alison irons while Jimmy Porter rants – and there were little obvious signs that female playwrights of the sixties were building on the few earlier examples of drama by women such as Shelagh Delaney (*A Taste of Honey* (1956), *The Lion in Love* (1960)) and Ann Jellicoe (*The Sport of My Mad Mother* (1958), *The Knack* (1961)). Admittedly, both Doris Lessing (*Play with a Tiger* (1962)) and Iris Murdoch (*The Severed Head* (1963)) had enjoyed some success, but the flirting of these novelists with drama was brief and merely served to highlight the absence of new female playwrights dedicated to theatre. Indeed, by the end of the sixties there were less women having drama produced than ten years previously and the eras of Agatha Christie (whose 1952 *The Mousetrap* is now the world's longest-running play) and Dodie Smith (one of the most fashionable and prolific dramatists of the thirties) seemed like halcyon days. As Lib Taylor points out, it would take the development of the Women's Liberation Movement, the creation of more radical theatre groups after the removal of censorship and the confidence derived from political empowerment to move drama by women into the spotlight.[86] There were monumental actresses (Peggy Ashcroft), world-renowned directors (Joan Littlewood), even – eventually – female theatre critics (Penelope Gilliatt): it seemed an anachronism that female dramatists were still lagging behind.

Television Drama

A final late developer to mention at this time offered both opportunities and dangers for the theatre: television. As an increasingly sophisticated and popular medium it represented a further competitor for people's leisure time, but as the audience of 6,380,000 viewers for Harold Pinter's 1960 televised production, *A Night Out*, proved, it could also serve as a way of stimulating interest in drama, as well as offering writers a new forum for their scripts. British theatre had been threatened by the arrival of the 'Talkies' in the thirties, but would quickly develop a more symbiotic relationship with the younger medium.

Television in Britain had come of age in 1953 with the broadcast of the coronation of Queen Elizabeth. Television drama came of age with the appointment of both Michael Barry as Head of BBC Drama and Donald Wilson as Head of the Script Department and their policy of appointing writers to the staff. Previously, plays had been beamed direct from theatres (the earliest being Pirandello's *The Man with a Flower in his Mouth* in 1930), with all the technical limitations that a static camera implied. Now, however, writers were encouraged to consider writing for this medium as a new technical challenge, and this resulted in ground-breaking popular programmes, such as Nigel Kneale's science fiction series, *The Quatermass Experiment* (1953–9) and Ted Willis's reassuring and conservative depiction of police life, *Dixon of Dock Green* (1954). The advent of independent television in 1955 increased the demand for scripts and also saw the arrival of Sydney Newman, a Canadian producer, first as Head of ABC, and, from 1963, as Head of Drama at the BBC. Newman's stress on contemporaneity – 'I think great art has to stem from, and its essence must come out of, the period in which it is created'[87] – created a hugely supportive environment for writers of drama keen to take advantage of the new possibilities, including Alun Owen, Bill Naughton, Clive Exton and Giles Cooper, and this matched the concomitant mood in the London theatre. The *Armchair Theatre* slot and then the *Wednesday Play* on BBC1 became the principal showcases for this movement, and resulted in the work that epitomised the trend towards verisimilitude and docudrama, *Cathy Come Home*. Broadcast on 16 November 1966, Jeremy Sandford's play (directed by the socially aware Ken Loach) focused on the misery of homelessness, and its gritty realism, poignant depiction of Cathy's attempt to be reunited with her husband and children and lambasting of a complacent society created a national outcry. Such was its power that it resulted in the founding of the charity for action on homelessness, Shelter.

By 1968, three trends of realism could be detected in television drama: plays written specifically for the medium that emphasised social reality; soap operas, such as *Coronation Street* (Britain's longest running soap, started in 1960), that were rooted in realism but strove to entertain – in this category also belonged the police serial *Z Cars* (1962), a harder, less nostalgic counterpart to *Dixon of Dock Green*; and situation comedies, such as *Till Death Us Do Part* (1965), that based their humour on exploiting and often parodying contemporary prejudices (in this case, racism and even homophobia). This tradition of British television comedy could trace its roots back to Tony Hancock's intelligent, sardonic comedy series of the fifties, *Hancock's Half Hour*, and still endures today.

A new generation was also now emerging of playwrights who were able to write for both theatre and television. Some, like Trevor Griffiths, eventually preferred to concentrate on television because of its wider reach, but Alan Plater, Jack Rosenthal, David Mercer, Peter Nichols and Dennis Potter continued to produce successes in both media. One crucial, and appealing, difference for television writers was frequently remarked upon, though – the absence of an all-powerful official censor.

The End of the Lord Chamberlain's Blue Pencil

An Indefensible Position (Matron)

By the early sixties it was evident to all concerned with the theatre that the most influential arbiter of dramatic activity was an officer of the Court. His dead hand, according to the innovative producer, Michael White, had overshadowed everything since the end of the Second World War: 'British theatrical life [had been] dominated not by great acting stars, mercurial playwrights or adventurous producers but by the far less well-known figure of the Lord Chamberlain'.[88]

The Lord Chamberlain's anonymity and the respect, no matter how disdainful, that had been accorded to his enormous power in the fifties, began to be challenged in the following decade. On the broadest level, people began to question whether the office of a censor was compatible with a healthy democracy. The expanding range of subject-matter that the liberalising of social attitudes afforded dramatists (sexuality, violence, individual freedom) brought them into increasing conflict with the rigidities of the censor's remit. The arbitrary way that the edicts were interpreted and the almost non-existent explanations as to why licenses were refused provoked immense frustration, as did the Lord Chamberlain's pretence that his was a licensing authority rather than a censoring one. The obvious anomaly that allowed identical scenes to be transmitted on television but banned in the theatre emphasised the farcical nature of the system, and this was plainly illustrated in 1963 when a satirical revue, entitled *See You Inside*, had its licence withdrawn by the Lord Chamberlain shortly before curtain-up, because it contained a disrespectful sketch featuring Queen Elizabeth and Prince Philip setting out for Australia and being ship-wrecked in a London dock.[89] The 450 audience members at the Duchess Theatre were deprived of seeing what eleven million viewers had witnessed earlier on BBC television.

To the recognition of the ludicrousness of this situation was added a growing anger at the restriction of civil liberties and the Lord Chamberlain's lack of accountability. British society was slowly moving towards two pieces of social legislation that would give the individual more choice in matters of personal behaviour – ten years after the Wolfenden report of 1957, the Sexual Offences Act of 1967 would decriminalise homosexuality for consenting adults over the age of twenty-one, and abortion was legalised in the same year. Not surprisingly, the theatre demanded a similarly mature treatment. The furore surrounding the 'dirty plays' controversy of 1964 emphasised how important – and how enervating – matters such

as good taste still were for the British theatre. Kenneth Tynan, in a witty article entitled 'The Royal Smut Hound' (1965), highlighted the futile and dis-
tracting nature of the Lord Chamberlain's scrutiny:

> Since he is always recruited from the peerage, he naturally tends to for-
> bid attacks on institutions like the Church and the Crown. He never
> permits plays about eminent British subjects, living or recently dead, no
> matter how harmless the content and despite the fact that Britain's libel
> laws are the strictest on earth. Above all, he feels a paternal need to
> protect his flock from exposure to words or gestures relating to bodily
> functions below the navel and above the upper thigh. This – the bed-
> ding-*cum*-liquid-and-solid-eliminating area – is what preoccupies him
> most, and involves the writers and producers who have to deal with
> him in the largest amount of wasted time.[90]

Even the House of Commons timidly discussed the possibility of
loosening the noose. In December 1962, Dingle Foot MP was refused permission to introduce a Private Member's bill concerning censorship, but
his very intention was painfully inadequate – he simply wished to make it
optional to submit scripts to the Lord Chamberlain.

By 1965, however, Lord Cobbold, a former Governor of the Bank of
England and the Lord Chamberlain since 1963, was beginning to feel the
winds of change. In April of that year he granted an unprecedented interview to J.W. Lambert of the *Sunday Times*, in which he adopted an air of
injured innocence in setting out his credo. Defining his personal view of
the censor's function as the need 'to assess the norm of educated, adult
opinion', he sought to stress both his reasonableness – he always employed
'a good deal of give and take' – and his refusal to interfere in the creative
process: 'When we ask for a phrase to be altered we never, as is often
alleged, ourselves suggest an alternative text' (a palpably untrue statement
if one examines the Readers' Reports kept at the British Library). Playwrights were often perplexing in their lack of good taste – 'You'd be
surprised to see the number of four-letter words, and I think I can say
obscenities, that are sometimes included in scripts by the most reputable
people' – and they frequently caused him difficulties when wishing to deal
with 'abortion…, farces about artificial insemination, physical contact
between homosexuals and such like': all serious issues of the day. Intriguingly, Lord Cobbold concluded the interview with some observations on
club theatres, which in hindsight were a clear shot across the bows of the
Royal Court. Whilst (rather unconvincingly) claiming that he was very
much in favour of venues where unlicensed plays could be produced –
'They give selective and interested audiences a chance to see experimental

work' – he strongly disapproved of managements using them to put on works that had been refused a license, and gravely commented:

> I very much hope myself that managements will have the good sense not to force the issue on this point, which might well involve difficulties for all theatre clubs and which would, in my view, be harmful to the general interests of the theatre.[91]

Lord Cobbold's concerns were prophetic, since by forcing the issue with Edward Bond's *Saved* (1965) and John Osborne's *A Patriot for Me* (1965), the Royal Court was to strike a significant blow against his powers to censor and therefore hasten the emancipation of British theatre.

A Patriot for Me (1965)

It would be inappropriate to describe *A Patriot for Me* as a ground-breaking play, given its implicit reiteration of the view that homosexuals are neurotic, inherently unhappy people (one only need compare Osborne's depiction of the self-repressed Redl with Orton's creation of the confident Hal in *Loot*, for example). Its true significance for the history of post-war British theatre is that the Lord Chamberlain's inability to persuade the Director of Public Prosecutions to mount a symbolic prosecution marked the first official confirmation that the establishment – and, in particular, the newly elected Labour government – were becoming more reticent in defending theatre censorship.

The play reflects Osborne's shift away from the realism of *Look Back in Anger* to the more panoramic history play, a pattern first evident in *Luther* (1961). Set in Galicia in the 1890s, it focuses on the career of an Austrian officer, Alfred Redl, who is first seen as a second in a duel between the aristocratic Kupfer and a Jewish officer, Siczynski. Redl's support of the latter, who is killed, is represented as both dangerous to Redl's career prospects and emblematic of his true sexuality and Redl's lack of connections, and his vigorously repressed homosexuality (most painfully evident in his uneasy relationship with his Commanding Officer's informant, Countess Delyanoff) emphasise how he, too, is an outsider and runs the risk of being marginalised. Initially, however, he achieves rapid promotion, but his inability to maintain the charade is highlighted in the last scene of the first act where Redl sleeps with a Private Soldier (significantly refusing to turn the light on), finds the experience liberating – 'Why did I wait – so long'[92] – but is then beaten and robbed by the soldier's friends. Positive depictions of homosexuality are absent in this work.

The second act is the one that caused the most controversy, because its first scene features a glittering transvestite ball, where a covert world of homosexual gatherings is revealed. In the opening production, George Devine played the cameo role of Baron von Epp to some acclaim. At the ball, Redl hears of a Viennese psychologist, Dr Schoepfer, who specialises in the homosexual 'condition', but the possibility of taking advantage of this dubious therapy is overtaken by being approached by the Russians with evidence of his increasingly promiscuous behaviour. Succumbing to blackmail (and with more than a glance at contemporary British spy scandals involving, amongst others, the gay Guy Burgess), Redl becomes increasingly desperate and, in a depressingly familiar end to a work involving homosexuality, takes advantage of the option of committing suicide when his duplicity is discovered by his superiors.

Although *A Patriot for Me* was a work of tendentious quality, Devine's tenacity in seeking to stage it was admirable. The Lord Chamberlain's reader, C. Herriot, was quite convinced of its unsuitability for licensing, even though, in an ironically pertinent observation, he had written that 'this is a serious but not a good play about homosexuality'. There were three principle and indefatigable objections: the transvestite ball; Osborne's tone, which was intriguingly interpreted as being designed to inflame the Lord Chamberlain's readers – 'Mr Osborne's overweening conceit and blatant authoritarianism causes him to write in a deliberately provocative way. He almost never misses a chance to be offensive'; and the familiar and dubious fear that the play would deleteriously influence an audience's sexual behaviour:

> If the company wish to try again then the whole of Acts II and III must be drastically revised with the ball left out and the inverted eroticism toned down. The present text seems to be a perfect example of a piece which might corrupt, since it reveals nearly all the details of the homosexual life usually left blank even in the newspaper reports.[93]

Seeing that there was no possibility of obtaining a licence, Devine decided to turn the Royal Court into a club theatre, requiring intending spectators to sign up in advance to join the English Stage Society at a cost of five shillings. The public duly responded, and a month before the opening on 30 June 1965, membership had increased from 1,600 to almost 4,000,[94] but Devine was running a considerable risk. The decision to stage a club performance reduced the potential box-office take and the production costs were large; the possibility of a transfer was remote; British star actors were still nervous of appearing as gay men on the London stage (Maximilian Schell eventually played Redl); and the Lord Chamberlain in his *Sunday Times* interview had expressed his alarm at the policy of utilising the club proviso to stage unsuitable works.[95] The danger of prosecution was real.

As it happened, the play opened to critical acclaim and played to 95 per cent capacity. The ball scene was deemed a coup de théâtre, the work received the 1965 *Evening Standard* award for Best Play and the Lord Chamberlain was incandescent. The Assistant Comptroller, Sir John Johnston, had already written to the Director of Public Prosecutions, urging a pre-emptive legal action –

> The Lord Chamberlain would … wish to emphasise that he has no desire to interfere with the operations of genuine theatre clubs. He is solely concerned to avoid a position where the law can be brought into disrepute by what is no more than a subterfuge[96]

– but no prosecution was sanctioned and although the Lord Chamberlain succeeded in preventing a public performance the edifice was cracking.

Saved (1965)

Weary of the day-to-day grind of overseeing the company, Devine signalled his intention to resign as artistic director of the ESC in November 1964. His achievement had been immense and he is now viewed as one of the chief initiators of the reorientation of British theatre. He died two years later after a period of illness that stemmed from a heart attack that he had suffered in his dressing-room following one of the final performances of *A Patriot for Me*. Devine's successor at the Royal Court was eventually named as William Gaskill, a previous director at the ESC, whose standing had risen greatly during his five-year connection with the National Theatre.

Although not officially taking up his post until July 1965, Gaskill spent the early months of that year planning his first season. In a paper to the company's management committee, he provided a neat summary of the three major changes that had occurred in the British theatre over the previous ten years:

> 1. The emergence of two large-scale permanent companies – The National Theatre and the Royal Shakespeare, playing in repertoire modern as well as classical plays.
> 2. The decline of the West End Theatre as a home for straight plays.
> 3. The death of weekly rep. and the growth of two or three weekly rep. companies and the raising of the standard of plays (though not necessarily of the performance) in the provinces.[97]

Given these events, Gaskill intended to base the ethos of his ESC on the need to create a permanent company that played in repertoire (note the similarity to the National Theatre), and with the focus on contemporary work, since this was 'the only structure in which one can nurse failures, support successes and give new writers the right conditions for their work to be seen'.[98] Gaskill would be given an early opportunity to demonstrate this principle. As with Devine, the third production of his opening season was to prove a defining moment.

Edward Bond's *Saved* was originally intended to open Gaskill's first season, but the objections of the Lord Chamberlain sabotaged this plan. The play, located in South London, depicts the aimless, rootless and enervating existence of a group of young men, whose only relief from boredom is through (generally comic) attempts at sex, mocking jocularity or casual acts of violence. Stark and realistic in its language, unembarrassed in its depiction of the brutality of suburban lives (in both a literal and metaphorical manner) and graphic in its foregrounding of the implicit violence of Pinter, the action focuses on the initially humorous relationship between the twenty- three-year-old Pam (played by Barbara Ferris) and the twenty-one-year-old Len (John Castle). Their early attempts at sex are farcical, with the bravado of Len quickly lapsing into self-consciousness and evasion as Pam takes the lead. Indeed, the reversal of the gender stereotype of the passive woman and the assertive man is a feature of a work that is fast moving and unexpected. The living-room of Pam's parents in scene one is quickly replaced by a rowing-boat containing Len and Pam in scene two, with scene three transporting the audience to the suburban park where Len's bored mates hang out. The early structural pace is mirrored by the momentum of the narrative that powerfully contrasts with the stasis of the lives being depicted. In the second scene, Pam appears to be pregnant, although the probable father is not Len, but Fred, the real object of Pam's desire. Indeed, from now on Pam views Len as an impediment, albeit one that she cannot dispense with. By scene four, Len has moved in as the lodger of Pam's parents, Harry and Mary, and a physical claustrophobia is now added to the pervasive emotional one overhanging the play.

Far from simply aiming to shock or sensationalise, *Saved* aims to examine the impulses that lie behind irrational acts of violence. In a Brechtian manner, the work suggests that the environment in which the characters exist exerts a profound influence on their behaviour. In scene three, we learnt that one of the gang, Pete, has run over a child for kicks:

What a carry on! 'E come runnin' round be'ind the bus. Only a nipper. Like a flash I thought right yer nasty bastard. Only ten or twelve. I jumps right down on me revver an' bang I got 'im on me off-side an' 'e shoots right out under this lorry comin' straight on.[99]

In a comment that identifies the play as emanating from a period of full employment, Len laments the fact that he is in work, since it is so routine, and the gang's enjoyment of sexual repartee is seen as a way of masking the emptiness of their discourse.

Scene four is similarly depressing. The sterile marriage of Harry and Mary, the absence of meaningful communication between them and the juxtaposition of Pam's growing hysteria at Len's intrusive presence and the passivity of her father in refusing to ask him to leave, create a depressing sight. It is one of the achievements of the work that this depiction of inertia is so compelling. The beginning of the baby's off-stage crying at this point adds to the atmosphere of frayed nerves.

Rejected and verbally abused by Pam, Len endures this ritualistic humiliation and even poignantly attempts to bond the child to its loveless mother in scene five:

> PAM: … This dump gives me the 'ump. Put that away.
> LEN: Yer can't let it lie on its back all day. Someone's got a pick it up.
> PAM: Why should I worry? Its father don't give a damn. I could be dyin' an' 'e can't find ten minutes.
> LEN: I'm blowed if I'm goin'a put meself out if yer can't cooperate.
> *He tries to put the baby in her arms*
> PAM: I tol' yer take it back! Get off a me! Yer bloody lunatic! Bleedin' cheek!

Such economic writing brilliantly prepares the ground for the climactic scene six, which still remains one of the most disturbing and necessary scenes of post-war drama.

Pam, resentful of the child's existence and frustrated by her inability to attract Fred, takes the baby (dosed up with aspirin to prevent it crying) for a walk in its pram. Goaded by Fred's humiliating taunts ('Your's must be the only stiff outside the churchyard she ain' knocked off', he tells Mike), she eventually storms off, leaving the baby behind with the comment: 'yer can take yer bloody bastard round yer tart's! Tell 'er it's a present from me!'.

The pram now becomes the focus of attention. One by one the group becomes obsessed by its presence: it offers a new diversion and a source of transient interest. Barry begins to push it, Pete projects it violently back to Barry and Colin joins in to form a triangle. Because it has been drugged the baby cannot open its eyes, so Pete pulls its hair, Barry pinches it and then removes its nappy. The nappy is soiled, the three torturers recoil and our terror increases. Pete punches the child, as does Barry and almost immediately afterwards, Colin. Gaskill has remarked on the ritualistic nature of this action[100] and the primeval nature of their behaviour is suggested as the group begins to act as a collective unit. After Pete rubs the baby's face with its own excrement, the only member of the group to have remained remote from the action, the putative father, Fred, is tossed a stone by Colin. After Pete has stated that 'Yer don't get a chance like this everyday', Fred's first stone misses, but not the second nor the succession of projectiles that the group now hurl into the pram, including burning matches. The park bell sounds and the group prepare to leave, though not before Barry has taken 'a stone from the pram and throws it at point blank range'. It is a moment of supreme horror.

The scene concludes with Pam returning and without even looking at the baby she begins to talk to it. That she addresses her child in a tender manner that we have not observed before, merely compounds the audience's misery:

I might a know'd they'd a left yer. Lucky yer got someone t' look after yer. Muggins 'ere. … 'Oo's 'ad yer balloon. Thass a present from grannie. Goin' a keep me up 'alf the night? Go t' sleepies. Soon be 'ome. Nice an' warm, then. No one else wants yer. Nice an' warm. Soon be 'omies.

Bond is quite clear in his Author's Note to the play that the brutality of this scene is justified for the work's overall didactic purpose –

… the causes of human violence can easily be summed up. It occurs in situations of injustice. It is caused not only by physical threats, but even more significantly by threats to human dignity. That is why, in spite of all the physical benefits of affluence, violence flourishes under capitalism[101]

– and the rest of the play is devoted to depicting the degradation of human dignity. Scene seven again demonstrates the capacity of the work to surprise when we discover that Fred has been apprehended and is later convicted for his involvement. But little changes, for better or worse, in the lives of the protagonists. Pam remains devoted to Fred, Fred remains indifferent to her advances on his release from prison, and Len remains in Harry and Mary's house, although scene nine, where he darns a hole in Mary's stockings whilst she is wearing them suggests a possible sexual liasion (and was another unprecedented and shocking scene for a mid-sixties audience).

The entire dysfunctional family is seen trapped in a living hell in the final scene, when Pam reads the *Radio Times*, Harry busies himself with a stamp and envelope, Mary undertakes some tidying and Len mends a chair. The abject nature of their activities closes the play on a note of depressing stasis, but a viewing of the work leaves one finding it harder to corroborate Bond's belief that the play is 'almost irresponsibly optimistic'.[102] The conclusion conveys a sense of weary pragmatism and denuded emotions, and whilst Len's usefulness might promise a less fraught existence, one's sense at the curtain is more of a speck of hope in the face of a truly appalling, socially produced tragedy, than the guarantee of a gradual recovery.

That the play would prove controversial was well known to Gaskill. C.D. Heriot, in his confidential Reader's Report to the Lord Chamberlain,[103] had insisted on fifty-four changes, including the excision of the 'torture and death of the baby' and the 'gratuitously salacious' mending of Mary's stocking. Heriot actually recommended ('reluctantly') that if these cuts were agreed to then a licence should be granted, but there was clearly no chance of that. In any case, his prefatory summary made it plain that he hoped that the work would never see the light of day, since it was a

> revolting amateur play by one of those dramatists who write as it comes to them out of a heightened image of their experience. It is about a bunch of brainless, ape-like yobs with so little individuality that it is difficult to distinguish between them. They speak a kind of stylised Cockney but behave in an unreal way, not because what they do is false, but that their motivation is not sufficiently indicated. ... They are all moral imbeciles. ... The writing is vile and the language and conception worse. Whether this could ever be considered a work of art is a matter of opinion; but it does seem that the taste of Messrs. Devine and Richardson has gone rancid – though with all the public money at their disposal, I don't suppose anybody cares.[104]

There could be no repeat of the successfully evasive strategy used to stage *A Patriot for Me*. The Lord Chamberlain and his officers were evidently out to nail the Royal Court.

With a licence for an uncut version impossible to obtain, the Royal Court was again turned into a theatre club. The opening night took place on 3 November 1965 and whilst Penelope Gilliatt bravely championed the work in The *Observer*,[105] Irving Wardle reflected the views of the majority of critics when he wrote that the work 'amounts to a systematic degradation of the human animal',[106] but there had been an even more hostile member of the first-night audience. Amongst the Lord Chamberlain's papers at the British Library lies a deposition from an anonymous reader about his previous night's visit to the Royal Court:

> As instructed I went last night to the Royal Court Theatre and witnessed a performance of a stage play entitled SAVED. I purchased a programme and a seat (K.17), programme and seat counterfoil are attached.
>
> At the box office I asked for a stall and was asked if I was a member, I said 'yes' and was asked if I had a ticket: I again said 'yes' and produced my wallet and started to produce the ticket at which the box office lady did not look, so I did not complete the manoeuvre. The box office lady said 'I'm sorry we have to ask you'.

The spy also recorded that the action included aspects specifically disallowed by the Lord Chamberlain. For example, in the first scene:

> Pam lay on the couch and opened her legs quite wide, Len then got on top of her and she received him in the position of intercourse. It is true to say that the physical motions which ordinarily next follow were not indulged in and that both participants, except for shoes, were fully dressed.
>
> Len then put his hands on Pam's breasts and later put his hands inside her blouse so that when she got up off the couch (the progress of their armour [sic] having been interrupted), her blouse was open, showing a slip underneath.

In scene three, 'when Colin says "What yer scratchin", one of the actors is scratching his testicles through his trousers' and in scene six 'the torture and murder of the baby was enacted in full', although intriguingly the spy later observes in a contradictory fashion that it 'was quite horrible … [but] so badly played that one could not really believe there was a live baby in the perambulator'. He also conveys an interesting sense of the evening as a whole:

> The auditorium was two thirds full [overall the production played to 36.7 per cent capacity for its twenty-four performances[107]] and without exception, so far as I could see – in their various styles, the audience looked well dressed and affluent: far removed from the characters on the stage.
>
> … Only one woman walked out towards the end of the performance, which otherwise was received in dead silence except for a few sniggers at some of the more disgusting episodes, such as urinating in the

parson's tea cup. There was quite warm applause at the curtain call, intended I thought, for the actors rather than for the play.

... During the interval I went to the bar and bought a bottle of light ale. There was only one lady there, working like a demon. I was not asked to show my membership ticket and drinks were being bought quite indiscriminately, that is unless everyone present was a member, a most unlikely circumstance.

For this trivial violation of the licensing laws and for not completing the manoeuvre at the box office (in other words, for allowing a member of the audience who had not been a club member for over twenty-four hours to purchase a ticket), the Lord Chamberlain proceeded to mount a prosecution against Gaskill as artistic director, Greville Poke, the company secretary and Alfred Esdaile, the licensee, for presenting an unlicensed play contrary to section fifteen of the 1843 Theatres Act. At the second hearing of 7 March 1966, expert witnesses including Lord Harewood and an eloquent Laurence Olivier made an impassioned defence of the Royal Court, but at the final hearing on 1 April, the magistrate, Leo Gradwell, upheld the case. The punishment, however – a conditional discharge for the defendants and a nominal fine of fifty guineas – left nobody satisfied. The theatre was still left to the mercy of the whims of the censor, and the Lord Chamberlain had received only half-hearted backing from the law, since Gradwell had made clear his dissatisfaction at the state of affairs: 'I am tied to the rock of the law waiting for some Perseus to rescue me'[108] It soon became apparent, though, that in reality the Royal Court has achieved an important moral victory.

Indignant and increasingly organised, the theatre profession redoubled its campaigning to rescue drama from censorship, and in early 1967, the Joint Parliamentary Committee on Censorship advocated the abolition of the 1843 Act. Although the government dropped its support for new legislation in November 1967, pleading pressure of parliamentary time, George Strauss MP pledged to take up the unfinished business. The courage and tenacity of the Royal Court in staging what is now seen as a modern classic ensured that a new Theatres Act, removing the requirement for the Lord Chamberlain to license productions, was to reach the statute book on 26 September 1968. A new era had truly begun.

Chapter 4

1969–1979

After Censorship: More Gains than Losses

The flood of permissiveness that supporters of censorship feared would sweep the stage after the Theatres Act became law in 1968 failed to materialise. Indeed, the very first post-censorship show to escape the clutches of the Lord Chamberlain, the American 'love-rock' musical *Hair*, typified the generally restrained way in which the London stage sought to take advantage of its new freedom to portray sexuality. Twice refused a licence in the months preceding the new act on the grounds that the musical offered innumerable threats to sexual decency (a charge that had been levelled against the genre ever since the innocuous *South Pacific*),[1] the producer, James Verner, simply decided to wait until the act became law rather than fight the Lord Chamberlain. Thus *Hair* opened at the Shaftesbury Theatre on 27 September 1968 following a welter of advance publicity. With warnings of full-frontal nudity, intimations of the drug culture and promises that the boundaries of personal liberty would be explored, the musical needed little selling, but the fact that it premièred the day after the Lord Chamberlain ceased his jurisdiction over the London stage ensured that it could claim a special footnote in the history of British theatre. For all the hype and the general consensus that it was one of the best musicals of the decade, the presentation of matters sexual was rather tame by today's standards. The rejection of materialism and authoritarian constraint caught the mood of the time and paradoxically led to it becoming a commercial success, but the much trumpeted nudity was shyly presented with lights dimmed and movement restrained. Its effect at the time should not be undervalued, however: after decades of heavy-handed repression, it was viewed by many theatre professionals as a revelation.

Kenneth Tynan's erotic revue, *Oh! Calcutta!*, symbolises a more comical exploitation of the new freedom, although his intention to 'use artistic means to achieve erotic stimulation'[2] was a serious one. Tynan, who in addition to working at the National Theatre had been pursuing a journalistic career that included writing for *Playboy*, had seen the work premièred in June 1969 in New York, but the Lord Chamberlain's redundancy soon opened up the possibility of a London production. In July 1970 an amended version of the original was staged at the Roundhouse and the cornucopia of sketches about the history of underwear, sado-masochism and voyeurism, together with displays of simulated sexual contact and frequent nudity, further demonstrated the lack of inhibition that the theatre now enjoyed. Most critics, although viewing the material as banal (the contributions of Beckett, Mercer, Polanski and John Lennon notwithstanding), agreed that the production constituted an important projection of self-confidence. Irving Wardle of *The Times* went so far as to observe that

> I have seen better revues than *Oh!Calcutta!*, but none based on ideas that strike me as more sympathetic. Namely, that the ordinary human body is an object well worth attention: and that there is no reason why the public treatment of sex should not be extended to take in not only lyricism and personal emotion but also the rich harvest of bawdy jokes.[3]

Wardle's enthusiasm was shared by audiences world-wide who made *Oh!Calcutta!* a significant financial success, but it is important to note that there were several less minor consequences of the censor's absence for British theatre.

In addition to the freedom to explore any subject-matter that did not corrupt or deprave, the fact that writers no longer had to submit scripts for time-consuming vetting introduced a revolutionising spontaneity to seventies drama. Productions could be mounted immediately, small collaborative groups were formed, flourished and withered within a matter of days and new venues such as pubs, community centres, 'arts labs' and working men's clubs began to spring up to cater for the increasing demand. Whereas in London there were approximately half a dozen such venues in 1968, by the late seventies there were over a hundred, including the King's Head pub in Islington, the Half Moon in Aldgate, the Bush on Shepherd's Bush Green, the Mall of the Institute for Contemporary Arts (ICA) and the Royal Court's Theatre Upstairs, that have endured beyond the decade.[4] Capitalising on the late sixties trend to view drama as something more than a building-based experience, travelling companies, invigorated by the new dynamism, began to proliferate. Theatre-in-Education groups, puppet companies, performers devoted to explore improvisation (previously suppressed by the Lord Chamberlain) and organisations keen to advance a particular political perspective through drama quickly multiplied.

It has occasionally been argued that the abolition of censorship had an adverse effect on new writing because playwrights lacked the cutting edge created by the requirement to keep one step ahead of the censor. However, this is a false premise. The alleged diminution in the quality of the new playwrighting of the seventies, an arguable notion in itself, stemmed less from the absence of repression than the growing perception that drama was less about individualism than collective endeavour. It is also a misconception based on a comparison with a truly golden period between the mid-fifties and sixties. The diversity of theatrical performances in the seventies was a notable and welcome corollary to the abolition of censorship and this can be perceived no more clearly than in the realm of political theatre. Performers in the seventies wanted, above all, to be topical.

Political Theatre

The Panacea of Socialism?

The election of a Labour government in 1964 after fourteen years of Conservative rule was greeted by many Britons as a long-delayed opportunity to complete the unfinished business of Clement Attlee's post-war administration. Expectations were high that the new Prime Minister, Harold Wilson, riding the white heat of new technology and demonstrating that he kept his finger on the pulse of the popular culture of the period with gestures such as inviting the Beatles to Downing Street, would modernise the country, energise its young people and make it less class-bound. In the event, great progress was made in the area of social policy. In addition to legislation on abortion, censorship and homosexuality, capital punishment was abolished in 1965, but the sterling crisis of 1966, the subsequent devaluation of the pound in 1967 and the embarrassing withdrawal in 1969 of Barbara Castle's proposal to reform trade union law, *In Place of Strife*, all dented the credibility of the government and led to an avoidable General Election defeat in 1970. Around this time, several dramatists, including David Hare, Harold Brenton, David Edgar, Howard Barker, Trevor Griffiths and John McGrath, were emerging with a shared desire to create drama that would inspire political and social change. Although not a school of political dramatists, they were united in their disillusion with the Wilson administration for failing to create the conditions for a flourishing of true socialism. They were also disappointed that the

revolutionary potential of the Vietnam protests, the Civil Rights movements and 'les evenments of 1968' had not been exploited, and angered at
the complacency that had led to the election of a Conservative government
under Ted Heath. Ironically, Heath's election proved something of a blessing, since the industrial conflicts that scarred his administration, notably
the miners' strikes of 1972 and 1974 which set the tone for constant industrial unrest throughout the seventies, were to provide both the background
to and the inspiration for many of their works. For several of these writers,
only the panacea of pure socialism could rescue the country.

Avant-Garde or Agit Prop?: Portable, Joint Stock, 7:84

In his book on political drama of the seventies, *New British Political
Dramatists*,[5] John Bull identifies two principal strands to political theatre:
avant-garde and agitprop. Two other strands can also now be added – gay
drama and drama for and/or by women.

Adopting Bull's terminology, two significant writers of the avant-garde
were David Hare and Howard Brenton. Hare, a Cambridge graduate and
aspiring writer, had founded the Portable Theatre with Tony Bicât in 1968,
with the aim of taking 'theatre to places where it didn't normally go'.[6] The
early plays, such as Brenton's *Fruit* (1970) and *Revenge* (1969), were written with the limited resources of the company in mind, and aimed both to
disrupt complacency and attack excessive materialism. Portable's collaborative piece, *Lay-By*, co-authored by Brenton, Hare, Brian Clark, Trevor
Griffiths, Stephen Poliakoff, Hugh Stoddart and Snoo Wilson, typified the
company's work. Inspired by a case of wrongful conviction for rape, it
focuses on the dysfunctional behaviour of people alienated by a society
driven by consumption. The deliberately distasteful and violent nature of
the play was emblematic of Portable's methodology and made a commercial transfer after the 1971 Edinburgh Festival problematic.

A second important collaborative avant-garde group was founded in
1974 by William Gaskill, David Aukin and Hare: The Joint Stock Company. To the aim of producing work that was politically challenging was
now added the desire to investigate the involvement of writers in collaborative preparatory work with actors. Freed from the constraints of time
and administration following his departure from the Royal Court in 1972,
Gaskill was particularly attracted by the potential of this artistic synthesis
and a working method known as the 'Joint Stock process' was soon
devised. In Gaskill's words, this incorporated 'a workshop in which the
material was explored, researched and improvised around, a gap in which
the writer went away and wrote the play, and an extended rehearsal period
of a more conventional kind'.[7] The workshop would typically last four

weeks, with the actors, writer(s) and director investigating ideas, hearing talks by experts and undergoing training in relevant professional skills – all with a view to producing material for a script. The writer then departed to compose the piece and the group worked with the resultant draft to create a production after six weeks of rehearsal.[8] Gaskill believed that this modus vivendi allowed the actors to 'share an understanding of the political responsibility of the play; they are not just there to serve the writer but, together with the writer, are making a statement,'[9] and it is evident that Gaskill's long-standing admiration for Epic Theatre was as strong as ever. Joint Stock's second production, David Hare's *Fanshen* (1975), a documentary play about the processes of the Chinese revolution, is the best example of this approach and did much to publicise the company's method.

By the mid-seventies, Hare and Brenton were beginning to cross over into the mainstream. Both Portable and Joint Stock had comprised a large number of articulate writers, actors and directors and had tended to oper-ate in arts centres, university theatres and fringe theatres for middle-class audiences and their entry into the pantheon of the subsidised theatre, the National, was perhaps inevitable. Brenton's *Weapons of Happiness* became the first piece of new writing to be performed at the National's South Bank complex in 1976, and although it simultaneously commended com-munism and denigrated Christ, it was questionable whether this was an assimilation by the establishment or a takeover by the revolutionaries. Brenton himself viewed the process as one of entryism – 'David [Hare, who directed the play] and I regard ourselves and our cast and our production team as an armoured charabanc full of people parked within the National walls',[10] – echoing Hare's assertion in 1975 that politically didactic writers should exist wherever they are best able: '… if you can possibly survive in the commercial theatre you should, because otherwise you're just blocking up the subsidized theatres for new writers'.[11] For Hare, who would become both the National's house dramatist in the late eighties and nineties with his 'State of the Nation' plays and a writer who would consistently be subjected to the taunt that he purveys 'public school socialism',[12] this would prove an oft-cited validation of his practice.

If the provocative nature of these avant-garde groups was dulled by their contact with the mainstream (although, as will be seen later, the National was to stage a couple of seventies works that advocated revolu-tionary socialist ideals), there was no danger of a similar appropriation for agitprop groups of the period. Aiming to educate and enlighten, eager to perform to working-class audiences in areas and venues rarely exposed to drama and often basing their productions on the history, struggles and experience of the audiences present, groups such as Agit-Prop, CAST

(Cartoon Archetypical Slogan Theatre), General Will and 7:84 were suspicious of institutions such as the National since they represented
the 'enemy' of the establishment. 'I'd rather have a bad night in Bootle',
John McGrath observed. 'You get more from it if somebody's going to
come up at the end and say, do you know what's happening in Bootle?'[13]
Such groups' didacticism was generally based on a Marxist analysis
of class struggle and was more politically focused than that of the avant-
garde's.

John McGrath's 7:84 group was a pre-eminent company in this strand
of political theatre. Having found success as a television dramatist in the
mid-sixties, McGrath began to tire of the approach that Brenton was to
embrace – fighting the ideological enemy from within its own ranks. Interviewed in 1975, he explained that

> I finally came to the conclusion that the mass media, at the moment, are
> so penetrated by the ruling-class ideology, that to try to dedicate your
> whole life – as distinct from occasional forays and skirmishes – to fight-
> ing within them is going to drive you mad.[14]

To preserve his sanity he founded 7:84 in 1971, its very name trumpeting
its didactic purpose, since at that time 7 per cent of the country's
population owned 84 per cent of the country's wealth. Receiving a small
amount of Arts Council funding, the company first played arts centres in
Aberdeen, Stirling and Lancaster with McGrath's own *Trees in the Wind*
and established its policy of taking material to audiences who can
empathise with what is being portrayed. A second group, 7:84 Scotland
Company, mounted the group's most famous production in 1973, *The
Cheviot, the Stag and the Black, Black Oil*: a musical that took its melodic
inspiration from the Highland ceilidh. The work is a historical panorama
that chronicles the exploitation of the Highlands of Scotland from the
clearances of the nineteenth century, which led to the forced migration of
the inhabitants, through the eviction of the population to secure land for
grouse shooting, to the development of North Sea Oil (which was just
coming on tap at this time and fuelling the Scottish Nationalist movement
which felt that England was exploiting a resource belonging to Scotland).
Throughout all these episodes, the resistance of the working class is seen
as heroic and deserving of celebration.

Energetic, fun and acerbic, the production rejected solutions pre-
scribed by official channels, dismissed the efficacy of the parliamentary
process and sought to introduce an historical overview to contemporary
dilemmas (an approach that would be increasingly copied). In its mixture
of raw entertainment and social questioning, the company bore similari-

ties to Theatre Workshop, but in its political immediacy it created its own distinct identity.

The disintegration of industrial relations during the Heath government (1970–74), the oil crisis in the middle east (1973) and the world economic recession (from 1974) gave companies such as Agit-Prop an almost endless source of material upon which to base their clarion call for political and economic reorientation, but it was this very economic recession that provided the Fringe and political groups with their severest challenges. Firstly, for the first time in ten years the Arts Council grant for drama did not increase (in 1975). Secondly, with financial belts being tightened, right-wing critics of subsidy began to question whether public money should be allocated to companies seeking to undermine the very establishment from which these funds had been allocated; and thirdly, the country's increasing frustration with strikes, over-mighty unions and failed consensus politics would result in the election in May 1979 of Margaret Thatcher – and her administrations would adopt a very different attitude to the arts as a whole, and the theatre in particular.

Gay Sweatshop and *Bent* (1979)

In the light of the policy of the Thatcher governments, the political certainty on the part of the agitprop and avant-garde movements of the inevitability of socialist change now seems naive, but one strand of political theatre, that based on the wish to challenge the continued repression of individuals on the grounds of their sexuality, has proved more durable and relevant in the twenty years since its emergence.

Emanating from the Gay Liberation movement of the late sixties, Gay Sweatshop was formed in 1975, following a series of plays presented by Ed Berman at the Almost Free Theatre. They aimed to challenge the pejorative stereotyping of the gay lifestyle and to present a more positive depiction of homosexual love. One of its founders, Nancy Diuguid, also revealed the implicit political dimension of the company's remit:

> We hope to make an artistic contribution to the theatrical scene; if we can attract people to us, professional theatre people and others, who are *not* ashamed of being gay, or see no horror in being assumed to be gay, then we shall have made a political contribution also.[15]

Two early pieces, Drew Griffiths and Roger Baker's *Mister X* (1975) and Jill Posener's *Any Woman Can* (1975) confirmed the group's rationale: to reassure gay and lesbian members of the audience that they were not alone, to engender solidarity, and to demand that gay people enjoy the same civil rights as other citizens. Conceived for touring and therefore employing few props other than a table, a tape recorder and some chairs (in the tradition of agitprop), *Mister X* was the first in a long line of 'coming out' plays. Divided into six sections and employing a revue form, each member of the cast relates their own individual experiences and conveys their changing perspective towards their own sexuality. The disarming use of humour to break down prejudice was copied by many subsequent writers dealing with a similar theme and has helped ensure that *Mister X* is now viewed as a seminal work of its type.

Any Woman Can was equally cathartic and dealt with the experience of lesbians. Ginnie, the main protagonist, narrates events from her life, including her unhappy time at school, taunted by her fellow pupils, her maltreatment at the hands of a malicious headmistress, a suicide attempt, her earliest affairs, the painful separation from a girlfriend reclaimed by her boyfriend, and her crucial moving beyond the primacy of sex to a conviction that being a lesbian is about enjoying women as friends as well as sexual partners. Resolutely unromantic, the overall tone is one of defiant assertion of one's individuality.

The open depiction in these plays of heartfelt feelings about a matter previously the preserve of innuendo or sniggering humour had an enormous impact on the audiences – straight and gay alike – that witnessed them during their year-long tour of fringe venues. As a consequence of the success of *Mister X*, a season of gay plays was presented at the Institute for Contemporary Arts (ICA), to be quickly followed by *As Time Goes By* (1977) – a study of gay repression over three different periods – co-written by Drew Griffiths and Noel Greig, the prolific dramatist who was to be associated as a director with Gay Sweatshop between 1977 and 1987. The subject matter of *As Time Goes By* had a resonance for a community which had had the threat of imprisonment for same-sex relationships removed only in 1967: its reworking by Martin Sherman in *Bent* was to provide gay theatre in Britain with its most notable exposure thus far.

That a critic of the quality of Christopher Innes can write in 1992 of the 'melodramatically inflated equation of homosexual persecution with the Holocaust and Nazi death-camps in *Bent*'[16] illustrates that Gay Sweatshop's task of education is far from complete. Picking up on the historical fact that in the concentration camps the bearer of the pink triangle (signifying homosexual) was considered to rank beneath the bearer of the yellow star (the Jew), Sherman's target is the mind-set that chooses to rank people for what they are rather than who they are. He also stresses the importance of the homosexual acknowledging to himself first and foremost his own sexuality and deriving strength from this; as well as revealing the possibility of humanity in even the most dismal of situations.

Bent is divided into two acts. In the first, set in pre-war Berlin, we witness the docu-drama format already familiar from *As Time Goes By* and *Mister X*, where the accession of the Nazis gradually threatens the existence of Max and his lover Rudy, until both are forced to go on the run before being finally apprehended. In a harrowing, proleptic scene, Max is compelled to witness the torture of Rudy, whilst the guards scrutinise him for any sign of emotion. Max's statuesque appearance ensures that he escapes a similar fate, but Rudy is beaten to death.

Act Two is set in Dachau. Max prefers to wear the yellow star that he has procured rather than the pink triangle which has been assigned to him, but his growing friendship with Horst, brilliantly depicted over five scenes in which the two men futilely carry rocks from one side of the stage to the other, provides a compelling tenderness one would have thought impossible in such a situation. Gradually the men fall in love, but they cannot touch or even look at each other. In a remarkable scene, they bring each other to orgasm through verbal love-making, but their companionship is destined to bring about their tragedy. With Horst succumbing to illness, Max manages to obtain medicine by prostituting himself to the Lieutenant (the brutal hypocrisy of this 'straight' man being self-evident), but the Lieutenant's discovery that the medication is destined for Horst leads to a sadistic game, whereby the guard throws his hat over the electric perimeter fence and compels the sick man to fetch it.

It is only after Horst has been killed that Max can touch him and for the first time Max is able to accept his true identity, even though he recognises the consequences. Only by such individual gestures, Sherman is arguing, will progress be made towards gay emancipation. Max replaces his fraudulent yellow star with Horst's pink triangle and walks voluntarily onto the electric fence.

The play is significant, not just because of its quality (in addition to the love-making scene, the episode between Max and his closeted Uncle Freddie is a model of poignant dramatic writing), but because it represented the first step for gay theatre from fringe venues to the mainstream of subsidised theatre. Premièred on 3 May 1979 at the Royal Court, the production featured the renowned actor from the Royal Shakespeare Company, Ian McKellen – then compelled to disguise his homosexuality from public acknowledgment (although he later became a prominent figure in the campaigning group Stonewall). Audiences gasped in the first act when a gay man walked naked across the stage having stayed the night with Max and were amazed, thrilled and disconcerted by the verbal love-making: nothing like this had been seen on the British stage. Nicholas de Jongh, the critic of the *Evening Standard*, recalled in 1992 'the unique

sense of raw shock and disgust that Bent engendered. It returned the elec-
tricity of surprise to the stage and a physical sense of revulsion and horror
I have never experienced before or since'.[17] Michael Billington's contemporaneous review for the *Guardian* admired 'the way it puts the case for
the declaration of one's feelings in such a sane, measured and eloquent
way',[18] but most critics found the presentation too unsettling and
identified with John Barber's belief that the play regrettably sought 'to
glamorise homosexual love by presenting it as coming to valiant birth
amidst the most succulent horrors in recent history'.[19] Far from being
born, gay drama had just come of age.

Female Playwrights

It would be hard to argue that during this decade female playwrights
achieved the breakthrough they deserved in terms of widely acknowledged success. Indeed, even by the end of the nineties, despite over fifty
per cent of audiences being women, a majority of theatre workers being
female and the gradual introduction of women into positions of power in
the subsidised sector (witness Genista Mackintosh at the National, Jude
Kelly at the West Yorkshire Playhouse, Deborah Paige at the Crucible and
Helena Kaut-Howson at Theatr Clwyd), it would be fallacious to claim
that women had achieved equality of opportunity in the theatrical profession. Although the Equal Pay Act of 1975 had outlawed pay discrimination
on the basis of gender, a 1994 survey for the actors' union, Equity,
revealed that women still earned less in subsidised theatre than men.[20]
Even the early and justifiable commercial success of playwrights such as
Caryl Churchill and Pam Gems proved a double-edged sword in that it
obscured for some the imperative of continually demanding that women
receive the same encouragement and access to venues as men. This said,
the trend towards collaborative theatre; the foundation of women's
theatre groups confidently demanding emancipation (signalled by the
protest of the Women's Street Theatre Group at the 1970 Miss World
competition in London); the creation of women-centred collectives and
the emergence of plays dedicated to challenging orthodox views on
gender, such as the Women Theatre Group's *My Mother Says I Never
Should* (1974), ensured that women's voices could be heard rather more
frequently in the theatre, if mainly on the fringe. This also led, in the
words of Lizbeth Goodman, to drama that sought 'to achieve positive re-
evaluation of women's roles and/or to effect social change, and which
[was] informed in this project by broadly feminist ideas'.[21]

Caryl Churchill's connection with the collective approach to writing of
Joint Stock led to *Light Shining in Buckinghamshire* (1976), a play about the

civil war in the seventeenth century, and Monstrous Regiment, a group dedicated to raising the profile of female practitioners and making 'exciting political theatre based on women's experiences',[22] commissioned her to write *Vinegar Tom* (1976), which examines the persecution of women as witches in the same century. *Cloud Nine* (1979), her second collaboration with Joint Stock, challenges sexual stereotyping by hilariously cross-casting and examines how a patriarchal Victorian family reacts to being transported to the end of the twentieth century.

Pam Gems' early work was also associated with an early theatre collective. *Go West Young Woman* (1974) was staged by the Women's Theatre Company (its early performances being interruptedby a group of radical feminists who objected to the presence of men in the cast[23]), but it is another historical/chronicle work (a feature of many plays by women dramatists in the seventies) that is her best known piece from this period. *Piaf* (1978) seeks to interrogate the myth that has grown up around the singer and, along with her rise to fame, charts the pitfalls of success, as well as one woman's struggle to gain sexual and economic independence. Its première at the RSC studio theatre and subsequent Broadway transfer brought Gems to wider public prominence, but it would not be until the eighties that more female playwrights would make the transition from the fringe to the centre.

Black and Asian Theatre in Britain

A final form of political theatre that emerged in the seventies was Black and Asian Theatre. The desire to eliminate prejudice on the grounds of race would prove as problematic as the attempt to remove prejudice on the grounds of sexuality, but the early seventies provided the first signs that Black and Asian practitioners viewed drama as an opportunity for celebrating their culture, as well as making positive political statements. Errol John's production of *Moon on a Rainbow Shawl* had proved a token event at the Royal Court in 1956, but the creation of black groups such as Temba and the Dark and Light Club (which avowedly sought to increase the employment prospects for Black practitioners) sowed the seeds that would principally be harvested in the eighties by Black performers and playwrights.

The establishment of Asian theatre slightly preceded this period, with the birth in 1977 of the Tara Arts Group (now greatly admired for productions such as Jatinder Verma's transplantation of Molière's *Tartuffe* to a Moghul Indian setting at the National in 1990). Its political intent was clear from the start, since it was founded as a reaction to the murder of Gurdip Singh Chaggar on the grounds of his colour, and Tara's early agitprop productions focused on racism in schools (*Fuse*, 1978) and the tensions at home caused by living in an uneasily multi-racial society (*Playing with Fire*). Drama's efficacy in changing long-held opinions, aided by subsidy and the absence of censorship, was cherished by many minority groups in the seventies, and in the flourishing of spontaneous community groups, this proved to be a halcyon period.

The End of an Era: The National Theatre, Olivier's Reign Phase 2 1969–1973

The proliferation of new theatre groups coincided with two further events in 1973 that signalled the end of an era: the death of the ubiquitous Binkie Beaumont and the departure from the National Theatre of Laurence Olivier. The second phase of Olivier's reign had proved to be more dogged by controversy than the first. Difficulties first started to arise when John Dexter, one of the original directorate, departed in 1967 after Olivier thwarted his plan for an all-male *As You Like It*, and this was quickly followed by the tortuous arguments about the intended production of Rolf Hochhuth's *Soldiers*. From today's perspective, the row seems bizarre, but Tynan's campaign to have it staged, the board's refusal to sanction this and Olivier's persistent defence of his dramaturg was a metaphor for a country pulled between an overweening respect for the past that was preserved by a protective establishment and a desire to modernise its ageing institutions, even if this was seen by some as condoning irreverence. The objection of the chairman of the governors to the play, which was set in 1943, was not to its debate about the morality of saturation bombing during wartime (which it reluctantly endorsed) but to the implication in the sub-plot that the head of the Polish government in exile, General Sikorski, had been murdered with the tacit approval of Winston Churchill, to prevent a rupturing of relations with the Russians. Lord Chandos, as Oliver Lyttleton, had been a member of Churchill's war-cabinet, and was outraged by what he perceived to be an unwarranted slur on the memory of the wartime leader, who had only recently died in 1965. Tynan, ever eager to demonstrate that the National could match the daring of the RSC, was equally convinced that the play not only deserved an airing, but was fashionably provocative and based on fact (a claim he later struggled to substantiate). On 24 April 1967, the board unanimously agreed that the play insulted Churchill and was unsuitable for production at the National. Olivier asked for it to be minuted that he was 'unhappy' with this decision.[24]

Several issues now arose. What were the powers of the board to override the artistic director? What constituted a suitable play for this flagship institution? Should the board be able to function as a de facto censor? Where did the bruising row leave Tynan? Chandos clearly wanted the dramaturg to leave, but again Olivier was fiercely loyal and prevented him firing the irritant and causing further bad publicity. Tynan himself mounted the play at the New Theatre in 1968 as a commercial venture in association with Michael White, but the critical reception made the whole business seem a terrible waste of effort – worthy but dull, seemed to be the general verdict. Joe Orton's *What the Butler Saw* (1969), where certain body parts from an exploding statue of Churchill are embedded in the body of a woman, was much more racily irreverent.

Three years of battle over a principle left Tynan in a very much weaker position at the National. At the end of 1969 his post was redefined as being that of a literary consultant, and from 1970 he was to share this position with Derek Granger. It was a clear and public demotion, and marked the beginning of the end for the Tynan/Olivier partnership.

The backstage turmoil that *Soldiers* created and the resultant bad publicity meant that the National was treated to ever increasing scrutiny by the press. From 1967 audiences began to dip, with the average attendance of 97 per cent in 1967 declining to 79 per cent in 1971/2.[25] Peter Nichols' *The National Health* (1969), a comic satire about the fear of pain and death set in a hospital ward, and Olivier's performance as Shylock in Jonathan Miller's production of *The Merchant of Venice* (1970) (for which Olivier had his teeth altered and finally managed to conquer his stage fright) demonstrated that the company could still mount significant productions, but there seemed a general lack of direction, coupled with a collective loss of confidence. The stupendous performances of John Gielgud and Ralph Richardson in David Storey's *Home* at the Royal Court in 1970 (before transfers to the West End and Broadway) raised the old suspicions that Olivier actively refused to employ actors of equal stature to himself out of competitive envy (it widely being felt that Olivier had never forgiven Gielgud for upstaging him in their alternating roles as Romeo and Mercutio in the 1935 production of *Romeo and Juliet* at the New Theatre). People also pointed to the continued absence of Alec Guinness, but such carping was temporarily silenced when real disaster struck in August 1970 with Olivier suffering a major thrombosis in his leg.

Olivier's powers of recuperation were legendary – he had conquered pneumonia, appendicitis, cancer of the prostate and loss of memory over the previous decade – but his incapacity now contributed to the sense of drift. After Olivier had stated the impossibility of continuing to work with him, Lord Chandos was succeeded as Chairman by Sir Max Rayne in a messily handled putsch. There was disconcertion at the Brechtian treatment of Shakespeare's *Coriolanus* (1971) by two directors from the

Berliner Ensemble, Manfred Werkerth and Joachim Tenshcert (Brecht had actually written his own version of the work); confusion reigned about the official role of Frank Dunlop, who administered the company for three years in Olivier's place, but whom Olivier could never concede was his deputy; and the decision to expand by taking over the New Theatre in addition to the Old Vic was initially a disaster.

Incredibly, it was in this climate that Olivier was to give one of his finest ever performances. The last production at the New in 1971 was of Eugene O'Neill's *Long Day's Journey into Night* and his phoenix-like performance as James Tyrone was greeted with adulation ('a massive performance. ... For a genuinely great actor to play a nearly-great actor is the hardest technical feat of all: Olivier does it to perfection'[26]) and relief. Relief at his return to health and form, and relief that the National had arrested its decline. The respite from a critical press was temporary, however, since the board, keen to identify an eventual successor to Olivier, now began discreet negotiations with the man Olivier least wished to see don his mantle: Peter Hall. The obfuscations surrounding these soundings; the decision to keep Olivier in the dark; the demands of Hall (who had resigned as the director at Glyndebourne) for a salary twice the size of Olivier's and greater freedom to pursue outside work; the dismissal of Tynan; Hall's tentative examination of the possibility of merging with the RSC; and the inevitable leaks to journalists created a welter of bad feeling within the company and disastrous public relations outside. The succession confirmed, nobody was particularly happy with the decision that Hall would join the National in 1973 to 'work with Olivier and the artistic executive and take over after the new building opened in 1974'.[27] That the new South Bank complex was not to open until 1976 was but one of the many problems to confront Hall on his accession.

The inter-regnum period at the National contained two significant productions. Peter Shaffer's *Equus* (1973), inspirationally directed by John Dexter, about the psychiatric mystery of why a stable boy blinds six horses, helped erase the company's previous financial deficit and reminded critics that Olivier's National Theatre had been responsible for showcasing several quality pieces of new writing. Trevor Griffiths' *The Party* (1973) marked Olivier's last ever stage performance. His decision to play the part of the Trotskyist, John Tagg, seems strange now, but it stemmed both from the period's obsession with plays that investigated the potential for revolutionary change (the work's fifteen minute political monologues and dialectical episodes seem devoid of dramatic tension today) and Olivier's fascination with the technical challenge of mastering Joe Tagg's Glaswegian accent. In his approach to performance, this consummate technician was consistent to the last.

Although unhealthily indecisive about his intentions to retire from the National, the clumsy way that Olivier was eased out of the company that he had built up into a world-class organisation for money that was a pittance of what he could have earned elsewhere, symbolised both the sense of crisis that was besetting the country economically and the insecurity that began to grip the theatre world.

Commercial Angst, Subsidised Joy?

For all the travails of the National, the subsidised sector appeared in ruder health than the commercial during the early seventies. The Royal Court continued to demonstrate its commitment to new writing by producing Storey's *Home* (1970), Bond's *Lear* (1971) and Portable's collaborative piece, *England's Ireland* (1972). Bond described *Lear* as being an attack on Stalinism and on bourgeois culture as expressed in Shakespeare's *King Lear*, and the work is a further example of a dramatic quest for the form of socialism appropriate to Britain's condition. It also highlights the appeal that the mix of political analysis, historical setting and literary appropriation held for many seventies playwrights.

England's Ireland was more directly linked to the contemporary political scene. The nightmare of Britain's involvement in Northern Ireland had been reawakened by the deployment of troops in Londonderry in 1969 and the situation degenerated further in 1972 with the suspension of the Northern Ireland parliament at Stormont and the beginning of direct rule from London. Portable's multi-authored production sought to throw the spotlight on the social injustices manifest in the province, as well as the religious bigotry. It criticised the laconic attitude of the British to the province before the violence erupted, questioned how 'normality' could return to areas where unemployment was running at forty-three per cent of the population and argued that the refusal to negotiate with terrorists was historically anachronistic. This contentious notion (which still remained a barrier to peace negotiations after the second IRA ceasefire of 1997) proved too dangerous for over fifty theatres, and even though the production eschewed agitprop and attempted to raise questions rather than prescribe answers, it was only to run for a few performances at the Royal Court.

John Arden and Margaretta D'Arcy's *The Ballygombeen Bequest* (1972), about an absentee English landlord's attempts to evict a tenant from his Irish estate, also acknowledged that Northern Ireland was now proving to be a major political crisis, but its tour of Belfast, Edinburgh and the Bush theatre, London, was halted by a libel writ – a powerful reminder that the departure of the Lord Chamberlain had not necessarily removed the obstacle of censorship. One of the authors of *England's Ireland*, Howard Brenton, would return to the ever sensitive topic of Ireland with even more controversial results in 1980 with *The Romans in Britain* at the National.

Whether one was inspired by the radicalism of these works or infuriated by their heresy, the risks in staging them contrasted markedly with the inertia of the West End. Indeed, the roll-call in 1972 of new works that emerged from subsidised venues continued to impress, with Stoppard's *Jumpers* (Old Vic), Charles Wood's *Veterans*, Wesker's *The Old Ones* and Osborne's *A Sense of Detachment* (all Royal Court), highlighting the anaemia of the dismal bedroom farces, such as *The Mating Game*, that the West End was offering. The finest ever Aldwych season in 1971 saw the RSC present Peter Brook's iconographic production of *A Midsummer Night's Dream* and Pinter's *Old Times*, happily confirming Binkie Beaumont's earliest fears about a subsidised London base overshadowing the work of commercial companies. Beaumont's death in 1973, together with that of Noel Coward and the demise of the World Theatre season, added to the West End's uncertainty.

The year 1973, however, would subsequently prove a watershed for theatre as a whole. The oil crisis and subsequent world recession pointed to domestic cutbacks that would reduce subsidy. The industrial unrest of the miners' strike in 1972 foreshadowed several years of conflict from which the theatre world would not escape and the inability of the Labour government (elected with a precarious majority in a second general election of 1974) to achieve either the socialist reorientation demanded by left-wing radicals or a constructive working arrangement with over-mighty unions, eventually created the political mood that would lead to the election of an administration for eighteen years that would have a much more market-orientated approach to the arts.

Peter Hall's accession to the Director's post at the National in 1973 was meant to coincide with the opening of the company's brand new home on the South Bank, but industrial disputes, spiralling costs and administrative bureaucracy delayed the opening of the three-theatre complex until 1976. The whole site would become a convenient target for the growing number of critics who wished to question the notion not just of taxpayers funding large artistic complexes but of the principle that plays that questioned orthodoxy should be funded by the state at all. No wonder Hall's memoirs devoted to this period are contained within a chapter entitled 'The War That Had To Be Won'. The golden days of rising subsidy were about to end.

The chill wind that would shortly blow was not yet quite in evidence. Trevor Griffiths' *Comedians* (1975) was first produced at the Nottingham

Playhouse, and signalled a shift of emphasis in his political writing. The play follows in real time the preparations of a group of comedians for their debuts in a talent competition in front of a London agent. Less directly proselytizing than *The Party*, the play is fraught with dramatic tension. The teacher, former comic, Eddie Waters, wants his charges to employ humour that is didactic and intelligent, whereas Bert Challoner, the talent scout and competition judge, believes that successful comedy always appeals to the lowest common denominator. The second act of the work traces the pupils' routines, with those comics who reject Waters' beliefs, such as the Jewish Matthews, who tells a succession of sexist and racist jokes to salvage his act, being offered contracts by Challoner. Part of the brilliance of the play lies in the fact that the real audience may also find these gags amusing and the embarrassment of acknowledging this is compounded by the manic, slightly terrifying and deliberately alienating routine that Gethin Price, Waters' most promising charge, performs. Back at the adult education centre, Waters praises the hardness and edge of this routine (which inevitably repulsed Challoner), but his enthusiasm is disturbing, since his response reminds him of an earlier visit to a Nazi concentration camp just after the war. The play thus becomes a fascinating examination of the power and nature of comedy and *Comedians* is now rightly regarded as a masterpiece of this period.

Transferred to the Old Vic for a National Theatre production, the dialectical approach of the work, again refusing to dictate an interpretation, and the consummate performance of Jonathan Pryce as Gethin, drew much admiration. This policy of subsidised transfers to London was particularly evident in 1975, with nineteen out of thirty-four West End productions following this route. But as well as highlighting the vibrancy of subsidised theatre, this osmosis also confirmed the sclerotic nature of the West End. The National's fight-back in 1975, the architectural innovation of the newly-built Royal Exchange in Manchester in 1976, the brilliance of the RSC season of 1977 and Hare's *Plenty*, Bond's *The Woman*, and Stoppard's *Every Good Boy Deserves Favour* from 1978 created an impression of dominance, but it also masked worrying signs throughout the country as a whole. From 1977, regional theatres began to close for the summer and studio spaces went dark for longer periods. The success of the big institutions and successful playwrights was concealing worrying trends elsewhere. At the end of the decade, however, the really sick man of theatre was the West End. Michael Billington wrote in October 1979 that unless the sector ceased to be 'a shop-window for goods purchased from the subsidised sector and Broadway' and earning its 'living off other people's initiatives', it would continue to decline. His solution was revealing, in the light of the eighties:

... the salvation of the West End theatre does not lie in simply grabbing whatever is available from other quarters. It also lies in recapturing a touch of the sheer showbiz instinct and creative flair that for the moment seems to have passed from the so-called tycoons to the ex-University graduates who run our subsidised theatres up and down the land.[28]

Commercial salvation would come for the West End, but in a form that Billington neither envisaged nor desired: the musical.

War: Peter Hall at the National Theatre (1973–1979)

Amadeus (1979)

It was a work with a musical theme that marked a turning point in the fortunes of Peter Hall's turbulent early tenure at the National. Fifteen years after *The Royal Hunt of the Sun*, Peter Shaffer was to provide the theatre with an equally important success that again emphasised his interest in theatricality over political analysis and set him apart from recent National dramatists such as Brenton, Hare and Griffiths. *Amadeus* (1979) examines the fortunes of two composers: the scabrous genius, Mozart, and the competent, unspectacular court composer Salieri, who cannot understand why his greater worthiness has not been blessed by God with the possession of greater talent. It had originally been intended that John Dexter would renew his successful partnership with Shaffer but Dexter's increasing disagreements with the playwright, and a growing disenchantment with the South Bank, meant that Shaffer asked Hall to direct the new piece instead. This fortuitous situation was propitious: Hall had previously been employed at Glyndebourne and an opera-style production of *Amadeus* was guaranteed. To prevent the evening becoming a reverie of beautiful music, Harrison Birtwhistle composed electronic versions of Mozart's melodies; John Bury's design of a gilt proscenium arch at the back of the Olivier stage created the courtly atmosphere; and an opening scene of overlapping whispers, representing the gossiping Viennese courtiers speculating whether Salieri had poisoned his more talented rival conveyed the atmosphere of intrigue and uncertainty that riveted the first-night audience.

Some critics were disconcerted by the bawdy, crude and immature behaviour of Shaffer's Mozart. James Fenton of the *Sunday Times* argued that 'Shaffer's Mozart is depicted in an offensive and banal way because he is seen through the eyes of a very, very bad dramatist indeed'.[29] This adumbrated initial public reaction in Britain to the hugely successful film adaptation in 1984 which featured the composer with an American accent, but such snobbery was, in effect, a compliment to Shaffer's intriguing conception of genius that perfection in one aspect of life need not imply perfection in all others. Most reviews of the original National production, however, were full of admiration for the impulsive, energetic, giggly, hopping performance of Simon Callow as Mozart and the frustrated, personal antipathy of Salieri, so superbly conveyed by Paul Scofield. John Barber commended Callow in the *Daily Telegraph*

> Simon Callow as Mozart goes to the harpsichord and astonishes everyone by playing a march just composed by Salieri. Then, under his fingers, Mozart adjusts the pedestrian little tune until it melts into the delicious *Non piu andrai* from *Fiagro*. You can feel Salieri's glassy appreciation turn to black bile within him.[30]

This was matched by the admiration for Paul Scofield's performance of Michael Billington, fast becoming the most perceptive and stimulating critic of his generation:

> His cracked-bell voice slides effortlessly between private hatred and public ingratiation: his seamed, pouched features alternate between haggard distinction and slit-eyed envy; and his hands are forever stroking and caressing the air as if only the severest effort prevented him strangling Mozart. It is a stunning performance.[31]

In *Being an Actor* Callow writes:

> From the first preview there was never any question that, whatever the critics might say, the effect of the play on the public was going to be enormous. Playing it I had again the experience I've only had on two or three previous occasions: a hunger from the audience, a feeling that they were getting something they'd done without for too long. Everyone who appears in the play feels the same thing: there's a magnetic pull coming from the auditorium.[32]

These observations are instructive, in that they suggest that a new era which ranked theatricality above political commitment was in sight on the eve of the eighties. The production certainly marked a turning point in Hall's reign. Sold out for 129 performances, transferred to the West End and abroad and made into an Oscar-winning film, *Amadeus* reaped the

National almost £500,000, rescuing it from a financial crisis brought about by a stagehands' strike earlier in the year and showing that work of excellence could still be achieved by the company. Although the *Sunday Times* would fan controversy in 1986 by questioning the amount that Hall had earned personally from the transfers (erroneously putting the figure at above £2 million when it was nearer £720,000), *Amadeus* brought much needed respite for the beleaguered director.

Last Days at the Old Vic

Hall's accession in 1973 had been clouded by the botched departure of Olivier and his early years at the National were occupied with countering the opprobrium that had been generated by this, creating an organisation familiar with his working methods, ensuring that an expanded company could finally settle into its interminably delayed South Bank home, striving to balance the books in an era of financial constraint and dealing with two serious industrial disputes – not to mention presenting work of quality to justify the 'national' tag. With hindsight, his achievement during this period in simply bedding down the company in three new theatres – the Olivier, the Lyttleton and the Cottesloe – was an impressive one.

The early omens were inauspicious. Fourteen theatre directors wrote to *The Times* in 1974 (including, ironically, Hall's eventual successor, Richard Eyre) expressing concern that the National might cream off a disproportionate amount of grant money at the expense of regional theatres, as well as claiming that Hall was poaching technicians with salaries that no other organisation could afford to match.[33] The National's detractors received further ammunition from a disappointing opening season, which featured an anti-climactic *Tempest*, with John Gielgud being unable to recreate his memorable Prospero. It was this policy of recruiting star actors, however, which would soon compensate for the departure of several of Olivier's old guard, including John Dexter, Jonathan Miller and Olivier himself (who left on 21 March 1974). The incorporation of star actors into the company had been something that Olivier had refused to countenance and this therefore marked an immediate change of emphasis. Ibsen's *John Gabriel Borkman* boasted Ralph Richardson, Peggy Ashcroft and Wendy Hiller, Beckett's *Happy Days*, which the playwright oversaw himself, featured Ashcroft buried up to her neck in earth as Winnie and Pinter's new work, *No Man's Land*, again coupled John Gielgud and Ralph Richardson. This latter production reminded people that Hall himself was the definitive interpreter of Pinter. The 'precision, understanding and ear for musical nuances of Peter Hall's direction are masterly'[34] wrote Frank Marcus in the *Sunday Telegraph*, and there was a definite sense that Hall was beginning to earn his spurs. Nevertheless, the move to the new home by the Thames still needed to be negotiated.

The South Bank

Twenty years after the third of the National's three new theatres, the Cottesloe, had finally been occupied in March 1977, plans were being discussed to alter the appearance of the South Bank complex. As part of the country's millennium celebrations, the architect, Sir Richard Rogers, proposed to cover the Royal Festival Hall, the National Film Theatre, the Queen Elizabeth Hall, the Hayward Gallery and the adjacent National Theatre complex with a gigantic glass roof to improve the aesthetics of the South Bank. Over the years, the physical appearance of the new National Theatre has attracted almost as much comment as some of the productions, but its concrete brutalism was of less concern to Hall in 1976 than its eventual inhabitation. Conceived by the architect Denys Lasdun at a time when energy prices were low, construction had begun in 1969 (with Jennie Lee pouring the first shovel of cement), but soaring costs as inflation began to spiral, technical difficulties in installing stage machinery such as the Olivier's revolving drum stage (which was not fully functional until 1988) and intermittent labour shortages all conspired to delay the opening until 1976. Its final cost was an unimagined £16 million.

Although the delays were immensely frustrating for Hall and the company at the time, a fine theatre building had actually been created, at least for audiences, who have grown to appreciate the complex as the years have passed. All three venues are loosely modelled on theatrical spaces from past eras. The largest, the Olivier theatre, drew some inspiration via the Chichester space from the Greek amphitheatre at Epidaurus, in that it is fan-shaped, open-staged and contains steeply raked seats. Obviously much smaller than the Greek prototype, it nevertheless contains 1,160 seats and a feeling of spaciousness inspires awe when one enters the auditorium. The Lyttleton theatre, also named after a recently ejected personality, this time the first chairman of the board, Oliver Lyttleton, is a more conventional proscenium-arch theatre that can hold 890 people in two simple levels of seating. Of the three venues, it is considered the most conservative. The final space, named after the chairman of the South Bank Board, which was responsible for the construction of the new National Theatre, has proved to be the most innovative, experimental venue. Housing 200 to 400 people, depending on the configuration required by the production, the Cottesloe is simply a rectangular box, with two tiers of flexible seating and an easily adapted floor space. Its antecedent was the inn space of the Tudor period.

Occupancy of the new venue was gradual. On 22 September 1975, Hall formed an advance guard and took possession of his office amid continuing attempts to complete the interior. On 8 March 1976, *Happy Days* began previews in the Lyttleton prior to the official opening of this theatre on 16 March 1976, with Albert Finney in *Hamlet* in a deliberate echo of the first NT production at the Old Vic. Finney fared better than O'Toole, in spite of having to cope with the death of his own father during rehearsal. The swift pace of the uncut production was admired, and even allowing for the inevitable quibbles about any performance of this statuesque work, Finney's interpretation seemed energetic and plausible. The much delayed Olivier began its operational life on 4 October, with Finney again in a lead role, this time as Marlowe's *Tamburlaine*, and the whole complex was inaugurated five months later on 4 March 1977 when Ken Campbell and Chris Langham's eight-and-a-half-hour epic, *Illuminatus*, christened the Cottesloe. Separating this event from the industrial turmoils that were beginning to engulf the NT, it was a climactic moment in the struggle for a flagship theatre.

Hall's early policy of employing star performers to bid farewell to the Old Vic (the last NT performance being in honour of Lilian Baylis – *A Tribute to the Lady* – on 28 February 1976) and to inaugurate the new venue had been successful, but there were looming problems ahead. Continual carping about the building, sporadic strikes and financial crises all added to the difficulty of establishing his vision for the repertoire.

Crises Off–Stage, New Writing On–: 1977–1979

Between 1977 and 1979 events off-stage at the National often appeared as dramatic as those on-stage. Industrial relations in Britain deteriorated during this period and the National was not immune. The stagehands' strike of 1976 was followed by a walkout in May 1977 by 100 backstage workers over the dismissal of a plumber for failing to repair two wash-basins. The dispute, typical of the actions of the time when unions sought to establish their primacy over management, lasted six days and the disastrous publicity that resulted from this absurd altercation stoked up criticism about the amount that the National was taking from the public purse. By the end of the year it was apparent that the venture was facing severe financial difficulties. The deficit from construction delays had risen to £500,000 and it was announced that the whole complex would require a staggering £1 million a year to run.[35] A one-off government grant was allocated to stave off closure, but Hall was no longer able to host visiting companies in the theatre.

The next two years followed a similar pattern. Comparisons were frequently (and unfairly) made with the value for money that the RSC was providing on a third of the budget, with its thirty-five productions a year to the National's twenty-three. The continued technological difficulties, not least the employment of extra stage crew to replace the computer-controlled flying system that did not work, were manna for the critics of the whole enterprise and the overtime ban and unofficial strikes by maintenance staff over pay in 1978 were followed by a second unofficial dispute in March 1979 which closed all three theatres.

This second strike dragged on for two months and dealt a near fatal blow to the besieged complex. Its tortuous course is exhaustively documented in the diaries that Hall kept at the time and which he published in 1983. In many ways, this dispute, with its sporadic violence, interrupted performances and sheer bloody-mindedness, symbolised what many former socialists were rejecting when they reluctantly elected Margaret Thatcher on 3 May 1979. Her promise of strong action to control the seemingly unfettered power of organised labour was highly appealing after the numerous strikes of the 'Winter of Discontent' in 1978/9. Even Peter Hall was reluctantly forced to vote Conservative for the first time.

In spite of these turmoils, good productions were staged. To his early policy of employing stars during the transition period, Hall now added a desire to fill every public area of the complex with some form of performance, an embracing of cross-fertilisation by staging previously ignored examples of European drama by visiting companies and a commitment to new writing. Thus, free musical performances were given in the Lyttleton foyer, art exhibitions (commencing with a display of Denys Lasdun's work) were displayed outside the auditoriums and *The Crucifixion* was staged on the terraces overlooking the Thames on Easter Sunday 1977. From this event was to emerge *The Mysteries* in 1985, Tony Harrison's version of the York Mystery Plays.

The year 1977 saw a brief flourishing of performances by visiting companies, before financial cutbacks curtailed this policy. Maximilian Schell directed von Horváth's *Tales from the Vienna Woods* in a translation by Christopher Hampton, Peter Stein presented a production of Gorki's *Summerfolk*, and Victor Garcia directed de Valle Inclán's *Divinas Palabras*. There were also visits from the Phoenix Theatre, Leicester, the Library Theatre, Manchester, the Birmingham Repertory Theatre and Paine's Plough which demonstrated a willingness to reach out to the regions, not an intention generally recognised by Hall's detractors.

It was the third policy strand, however, that placed the National back on the road to recovery. Hall had originally commissioned six writers to provide new plays for the South Bank's first season but the plan was fragmented by the numerous delays. Pinter's *No Man's Land*, already premièred at the Old Vic, briefly flourished at the Lyttleton in 1976 before a Broadway transfer, and Osborne's *Watch it Come Down* also opened at the old home, yet enjoyed a run of a mere twenty-nine performances when transferred to the Lyttleton. Howard Brenton's *Weapons of Happiness* was of greater significance in that it marked not just the Lyttleton's first production of a new work but the start of a collaboration between the playwright and the National that would lead to the fireworks of *The Romans in Britain* (1980) and the acerbic satire of *Pravda* (1985). This latter play would be co-authored with his former Portable collaborator David Hare, whose 1978 *Plenty* (much hailed for the rarity of a substantial female role – Susan Treherne, played by Kate Nelligan) was the beginning of perhaps the most fruitful connection between a playwright and the National thus far. A further new work, *State of Revolution* (1977) by a playwright of the fifties, Robert Bolt, was less enduring but Alan Ayckbourn's *Bedroom Farce* (1977) confirmed him as the most popular playwright in the country.

This flourishing of new work, combined with polished revivals of Travers' *Plunder* (1976) and Jonson's *Volpone* (1977), featuring a red-wigged Paul Scofield making his first NT appearance; ingenious adaptations that included Keith Dewhurst's treatment of Flora Thompson's mosaic of village life, *Lark Rise* (1978); and other innovative promenade productions in the Cottesloe staged by Bill Bryden illustrated that there was more to praise than lament during this difficult period, even if this was not immediately apparent at the time.

Alan Ayckbourn

By the end of the seventies, Alan Ayckbourn was the West End theatre's most commercial playwright and it was not surprising that Peter Hall had viewed the playwright's debut at the National with *Bedroom Farce* in 1977 as a surefire box-office success. Following a recommendation from his schoolmaster at Haileybury, Ayckbourn had joined the company of the renowned Shakespearean actor, Donald Wolfit, as Assistant Stage Manager in 1956. He then proceeded to tour the repertory circuit, before becoming a member of Stephen Joseph's theatre-in-the-round company based at Scarborough. This marked the start of a remarkable liaison with the theatre in this northern coastal town that saw Ayckbourn eventually presiding in 1997 over the inauguration of a new venue (a converted Odeon cinema) as Director of Productions. Ayckbourn had achieved this position in 1970 after three important encounters: with Stephen Joseph himself, in whose company he was an actor-writer; with Peter Cheeseman at the Victoria Theatre, Stoke for whom he worked between 1962 and 1964 as an associate director, whilst writing some early plays; and with the BBC in Leeds, where he was employed as a radio drama producer between 1964 and 1970. He underwent, therefore, an enviable apprenticeship that gave him a valuable insight into the technical, writing and performance sides of theatre.

Being based at Scarborough, Ayckbourn has conceived all his works with that venue in mind and this leads to an economy of approach that has made his works hugely appealing for generations of amateur drama groups working within tight budgets and numerically restricted casts. In his preface to *The Norman Conquests* (1973) he is perfectly frank about his pragmatic attitude. The three parts of the trilogy had to 'be able to stand independently' given that it was unlikely that a holiday-maker spending a week in Scarborough would willingly give up three separate evenings at the theatre, 'yet not so [independently] that people's curiosity as to what was happening on the other two nights wasn't a little aroused'.[36] Because the company could only afford six actors, there would only be six characters and the inability of the performer who Ayckbourn wished to take the leading role of Norman to arrive for rehearsal until the first few days of the season, meant that the character's entry had to be delayed in the script. Finally, the stage entrances could only number two as no more were possible at the Library Theatre.

Ayckbourn was completely unapologetic about his methodology: 'If this all makes me sound like a writer who performs to order, I suppose it's true. I thrive when working under a series of pre-conditions, preferably over which I have total control.'[37]

His ability to make a virtue of necessity has attracted admiration, envy and a misguided tendency (that is lessening now) to belittle his work as undemanding entertainment for the middle-classes. The fact that he consistently proves so popular with commercial audiences further infuriates his detractors. What is incontrovertible is that the opportunity to direct his own works and cast his own choice of actors in his own familiar space is the main reason Ayckbourn has remained so resolutely loyal to the Scarborough Theatre – an unparalleled state of affairs in post-war theatre.

Ayckbourn's first West End success came in 1967, when *Relatively Speaking* opened at the Duke of York's, having first been seen in Scarborough under the title *Meet My Father*. Its conception was typically utilitarian:

Stephen asked me simply for a play which would make people laugh when their seaside summer holidays were spoiled by the rain and they came into the theatre to get dry before trudging back to their landladies. This seemed as worthwhile a reason for writing a play as any so I tried to comply.[38]

Its mixture of misunderstandings, suggested infidelity, gentle suburban satire and technical brilliance created a template that would remain enormously popular for the next three decades. A number of themes that Ayckbourn has reworked and developed were contained in this early hit which ran for 355 performances. These included a gentle scepticism about marriage, that has hardened in later works ('Look at the Coopers. Married nearly thirty years. Couldn't have a happier couple. I'm sure it's because he spends nine months of the year in Rio de Janeiro'[39]); a wry observation of the British obsession with social status and appearance; an approving empathy with people unable to scheme or calculate; and a documentation of middle-class concerns and pursuits. In *Relatively Speaking* this covers the ritual of Sunday lunch, the unwillingness to offend, even when total strangers intrude into Sheila's home, and polite discussions about weather, gardens and prospects to prevent embarrassing lapses of conversations. Michael Billington's description of Ayckbourn's dramaturgy creating a 'Theatre of Recognition'[40] for the middle classes, gently mocking, observing and condoning them, seems very apt.

At times in the 1970s, it seemed as if Ayckbourn's works alone were sustaining a soporific West End. *Absurd Person Singular* (Scarborough, 1972; London, 1973) was an immediate success and introduced a new type of Ayckbourn character, whom the playwright would subject to increasing scrutiny in his eighties work – the unethical, socially ambitious entrepreneur. Written in three acts, with each act set in the kitchen of a different couple on successive Christmas Eves, the play charts the rise and fall in the fortunes of three couples – the humourless shop-owner, Sydney, and his subservient wife, Jane, who obsessively cleans everything in sight; the libidinous architect, Geoffrey, and his neglected, suicidal wife, Eva; and the oleaginous banker, Ronald, and his two-faced, snobbish wife, Marion. In the first act, Sydney, who is only holding his social gathering to impress the two other men, revealingly betrays the shallowness of his personal credo through his use of redundant language:

SYDNEY: You see, as I envisage it, once I can get the necessary loan, that means I can put in a definite bid for the adjoining site – which hasn't incidentally come on to the market. I mean, as I said, this is all purely through personal contacts.
RONALD: Quite so, yes.
SYDNEY: I mean, the site value alone – just taking it as a site – you

follow me?
RONALD: Oh, yes.
SYDNEY: But it is a matter of striking while the iron's hot
before it goes off the boil …
RONALD: Mmm …
SYDNEY: I mean, in this world it's dog eat dog, isn't it? No place for sentiment. Not in business. I mean, alright, so on occasions you can scratch mine. I'll scratch yours.
RONALD: Beg your pardon?
SYDNEY: Tit for tat. But when the chips are down it's every man for himself and blow you, Jack, I regret to say …
RONALD: Exactly.

In Act Two, we learn that Geoffrey is also involved in the development of this shopping complex as its architect, but this information is deliberately concealed beneath brilliant farcical humour – Eva is trying to commit suicide and is inadvertently thwarted by all the guests. When she tries to gas herself in the oven, for example, Jane thinks that she is simply trying to clean it and resolves to lend a hand, scrubbing like a maniac.

The third act takes place the following Christmas. The odious Sydney and Jane, previously viewed by the others as existing at the outer limits of their social circle, have now become the most prosperous couple, albeit through property speculation and jerry building. Geoffrey wryly observes that 'Half [Stanley's] tenants are asking to be re-housed and they haven't even moved in yet'. Geoffrey's own professional reputation is ruined, since the roof of the shopping complex has fallen in and Ronald's financial advice to his bank to support the scheme has dented his reputation as well. In their personal lives, too, there has been a similar flux that is undetectable in Sydney's. Marion is now an alcoholic recluse, rarely leaving her room and although Eva has recovered her poise, she is motivated by denigrating her husband for his business failure. The reversal is completed when we observe that Geoffrey's earlier bravado has been replaced by a desperate need to recover his professional standing, with Sydney ironically representing his last chance of employment, and Ronald is reduced to chuckling over his teenage son's dirty books in an attempt to shut out reality. The play concludes with the newly empowered Sydney compelling everybody to play ghastly Christmas games.

Written at a time when a number of similar property scandals had been reported in the press, the play was topical and probing, although clearly less didactic than a piece by Brenton or Hare. From now on, Ayckbourn would continually be sniffed at for his popularity and even theatricality – *Absurd Person Singular* is a brilliant exploration of off-stage action, since the parties and gatherings take place in venues out of sight from the audience – but his standing with the general public continued to rise. *Absent Friends* (Scarborough, 1974, London, 1975) examines the well-meaning but ultimately disastrous decision by a group of friends to invite an old school acquaintance, Colin, to a social gathering to lift his spirits after the death of his fiancée. The strain of social interaction, the encounter with death and the boorish behaviour of the bereaved man expose the tensions within the relationships of the respective couples. In its blend of humour, precision and poignancy, it is quintessential Ayckbourn, and ensured that with the simultaneous running of *The Norman Conquests*, *Confusions* and *Absurd Person Singular*, 1974 would prove to be the dramatist's *annus mirabilis* of this decade.

Drama Away From London

Scotland

Ayckbourn's remarkable loyalty to Scarborough provides a timely reminder that drama can flourish away from London. This is no more apparent than when one considers the theatre in Scotland since the war – and with the establishment of a Scottish Parliament in the year 2000 there is every prospect that Scottish drama will continue to prosper.

As in England, important developments occurred during the Second World War that were to help shape the fortunes of post-war theatre in Scotland. In 1943 the playwright James Bridie, eager to propagate the notion of a Scottish National Theatre, founded the Citizens' Theatre. Boosted by financial support from CEMA, the company was initially based in the tiny Athenaeum Theatre, but in 1945 it moved to the Royal Princess's Theatre in the run-down Gorbals district of Glasgow, its home ever since. The Citz, as it is popularly known, has subsequently become one of Britain's most important theatrical venues.

Up until the end of the sixties, its policy was to produce the best of British and European drama and it also nurtured new Scottish playwrighting, but in the face of dwindling audiences, a new artistic director, Giles Havergal, together with co-directors Philip Prowse and Robert David Macdonald, initiated a radical policy in 1970. From now on, they aimed to reinvigorate familiar works, eschew naturalism and employ outrageous theatrical styles to freshen up familiar productions. By the end of the seventies, this approach, together with keen ticket-pricing, had brought an international reputation and regularly drew London critics to the venue. In September 1977, for example, Michael Billington conveyed a flavour of the Citz experience in a review for the *Guardian* that evoked comparisons with the Theater am Schiffbauerdamm, the home of the Berliner Ensemble in East Berlin:

> From the outside the Glasgow Citizens' Theatre looks none too inviting. It stands on a patch of razed Gorbals ground with only a bingo parlour and a huddle of shops for company. Yet inside it is almost voluptuously attractive. The beautiful, horseshoe shaped, 750-seater auditorium and the front-of-house area are painted a bordello-scarlet. And for the première of Noel Coward's *Semi-Monde* the place was packed from floor to ceiling; not surprisingly when you learn that all the seats cost 50p with half-price for students and free admission for old-age pensioners.

Although Billington was ambivalent about the play, he was enthraled by Prowse's set, which he described as

> a triumphant recreation of a vanished world. The stage is ringed by a wall of mirrors. A pianist (Robert David Macdonald) sits at a pink baby grand underscoring the action with Coward and Porter numbers. And leaping from table to table are men in double-breasted dinner-jackets and beautiful women in silk, chiffon, bangles and beads. It's like a vision of the damned, dressed by Erté.[41]

This type of interactive design, where the set might function dramatically with the production, was to become Prowse's (and the Citizens') hallmark. His talent both as a designer who could create intriguing visual fare from limited budgets, and as a director who could enliven the most familiar work, played a large part in cementing the Citizens' reputation as a venue of exploration and innovation.

Other important war-time and post-war Scottish theatres include John Stewart's Park Theatre (1940–49) and the Pitlochry Festival Theatre (1951 onwards), which is known as the 'theatre of the hills' and became a favourite destination of the critic, Harold Hobson; the Gateway theatre in Edinburgh, which was opened in 1946 by the Church of Scotland and rented out from 1953 for approximately eight months in the year to the playwright, Robert Kemp; and the Glasgow Unity Theatre (1941). This latter venue housed a left-wing theatre group that testified to the enduring popularity in Scotland of political, working-class theatre companies based in the main urban centres. Unity swiftly gained success with a production of Gorky's *The Lower Depths* that was presented in London, and in 1948 a full-time professional troupe was established that began to tour throughout Scotland. The embracing of touring is a policy that theatre groups have continued to this day, given the far-flung and isolated communities that, together with the major cities of Glasgow and Edinburgh, comprise the relatively small population of Scotland. Unity's most notable production was Robert Macleish's *The Gorbals Story* (1948), a study of poverty in an overcrowded slum, which was toured frequently, revived on several occasions and eventually filmed. Despite this success, however, Unity foundered in the early fifties, although, as with Theatre Workshop, its principles and traditions continued to be disseminated by its performers and it can now be seen as a precursor of 7:84 Scotland and Wildcat Stage Productions.

It might be argued that the subsequent development of Scottish drama is divided between those who wish to stress its independence from English traditions by propagating indigenous writing and performance that draw on native customs, history and popular culture, and those who seek international, non-English models, to provide templates for the fostering of a distinctive Scottishness in theatre. The first strand received a boost with the founding of an institution for the training of Scottish performers – the College of Dramatic Art in Glasgow (subsequently the Royal Scottish Academy of Dramatic Art) – by James Bridie in 1950; the creation of a separate Department of Drama at the University of Glasgow in 1966; and the establishment of the Scottish Theatre Archive in 1981. Similarly, dramatists such as Robert Kemp and Robert McLellan have written for a Scottish theatre. John McGrath's work with 7:84 Scotland has continued to demonstrate the philosophy articulated in his book, *A Good Night Out* (1981), that theatre should be popular and socialist, address working-class audiences in their own environment and help to advocate social change, and the theatre in the Old Tron Kirk in Glasgow, which was established in 1981, now specifically promotes new Scottish writing.

The second strand is best evidenced in the work of the Citizens' Theatre, the Traverse Theatre Club in Edinburgh and the world-famous Edinburgh Festival. The Traverse was opened in January 1963, primarily on account of the work of the American Jim Haynes, who was later to open the Arts Laboratory in London. The venue has been responsible for the premièring of many foreign productions in English, including plays by Jarry, Arrabel and Peter Weiss, but it has also devoted itself to developing native talent and has regularly contributed productions to the Edinburgh Festival. This cultural polymath, one of Europe's leading musical as well as theatrical events, takes place in August and September every year, and is famous for the quality of the dramatic productions performed by invited foreign companies. Past highlights have included the Renauld-Barrault Company's

Hamlet (1948), Feuillère's performance in *La Dame aux camélias* (1955), Thornton Wilder's *The Matchmaker* (1954), Athol Fugard's *Dimetos* (1975) and the Georgian Rustaveli Company's adaptation of *Richard III* (1979). What makes the Festival such a vibrant and exciting event today, however, is not necessarily its main attractions but the ever-growing Fringe, housing alternative comedians, student groups, experimental companies and a rich cornucopia of performers in rented church halls, school yards and broom cupboards. The prospect of discovering exciting new talent – and of being discovered – is what attracts audiences, critics and performers alike to the most unlikely and intriguing venues.

Whatever model of analysis one chooses to discuss Scottish theatre, its vibrancy and eclecticism during the post-war period is undeniable. Whether it be in the naming of Glasgow as the European City of Culture in 1990 or the recognition that a book deserves to be written about post-war Scottish theatre alone, its integrity is clear for all to see. The Glasgow academic Adrienne Scullion observes that 'because there has been a relative lack of engagement with Scottish theatre from the academy the critical agenda of contemporary historiography has little occupied Scottish theatre studies'.[42] This is a clarion call that can no longer be ignored – and it equally applies to the development of Welsh-language and English-language drama in Wales and theatrical activity in Belfast and Northern Ireland, particularly against the backdrop of the Troubles since 1969.

Regional

Whilst it is easy to pick out post-war milestones, such as the visit of the Berliner Ensemble to London in 1956, it is arguable that equally important work has been done over the past fifty years in regional venues catering for the needs of local communities throughout Britain. One example of a regional venue that pre-dates the Second World War but has continued to produce interesting work in the new era is the Maddermarket Theatre, Norwich. Built inside a dilapidated hall in 1921 by Nugent Monck, the venue comprises the replica of an Elizabethan interior and houses an amateur company that creates a new production every nine performances and maintains the anonymity of the cast. Monck himself performed in every single Shakespearean work before his retirement in 1952 and the Norwich Players, capitalising on their founder's fame, entered the seventies with an enlarged venue that held 300 people.

But perhaps *the* defining feature of post-war theatrical development in the regions has been the construction of new regional theatre buildings and the housing within them of new companies. After the unveiling of the Belgrade Theatre, Coventry, in 1958, Anthony Jackson argues in the invaluable reference book, *The Repertory Movement: A History of Regional Theatre in Britain*, that there are three identifiable phases of regional growth over the subsequent twenty-five years. The first phase is characterised by a conviction that the arts in general, and the theatre in particular, were a mark of a civilised society, and thus deserved the support and encouragement of government, local authorities and funding bodies, such as the Arts Council. This collective patronage led in the sixties to the redevelopment of the repertory theatres at Nottingham, Sheffield, Birmingham and Bristol, as well as the construction of completely new complexes in Stoke-on-Trent, Scarborough, Chichester, Pitlochry, Manchester (the Contact and Royal Exchange Theatres), Newcastle and Leicester. The drive away from conventional spaces and desire to experiment with new forms of drama also meant that many of these new sixties venues possessed studio spaces and facilities for TIE groups.[43] By 1970, twenty new theatres had been constructed.[44]

The second phase of regional growth in the early to mid-seventies was less building-based. Reflecting the trend towards exploring different modes of drama, alternative theatre groups for women, gays, local communities, political campaigns, ethnic minorities and young people sought new audiences in venues as diverse as street-corners, staff canteens, public houses and prison cells. The funding authorities were no longer perceived as beneficent bodies but integral parts of an establishment that was contesting the very social change these groups were demanding. Alternative and fringe theatre thrived on the tension that this created.

Phase three again saw the rationale of these new complexes being questioned, but this time on grounds of finance. The economic prosperity of the sixties had given way to the economic crisis of the seventies and from 1975 the increases in annual Arts Council grants were unable to keep pace with inflation. Several theatres, including the Theatre Royal, Lincoln and the Lyceum at Crewe, were forced to close and the running costs of many sixties buildings were seen as increasingly prohibitive. The industrial and financial difficulties that surrounded the construction of the National Theatre's South Bank complex also served to focus press criticism on the alleged 'white-elephant' status of these modern complexes.

It would be disingenuous to claim, however, that the golden era for individual regional theatres in the sixties was always followed by a downturn of fortunes in the seventies. If one considers the Nottingham Playhouse, for example, the halcyon period of John Neville's directorship (1963–8), which saw the matching of classic plays and contemporary drama to create, in his words, 'a pocket National Theatre for the region',[45] was followed by the directorship of Stuart Burge (1968–73), that witnessed the première of Peter Barnes' incisive satire of British class attitudes, *The*

Ruling Class, and Richard Eyre's tenureship (1973–8), that oversaw some of the most revitalising writing of the seventies: Hare and Brenton's *Brassneck*, Brenton's *Churchill Play* and, in particular, Griffiths' *Comedians*.

The truly depressing period for regional theatre, namely the years from 1983 onwards, is not covered in *The Repertory Movement: A History of Regional Theatre in Britain*. Phase four, the eighties, has seen the philosophy of subsidy eroded by the philosophy of the market-place and given that regional theatres' income is derived from the box office, Arts Council grants and Local Authority support, the reduction in the latter two has had an inevitable effect on the former. The election of the Labour government in 1997 may herald a revival of support, although current signs are mixed. What is clearer is that phase five has been ushered in less by renewed governmental support than by the arrival of the National Lottery, whose allocation of funds has already signalled a second wave of new theatre building for the millennium. The construction of the Salford Opera house is the most visible evidence of this.

Some theatre professionals argue that if lottery funds were released to support companies rather than buildings then the viability of regional theatre would be ensured and the pioneering conditions of the sixties could be recreated. Others are less sanguine, claiming that the original lottery legislation was designed in the early nineties to ensure that lottery money did not allow government to reduce the amount of support it gave to the arts in direct grant aid. This debate is ongoing.

Peter Cheeseman at Stoke

The resilience and value of regional theatre is no better illustrated than by the figure of Peter Cheeseman, the founder in 1962 of the Victoria Theatre in Stoke-on-Trent. By the time of his final project, *The Tempest* in March 1998, he could claim over 140 productions to his name and no one in Britain can rival his devotion to a single theatre and its surrounding community. Generally following a policy that stuck to three commitments – performances in-the-round (the area gained a new theatre-in-the-round in 1986), the juxtaposition of new work and classics and the history and contemporary problems of North Staffordshire – Cheeseman is best known for eleven documentaries on local issues, in the form of 'living newspapers' and in the tradition of Theatre Workshop.[46] These productions have featured the area's ailing mining, steel and potteries industries and have contributed to local political campaigns, as well as helping to keep alive the oral testimony that is so often lost in accounts of local struggles. Whilst Ayckbourn passed through Stoke on his way to Scarborough, London and great fame, Cheeseman remained and it would clearly be invidious to argue that for the theatre as a whole the one's work was less important than the other's.

Musicals

Even Alan Ayckbourn, a playwright not over-exposed to failure, did have one commercial flop during the seventies the musical *Jeeves* (1975). Over-elaborate, excessively long (it ran for four hours) and hyped to enormous proportions in its advance publicity, its failure still seems slightly odd now, given that his collaborator was the man who would join Ayckbourn in the eighties in helping to sustain the West End – Andrew Lloyd Webber. Intimations of what was to come were already apparent. Stephen Schwartz's rock musical *Godspell* (1971), Stephen Sondheim's treatment of marriage and solitude, *Company* (1972), the nostalgic reflection on the fifties by Jim Jacobs and Warren Casey, *Grease* (1972) and the ingenious *A Chorus Line* (1975), in which aspiring dancers were required to reveal their background and demonstrate their talent, provided salutary reminders that the American form of the genre was still pre-eminent in the West End. But the balance was shortly to be redressed. Taking advantage of the new freedom to portray religious episodes on-stage in the post-censorship era, the biblical musical, *Joseph and the Amazing Technicolor Dreamcoat* (originally 1968, and the start of the Lloyd Webber/Tim Rice collaboration), was much revived during the seventies and since, and proved a popular mixture of melodic tunes, cheeky irreverence and rock anthems (Pharoah was conceived as Elvis Presley). *Jesus Christ Superstar* (1972) adopted the same template, encompassing sinister pharisees, haunting musical laments sung by Mary Magdalene and a spectacular, anguished crucifixion, and *Evita* (1978), based on the career of Eva Peron, demonstrated both Lloyd Webber's unerring ability to write haunting tunes that stuck in the mind, in this case, 'Don't Cry for Me Argentina', and Rice's talent for creating economical, entertaining books. The technical precision of these musicals (which became *the* hallmark of later productions of Lloyd Webber's Really Useful Theatre Company) was lacking in *Jeeves*, but neither of its authors need have worried: a pared-down version opened in London in 1995 to a much more favourable reception.

The Royal Shakespeare Company 1969–1979

The experience of the Royal Shakespeare Company, Britain's 'other National Theatre', in the seventies served as a microcosm of developments within British theatre as a whole. The early struggle to establish an identity distinct from the practice of the sixties, the questioning of 'director's theatre', the move towards smaller, more exploratory venues, a fascination with the forms and subject matter of alternative theatre groups, financial crises brought about by the cuts of 1975, occasionally magnificent, innovative work that seems remarkable given the financial constraints under which it was produced, and the eventual recognition that commercial sponsorship would be needed to bridge the shortfall in subsidy – all these developments specific to this company also applied in general terms to theatre throughout the country.

Trevor Nunn Takes Charge

The ensemble system of performers that had been established so success-fully by Peter Hall continued under his successor, Trevor Nunn, and a new generation of actors began to emerge, which bode well for the new decade. These included Alan Howard, Helen Mirren, Ben Kingsley, Janet Suzman and Patrick Stewart (who would later achieve world-wide fame as the Star Trek captain, Jean-Luc Picard). A young director, Terry Hands, also joined the company from the Liverpool Everyman, resulting in a pool of four direc-tors: Nunn, Hands, David Jones and John Barton (the link with the old regime) who determined the company's policy during the seventies. Their first artistic decisions emphasised the immediate desire to carve out an identity distinct from the Hall era. For the 1970 season, a series of late Shakespearean plays was presented, marking the first thematic approach since 1960 and a shift away from the focus on the history plays. Allied to this was the scaling down of productions to explore a new simplicity of production (best seen in Nunn's 1976 production of *Macbeth* where the playing space was a circle etched inside a box with no scenery) and a new permanent set for the main theatre designed by Christopher Morley which resembled a giant, empty box. It was in this arena that Peter Brook's momentous production of *A Midsummer Night's Dream* was staged in 1971.

Peter Brook's *A Midsummer Night's Dream*

This coup de théâtre had tremendous ramifications, not just for the RSC itself but for the dramatic treatment of Shakespeare, and is now viewed as a seminal event of the last fifty years of British theatre. Rejecting the con-ventional approach to the work that emphasises enchanting fairies, delightful magic and bewitching melodies, Brook chose to explore the subliminal eroticism, violence and cruelty contained within the script. His fairies elided speeches and songs, chanted discordantly and grunted and growled where previously they might have whispered. Oberon and Puck swung from trapezes, highlighting the athleticism and physicality of the performers, and the characters were clad, not in the pastoral shades of old, but in satin costumes in the primary colours of Chinese tumblers. This utilisation of circus skills (which spawned many imitators in the following years) was viewed as particularly experimental and on the opening night the audience was on its feet applauding even by the interval, alert to the originality of what they were witnessing.

Ironically, this approach marked a rejection (first signalled in *Marat/Sade*) of Brook's past practice of 'director's theatre', where the concept was ruthlessly imposed by the controlling hand. In this production Brook spurned the methodology that had resulted in the forties' *Love's Labour's Lost* and the fifties *Titus Andronicus*, for a vision that relied on the company of actors embarking upon a voyage of discovery that drew strength from collaboration and the freedom to explore. Answers were generated from within rather than suggested from without, and the bare, brilliantly lit stage helped highlight the extent to which the performers were being encouraged to rely on their own resources. After the zenith of director's theatre under Hall in the sixties, the fact that one of its former devotees should be perceived as having publicly recanted was seen as highly significant.

The heterodoxy of Brook's *A Midsummer Night's Dream* drew great laudations – Clive Barnes stated that it was 'Without any equivocation whatsoever the greatest Shakespearean production of Shakespeare I have seen in my life'[47] – although, some, including Benedict Nightingale in the *New Statesman*, found the emphasis on physical theatre overpowering. Financially, though, the production was a life-line, with the Broadway transfer alone earning £70,000, and it ensured that the RSC was to end the 1970/1 season in surplus for the first time in its history.[48]

The Search for Smaller Spaces

Like the National in the sixties, the RSC spent the seventies waiting for a much-delayed new building to be completed. Nevertheless, the postponement of the opening of the Barbican complex until 1982 was probably a blessing in disguise, given the opprobrium that the South Bank complex drew to the National at a time of crisis. Few opportunities were lost to point out that the National's share of the Arts Council's drama budget rose from 12.5 per cent in 1972/3 to a mammoth 25 per cent in 1975/6,[49] and it is possible that one of the institutions might not have been able to survive the simultaneous unveiling of two cash-hungry complexes. Instead, in the interim the RSC decided to seek out more intimate venues to play in, reflecting the decade's trend towards smaller spaces. In 1971 the company occupied The Place for a supplementary season and performed Trevor Griffiths' study of Gramsci, *Occupations*, an early attempt by Griffiths to make socialist ideas more accessible, as well as a production of *Miss Julie* that was so realistic that one horrified critic was convinced that a real canary had been strangled on stage.[50] A more significant space was opened in 1974 and endures up to this day. A converted shed-like structure holding 140 people, the spartan nature of the Other Place at Stratford was in complete contrast to the thirties' grandeur of the RST. Its first artistic director, Buzz Goodbody, immediately illustrated the potential for pared-down exploratory work, and her suicide in 1975 was a terrible blow to the company.

Mid-Decade Crisis and Recovery

The 1972 season saw the RSC stage the second of Nunn's thematic cycles, this time of the Roman plays, but even the RSC was not immune to the general decline in the fortunes of drama during the mid-point of this decade. Under pressure from critical opinion that saw Stoppard's *Travesties* (1974) as a beacon in a sea of gloom (literally, in the West End's case, with theatre lights being dimmed in 1973 during the energy crisis), the cuts of 1975 brought pressure (just resisted) to close down the company's Aldwych base and severely restrict overall activity, but from this nadir was to come a recovery into what is now perceived as a golden period. Terry Hands' patriotic rendition of *Henry V* seemed appropriately nationalistic and evoked memories of Olivier's morale boosting film in the forties. The burningly contemporary *Destiny* (1976) by David Edgar, a study of fascism and racism that juxtaposes attitudes in the seventies to attitudes in the forties, confirmed that the RSC could still discover significant new writers and Trevor Nunn's *Macbeth* (1976) was to prove as significant for subsequent Shakespearean productions as Brook's *A Midsummer Night's Dream*.

Trevor Nunn's *Macbeth* (1976)

In this, his third production of *Macbeth*, first staged at the Other Place, Nunn finally decided that simplicity was all. A black circle was etched onto the floor around which characters sat observing and occasionally participating in the action. The stripping away of props and clutter, the focus on the performers' own capabilities and the immense theatricality of simple effects, such as a single lamp circling over Macbeth's head in the final scenes, brilliantly illustrated that drama was not the preserve of enormously expensive buildings, but could be staged to great effect in the barest of spaces. This simple visual reminder was hugely influential and demonstrated the new polarisation of venues in the country.

The production was particularly memorable for the performances of Ian McKellen, the rising star of the company, as Macbeth, and Judi Dench as his wife. Michael Billington's account in the *Guardian* conveys a flavour of the performance, which was brought alive for many schoolchildren (this author included) by a widely distributed video-recording. The production's very spartan nature seemed to demystify Shakespeare by allowing the performers to breathe:

[McKellen] is at his best … when after his coronation he assumes a mask of tight-lipped diplomatic courtesy broken wide open by the vision of Banquo's ghost; the long jaw slackens and judders, the cheeks puff in and out like bellows, the mouth foams as a once whole man is reduced to epileptic frenzy. The guests gone, he turns to Lady Macbeth, who slumps stricken to the ground; picking her up and setting her features as if she were a ventriloquist's dummy, he stumbles sightlessly into the black future that awaits him.

If this is not great acting, I don't know what is; and McKellen's study of evil bursting through a mask like a clown through a paper hoop is finely complemented by Judi Dench's Lady Macbeth, which is not some painted Gorgon but a portrait of a novice dabbling in Satanic powers. Invoking evil spirits in her first scene, she suddenly darts back with a stab of fear as if having made contact; and that one gesture gives us a clue to a woman who is half-fascinated, half-terrified by the pit she has entered. Miss Dench too shows the cracking open of the mask and the cry of remorse she utters in the sleep walking scene, apparently drawn from her very soul, is guaranteed to haunt one for nights to come.[51]

My own class 3G, wrestling with *Macbeth* as an O Level text, were both horrified and amazed by these performances. It was the ritualistic murder of Macduff's son, however, with a thin line of blood following a slowly drawn knife across a young neck, which provided the most chilling moment of a marvellously atmospheric production.

Terry Hands' *Henry VI* Trilogy

The RSC's revival, astonishing given external circumstances, continued into 1977. The Donmar Warehouse in London provided a studio base in the capital, the Aldwych season thrived on a diet of the new (Nichols' *Privates on Parade*), the old (Ibsen's *Pillars of Society*) and the enduring (Brecht's *The Days of the Commune*) and the first of the annual tours to Newcastle, signalling a policy of reaching out to the regions, was undertaken. All in all, Stratford saw 8 productions in this season, the Aldwych 11, the Other Place 5 and the Warehouse 9. No wonder the National looked lack-lustre in comparison with its expanding rival.

Terry Hands' *Henry VI* trilogy (1978) further emphasised the company's rude health. Conceived as the first production of the unadapted text since the Elizabethan period – and thereby marking a completely different approach to text from the *Wars of the Roses* project – it was played in its entirety from 10.30am to 11pm and highlighted the worth of nurturing acting talent on long-term contracts. Alan Howard's performance as Henry VI – 'a thing of beauty and wonder'[52] in Billington's view – made many feel that in its ability to unearth new acting talent the company was unrivalled in the world and the grounding in verse-speaking that John Barton's precise inculcation provided was seen as unsurpassed. Howard's performance as Coriolanus, making one of Shakespeare's least appealing protagonists empathetic, underlined this view.

For all its success, money was still an abiding worry for the RSC as the decade drew to a close, as it was for all theatres. The imbalance in state funding between the RSC and the National would continue into the next decade (in 1981, for instance, the NT received £6,030,000 compared to the RSC's £2,255,000) and it was evident that more money would have to be generated to make up for its income shortfall. The notion of a 'right to fail' now seemed an anachronism from the sixties in the light of economic circumstances and the election of Margaret Thatcher's government in May 1979 would make the climate even less temperate for the arts in general.

In 1978, the RSC embarked on an initiative that would have important consequences for British theatre in the eighties. For a regional tour of twenty-six towns, it entered into a sponsorship agreement with Hallmark cards in return for £12,000 in 1978, £25,000 in 1979 and £45,000 in 1980. The debate about the extent to which theatre would have to enter the market-place – a debate to rage for the entire duration of the incoming Conservative administration – had begun.

Chapter 5

1980–1997

From a critic's point of view, the history of twentieth century drama is the history of a collapsing vocabulary. Categories that were formally thought sacred and separate begin to melt and flow together like images in a dream. (Kenneth Tynan)

Continuity and Change: Institutions 3

A comparison between 1945 and 1985 of the health of the four major theatrical institutions in Britain illustrates the distance travelled in these years. Two had suffered a not unwelcome decline, one had prospered and the fourth was facing an uncertain future. H.M. Tennent Ltd had lost its stranglehold in a West End which was now no longer the pre-eminent forum for drama. The Lord Chamberlain was no longer empowered to censor. The Shakespeare Memorial Theatre, Stratford, had metamorphosed into the hub of a world-class theatrical company, whereas the Old Vic had endured a personal decline after the departure of the National Theatre to the South Bank. The history of post-war British theatre had inevitably been one of continuity and change and this was to continue between 1979 and 1997.

In addition, the eighties and nineties witnessed the following concomitant developments: new entrepreneurs have emerged to fill the vacuum left by Binkie Beaumont, specifically with blockbuster musicals produced by Andrew Lloyd Webber and Cameron Mackintosh in a West End reticent about staging new writing. The Lord Chamberlain may have been sidelined but drama still faced the threat of censorship from legal action in the courts (*The Romans in Britain* (1980)), government policy or the unsatisfactory allocation of funding. The Royal Shakespeare Company pioneered the concept of sponsorship with commercial companies

(Hallmark Cards, Guardian Royal Exchange), aided the trend towards large-scale adaptations, known as 'event theatre' (*Nicholas Nickleby* (1980), *Les Misérables* (1985)), and helped maintain Shakespeare as a symbol of national consciousness; and the Old Vic, having been home to a season of well-received repertory productions mounted by the Peter Hall Company (for example, *Waiting for Godot* with Ben Kingsley and Alan Howard), ended 1997 under the threat of closure after its Canadian owners, the Mirvish family, decided that they could no longer sustain its increasing losses. In short, theatrical activity under the two Conservative administrations of Margaret Thatcher (1979–90) and John Major (1990–97) was characterised by a mixture of financial crises, pessimistic prognoses and a feeling that drama was being forced to justify its very existence, alongside a rediscovery of the power of the actor, a plethora of new writers (most frequently nourished by the subsidised triumvirate of the National Theatre, the Royal Shakespeare Company and the Royal Court) and, above all, continuing demonstrations of the resilience of the profession.

The Problematics of Funding: Thatcherism, the National Lottery and 'Stabilisation' Grants

Margaret Thatcher became Leader of the Conservative Party in 1975 and the personal vision that she set out in her first party conference speech was one from which she did not deviate during her entire period of office as Prime Minister:

> Let me give you my vision: a man's right to work as he will, to spend what he earns, to own property, to have the state as servant and not as master – these are the British inheritance. … We must get private enterprise back on the road to recovery – not merely to give people more of their own money to spend as they choose, but to have more money to help the old and the sick and the handicapped. … I believe that, just as each of us has the obligation to make the best of his talents, so governments have an obligation to create the framework within which we can do so. … We can go on as we have been doing, we can continue down. Or we can stop and with a decisive act say 'Enough'.[1]

The conviction, determination, even simplicity of this was to prove instrumental in achieving three General Election victories (although it should be noted that a majority of Britons always voted against her). Her rejection of consensus, which had been held by many to be the cause of the industrial and economic turmoil in the seventies, would eventually lead to an atmosphere of spurious certainty ('This Lady is not for turning'), faction-alism (opponents were decried for not being 'One of Us') and selfishness ('There is no such thing as society'). This left the theatre, a medium designed to stimulate discussion, encourage debate and promote collec-tive endeavour, in an exposed position. Initial policy on the arts as a whole reflected the very different priorities of the new administration, and the stress on private enterprise and self-help meant that the notion of the state funding theatrical activity would be viewed with suspicion.

Although the principle of 'arms-length' funding, where the government decided the amount of the annual arts budget but left its allocation to the Arts Council, had been respected by previous administrations since the Council's inception in 1946, a glance at the changing titles of the Arts Council's annual reports betrays the new climate that prevailed. Whereas in the sixties the Council could speak cheerily of *A Brighter Project* or *An Urban Renaissance*, in the eighties it was necessary to write of *Making Arts Money Work Harder* and in the early nineties employ the rather desperate sounding *Keeping the Show on the Road*.[2] Within a year of Thatcher's first election in 1979, the Arts Minister, Norman St John Stevas, had cut the public subsidy for theatre and signalled the government's desire to see 'the private sector raising more money and bringing business acumen and effi-ciency to bear on the administration of cultural institutions'.[3] The securing of commercial sponsorship was possible for an organisation of the prestige of the Royal Shakespeare Company, which was to sign a lucrative agree-ment with the Guardian Royal Exchange in 1984, but more questionable for the numerous, less 'marketable' companies up and down the country. Ironically, however, state money was to follow private subsidy in that by 1986 both the National and the RSC were consuming over fifty per cent of the entire theatre allocation. Given that the overall budget was only £26 million (requiring an additional £16.2 million to restore funding to the levels of 1970[4]), it is obvious why many feared for the continuation of regional theatre. The feeling of siege mentality increased in the profession that year with the *Sunday Times* publishing an ill-researched article lambasting Peter Hall and Trevor Nunn for their earnings from transfers to the commercial sector, and many agreed with Michael Billington that they had become 'sacrificial victims' for subsidised theatre.[5]

In the same year (1986) the Arts Council set up a Theatre Enquiry chaired by Sir Kenneth Cork. This status report made disturbing reading: the subsidised sector was being subsidised by the very people who worked in it by means of their below-average wages; between 1971 and 1985 musi-cals had increased from 4 per cent to 9 per cent of the repertoire, new work decreased from 15 per cent to 11 per cent and classics (excluding Shakespeare) plummeted from 18 per cent to 8 per cent (the large casts they demanded were simply too expensive); and the two premier companies devoured 47 per cent of the budget in 1985–6, as opposed to 39 per cent in 1977–8 and 30 per cent in 1970–1.[6] Alas, the chances of the implementation of the Cork Report's main recommendations, that more money was needed to ensure diversity and that this could be raised by a one per cent levy on the television licence, were dashed by the third Conservative election victory in 1987. When the new Arts Minister, Richard Luce, stated shortly afterwards that 'the only test of our ability to succeed is whether or not we can attract enough customers',[7] confirmation was provided that the right to fail had been abolished. Theatre was now a product that needed to survive in the market-place.

The adminstration led from 1990 by John Major was always torn between stressing its ideological links with Thatcherism and attempting to emphasise its distinctiveness. This schizophrenia carried over into its theatre policy. In 1991, the first full year of John Major's premiership, the theatre received a very welcome pre-election increase of fourteen per cent in its grant. The appointment of an arts lover, David Mellor, to oversee the newly created Department of National Heritage, seemed to bode well, also, but Mellor's forced departure following a farcical sex scandal symbolised the Major government's inability to deliver its good intentions through a mixture of bad luck and incompetence. Its most significant legacy, however, may prove to be the most valuable of all for the theatre.

The creation of the National Lottery and the allocation of a substantial amount of its revenue to the arts (£250 million in 1996) promises to initiate the biggest expansion in cultural activity since the sixties. The swift relaxation of the original lottery rules by the last Heritage Secretary of the Conservative government, Virginia Bottomley, also conceded that arts organisations were in financial crisis, something that had previously been persistently denied. The 'stabilisation' programme instigated in 1997 offered a one-off chance for selected organisations to put their finances in order and, given that regional theatre alone had a deficit of £8 million, it is not surprising that 129 organisations applied for the fifteen places on the pilot scheme.

The fifteen that were finally chosen for a share of £15 million (a paltry sum when compared to the £78 million awarded for the controversial redevelopment of the Royal Opera House) included six projects connected to theatre: the Birmingham Rep., to help attract new audiences, and explore recording and broadcasting opportunities; the Bristol City Consortium, to link up the Arnolfini, the Bristol Old Vic and the Watershed Arts Trust; Hampshire Arts Centres Consortium, to help six arts centres plan for 'foreseeable reductions in subsidy' after local government reorganisation; the Junction, Cambridge, to enable this venue to produce riskier work; Tara Arts, London, to develop a permanent home for Asian theatre in the UK and the West Yorkshire Playhouse, to clear outstanding debts from the building of its new theatre in 1991.[8] All in all, a mixture of the innovative (Tara Arts, the Junction), the creative (Birmingham Rep.) and the desperate (Hampshire Arts, the West Yorkshire Playhouse), but a welcome, if small and belated, recognition of the consequence of years of inadequate funding.

The hope now invested in the lottery provides a valuable reminder that the history of British theatre since the medieval period has always been characterised by setbacks to be negotiated. The changing religious sensibilities that denied the Mystery Plays an audience; the plagues in Elizabethan England that shut the playhouses; the proscription of drama during the English Civil War which resulted in the closure of all public theatres between 1642 and 1660; the creation of a formal censor in 1737 to rein in satirical writers; the dominance of melodrama in the Victorian period to the exclusion of less sensational work – all these challenges have been taken up and overcome. Similarly, whilst the period between 1979 and 1997 has been one of struggle, it has also been one of achievement against great odds.

Musicals

The re-emergence of a genre popular in the fifties was the single most noticeable feature of the West End in the eighties, but instead of relying on American imports, London became famous for its efficient and profitable staging of home-grown musicals. Their dominance has drawn much adverse comment and they are regularly accused of variously blocking the entrance of new writing into the West End, restricting choice, driving up prices and being intellectually light-weight, but their enduring popularity testifies to their ability to entertain on a grand scale (often marrying impressive technical feats with soaring melodies), their capacity to reach beyond the normal pool of theatre-goers, and the ingenuity with which they are marketed. The fay little waif of *Les Misérables* is now an emblem recognisable throughout the world and such is the show's popularity that it can sustain the release in 1997 of an anniversary CD-ROM which supplies copious information about the productions and permits three-dimensional back-stage tours.

These new musicals were also a product appropriate to their time, in that, as with *Oklahoma!* in 1947, their glamour and panache were a welcome relief for a country recently racked by industrial unrest, low in self-confidence and now suffering from a recession.

The matriarch of eighties' musicals was *Cats*, based on T.S. Eliot's *Old Possum's Book of Practical Cats*, which initiated the trend for musical adaptations of literary works. Everything about the 1981 production was meticulously executed. Andrew Lloyd Webber's score aurally identified the characteristics of each individual cat. John Napier's rubbish-dump set, comprising dustbins, rusty old cars, discarded tyres and other detritus, provided a perfect arena for the cats to glide around. The choreography by Gillian Lynne was conceived to allow accomplished dancers, including Wayne Sleep, the maximum opportunity to display their virtuosity, and Trevor Nunn's direction, which integrated the audience by surrounding them with cats' eyes that dazzled in the dark, contributed to the feeling that this was theatre at its most alluring. Even the interpolation of Lloyd Webber's melodies with Eliot's original verse drew favourable comment. What supporters of the British musical found particularly cheering was the way that *Cats* compared favourably to the transfer from Broadway of the American blockbuster *Barnum* in the same year. Here, at last, was a British offering that could make the return journey with pride.

Lloyd Webber's skills as an entrepreneur who could identify a market, as much as a composer who devised memorable melodies, now ensured a succession of box-office winners. In 1982 he purchased the Palace Theatre (later to become the home of *Les Misérables*) as a signal of his dynastic intent and in 1984 *Starlight Express* took up residency at the Apollo Victoria. It was this work that critics cited as a regrettable triumph of bravado and glitz over substance and sense. A paean to the age of steam, the work required that the auditorium be fitted with a track that swooped and dived around the auditorium, allowing the performers dressed up as trains to roller-skate at frightening speeds. The production cost alone was £1.4 million. The combination of John Napier and Trevor Nunn resulted in several breath-taking races, large video screens that allowed the audience to follow the performers' progress and pounding disco beats designed to enhance the excitement. Most critics found the frenetic pace of the production less effective than the feline grace of *Cats*:

> In *Cats*, the balance between spectacle and emotion was well-nigh perfect and the final ascent to the skies lifted the spirits. But here when the cast finally hymn the 'Light at the End of the Tunnel', I was reminded of Raymond Briggs's classic remark that what that often signified was simply an oncoming train.[9]

Nevertheless, such comments did nothing to dent the confidence of the public at the box office.

The popularity of musicals was such that in 1985 the RSC decided to get in on the act by staging *Les Misérables*, one of Trevor Nunn's final productions as artistic director and another literary adaptation, this time of

Victor Hugo's novel. The National had enjoyed a huge success with a revived *Guys and Dolls* in 1982, but its own attempt at staging a new work had been a spectacular disaster, with *Jean Seberg* (1983) earning almost universal opprobrium. *Les Misérables*, therefore, was something of a calculated risk but one that the RSC was wise to take. Its commercial appeal led to a swift transfer from the Barbican to the Palace Theatre in the West End, before premièring triumphantly worldwide and seeming likely to survive into the new millennium. Its profitability led to questions about the propriety of Nunn benefiting personally from West End transfers, questions that again cast the spotlight on the two subsidised flagships, but of greater significance was the fact that *Les Misérables* heralded the arrival of a second West End impresario to rival Lloyd Webber: Cameron Mackintosh.

Blood Brothers (1983), *The Phantom of the Opera* (1986), *Chess* (1986), *Aspects of Love* (1989), *Miss Saigon* (1989), *Buddy* (1989), *Sunset Boulevard* (1993), *Martin Guerre* (1995), a revamped *Jeeves* (1995) and revived productions of *Me and My Girl* (1985), *Joseph* (1994) and *Jesus Christ Superstar* (1996) have all followed the lucrative path delineated by *Cats*. It would be no exaggeration to state that the arrival of this British phenomenon has proved the financial salvation of an otherwise parlous West End and helped create a worldwide reputation for a particular facet of British theatre in the same way that the emergence of new writing did thirty years earlier.

Crisis and Hope: The Return of Actors' Theatre 1979–1986

The funding cuts of 1980 began to bite in 1981 and the fact that by October twelve London playhouses lay dark – almost a third of the total – illustrated how dependent the West End was becoming on the blood transfusion of imports from the subsidised sector. The government's suspicion of all things subsidised was posing a serious threat to the theatre as a whole. How different from twenty years earlier when it was the H.M. Tennent transfers of Theatre Workshop's work that had hastened the demise of that (barely) funded company.

The current West End's reliance on old stars and new musicals, the premature deaths of the critic Kenneth Tynan and playwright David Mercer and the unfortunate profligacy of productions such as Alan Ayckbourn's *Way Upstream* (1982), which caused £125,000 worth of damage to the Lyttelton auditorium when the 6,000-gallon water-tank burst onstage, cast a pall at the start of the decade in tune with the sombre times. Bright moments in 1982 tended to emphasise the state of siege – the Mirvish purchase of the Old Vic secured its medium-term future and the Theatre

Museum was saved from closure after a rearguard action mounted by the Society for Theatre Research – and even the eventual opening of the RSC's new London home, the Barbican, was overshadowed by criticism of the maze-like nature of its walkway approaches and apprehension that it might prove as costly to run as the South Bank. In the midst of this gloom, however, it was evident that some fine acting performances were being given, in particular by Michael Gambon as Lear in the RSC's Stratford production and Judi Dench as Lady Bracknell in *The Importance of Being Earnest*. Although it was not unnoticed by critics that these were taking place in revivals of classics and rarely in the West End, they nevertheless signalled the return by the mid-eighties of an 'actors' theatre' to London, embracing both the commercial and subsidised wings, which supplanted the directors' theatre of the seventies and the playwrights' of the sixties. Thus the gloom of 1983 at the continuing closure of twelve playhouses was mitigated by Judi Dench in Hugh Whitemore's *Pack of Lies* at the Lyric, Penelope Keith in Coward's *Hay Fever* at the Queen's and the rising star of the RSC, Antony Sher, in David Edgar's *Maydays*. One of the most dramatic events in 1983 was the publication by Peter Hall of his diaries, which documented in frank and controversial detail the battles he had fought at the National in the seventies and early eighties. More scrutiny inevitably befell Hall and the South Bank.

Although Orwell's nightmare vision for 1984 failed to materialise, many viewed the simultaneous production of sixteen musicals in the West End as a depressing enough state of affairs. Ticket prices exceeded £10 for the first time, the continued survival of the Royal Court was in question and summer closures in regional theatres became the norm. Again, though, good performances (primarily at the RSC or NT) abounded. Antony Sher surpassed his previous achievements with a 'fleet and demonic'[10] Richard III in a production that would tour worldwide, Judi Dench emphasised her versatility and gravitas as Mother Courage and Sheila Gish was a fragile and poignant Blanche Dubois in *A Streetcar Named Desire*. The London fringe, which had struggled to adapt to an environment where recession and political disillusion had dulled the appetite for didactic theatre, also began to show signs of revival with the rise of the Bush Theatre in Shepherd's Bush, the Gate Theatre in Notting Hill and the Orange Tree, Richmond.

Perhaps of all the years in this decade, 1985 illustrated the truly ambiguous nature of the theatre's fortunes. On the one hand the government was mounting a further concerted attack on the subsidised sector, with the shortfall in grant being such that the National had to shut the Cottesloe for six months. Sheridan Morley, the critic in the *Spectator*, points out the myopia of this:

The irony here was, of course, that in the name of … Victorian values, notably self-sufficiency and chronic tight-fistedness, the Government through the Arts Council was waging an unprecedented war on sub-sidised companies at a time when the supposedly commercial West End was in fact being kept alive by these companies.[11]

The British public also seemed to be losing the habit of theatre-going, with forty-four per cent of West End audiences comprising overseas visitors; Paris was now perceived as overshadowing London as a centre of theatri-cal excellence; and Peter Brook's *The Mahabharata* at Avignon provided a painful reminder of what had been squandered.

On the other hand, the talent of indigenous performers was, at times, impressive, most notably in Sher's London transfer of *Richard III*, Antony Hopkins' sinister performance as the newspaper proprietor, Lambert Le Roux, in David Hare and Howard Brenton's *Pravda*, Alan Rickman's languorous Vimconte in Christopher Hampton's adaptation of Laclos' *Les Liaisons dangereuses* and Simon Callow's interpretation of the life of Charles Laughton. Actors' theatre had truly returned.

The standstill drama grant (a cut in real terms), the press row over Hall and Nunn's earnings, and the continuing difficulties of regional theatre supplied a depressing continuity to 1986, yet the increasingly familiar leitmotif of progress born of crisis was apparent in this year as well.

Gay Drama

Nowhere was this crisis more evident than in the shift from the fringe to the major London venues of plays that dealt with homosexuality. The contro-versy engendered by Brenton's *The Romans in Britain* (1980), and, in par-ticular, Mary Whitehouse's scurrilous prosecution of the play's director, Michael Bogdanov (see below), was a dismal reminder of the power of prej-udice. Yet the onset of the AIDS pandemic in the early eighties led to gay writers and playwrights, no longer content with half-hearted, apologetic depictions of the homosexual as an inevitable victim, going on the offensive. Larry Kramer's polemical American play, *The Normal Heart* (1986), was both a critique of a promiscuous gay lifestyle that had contributed to the spread of HIV and a powerful denunciation of the political and medical establishments for failing to act quickly enough in the face of a growing pub-lic health problem. That a gay writer was lacerating the US President, Ronald Reagan, and the Mayor of New York, Ed Koch, for treating gay peo-ple as second-class citizens as well as simultaneously condemning the unfet-tered hedonism of a section of the gay community – at one point, the protagonist, Ned Weeks, rails that 'All we've created is generations of guys who can't deal with each other as anything but erections' – introduced a refreshing dualism of approach absent in previous works. Undoubtedly melodramatic and at times simplistic (the comparison between the inertia of the authorities and the passivity of American Jews' attempts to save their kinsmen in Nazi Germany is too easily drawn), the London production at the Royal Court in 1986 was nevertheless completely sold out. Whether this was due to the casting of the film star Martin Sheen in the main role or the contemporaneity of the work seems a moot point, since the work's significance is that it enjoyed a well-received airing.

In the same year Hugh Whitemore's *Breaking the Code*, a poignant account of the life of Alan Turing, the British scientist who cracked the German Enigma code during the Second World War, opened with a bravura performance by Derek Jacobi. In its exploration of the public service and private repression of the post-war homosexual – Turing was feted for cracking the code but committed suicide after being threatened with the public exposure of a gay encounter – the work bore similarities to Julian Mitchell's *Another Country* (1981), where a public schoolboy's eventual decision to spy for Russia is traced back to the isolation he endured on account of his sexuality. Mitchell's play reached a large audience when it was popularised in a film version, starring Rupert Everett. Premièring shortly after the revelation of the treachery of the Queen's art advisor, Anthony Blunt, the parallels with the notorious fifties spy, Guy Burgess – equally rebellious, talented and gay – were plain for all to see.

Jonathan Harvey's *Beautiful Thing* (1994), Kevin Elyot's *My Night With Reg* (1994) and Mark Ravenhill's *Shopping and F***ing* (1996) demonstrate the continuing evolution of British drama with a gay theme. *Beautiful Thing* unashamedly appropriates the age-old boy meets girl, boy falls in love with girl format and substitutes two teenage boys on a South London housing estate as the young lovers. In its rejection of stereotypes – one boy, Ste, far from being the ostracised gay, is popular at school and keen on sport – and its eschewing of the polemic favoured by Gay Sweatshop – 'We don't have a picture of two boys hugging outside the Duke of York's theatre because that would put people off. Audiences go to the theatre to enjoy themselves. I want to help them to do that',[12] Harvey commented – *Beautiful Thing* is a romantic love story, conventional in everything but the sexuality of its protagonists. Its popularity led to the creation of a film, which was acclaimed for its feel-good factor (the holy grail of nineties Britain) in 1996.

Elyot's *My Night With Reg* is similarly unprovocative. It employs a comic format to investigate the friendship between six male friends who have all, it transpires, had a brief relationship with the recently deceased

Reg. That Reg has died from an AIDS-related illness supplies a melancholic edge to much of the comedy, but the script is full of humorous moments that filter the didactic import of some of the observations. Elyot clearly feels that the raising of gay issues is now more effectively done through suggestion rather than confrontation and the portrayal of contented as well as discontented gay men shows that plays with gay themes are no longer required to be written in code, as with Rattigan, or in anguish, as with Tennessee Williams. The very conventionality of Guy, the advertising copywriter, John, the ageing public schoolboy, Benny, the bus-driver and Daniel, the art dealer, mirrors the growing acceptance in nineties Britain that gay people can happily exist in all walks of life. John Peter in the *Sunday Times* wrote the most intelligent acclamation of the work, and highlighted the progress that gay drama had made since the foundation of Gay Sweatshop, when he observed that

> Elyot's play … suggests a maturity and understanding. Its presentation of love and lust, of pain and hope and tenacity has nothing to do with either exhibitionism or self-pity. There is nobody to hate. The gay condition is part of the human condition. This play is for adults only.[13]

Views such as Peter's easily eclipsed the anachronistic complaints of critics such as the elderly Milton Shulman, who under the headline 'Stop the plague of pink plays', querulously asked in the *Evening Standard* whether there was not something 'lop-sided about the British theatre when, in a country where only three per cent of the population are homosexuals, its playwrights and management are so fixated on a single theme?'[14] That Shulman had been succeeded by the out-gay Nicholas de Jongh as the *Evening Standard*'s theatre critic signified how obsolete such prejudice was becoming.

Shopping and F***ing is a more overt work in that the seamier sides of some gay lifestyles are depicted as a metaphor for an increasingly exploitative and materialistic society. The fact that the playwright Mark Ravenhill feels able to depict behaviour that one is unlikely to condone illustrates the increasing confidence gay writers possess in being able to move away from drama that simply pleads the case for homosexuality. The polemic of the gay liberation movement of the seventies might still be necessary in the nineties but would certainly be less effective on stage.

In the play, Lulu, Robbie and Mark all live and sleep together, but Mark's drug dependency means that he soon needs to leave to obtain treatment for his addiction. Lulu and Robbie, desperate to earn money, turn to selling drugs for the sinister Brian, but Robbie takes some ecstasy whilst dealing in a club and ends up losing the entire stock. Given one week by Brian to raise the £3,000 this would have fetched or risk being mutilated, Lulu and Robbie turn to selling telephone sex. This proves surprisingly lucrative and the sum is quickly raised. Having received drug counselling, Mark, too, discovers the power of money, when he seeks sex from a rent boy. Such is his desire to avoid emotional commitment that he wishes to engage in a 'transaction' that will have no emotional value. The particular service he desires is to rim the rent boy, an act performed on stage to the disconcertion of many audience members.

As the play reaches its denouement it emerges that all the characters are involved in some form of transaction, be it sexual or material. Emotional engagements are perceived as dangerous, materialism and the ownership of goods are viewed as the key to happiness (Mark and Gary embark on an orgy of shopping with stolen credit cards) and exploitation is both condoned and welcomed. Brian 'owns' Robbie and Lulu because they require the income his drugs can generate; the fourteen-year-old Gary is unable to discard the pain of the abuse he suffered from his step-father and, in a horrifying scene, demands to be buggered by a fork to expiate the humiliation that he feels at his experience; and Mark is controlled by the drugs that he is unable to dispense with. At the end of the work, the original threesome of Mark, Robbie and Lulu are reunited in a hell of frozen suppers, exploitative sex and yearning for money. As a comment on the depravity and corruption of the late nineties, it is intentionally shocking. As a play that employs exploitative same-sex encounters as a negative rather than a positive metaphor without being concerned that this might stir up prejudice, it illustrates the new resilience of gay drama.

An interesting footnote to this play occurred in September 1997 whilst the play was on tour at the West Yorkshire Playhouse, Leeds. In scene thirteen, Lulu asks Mark to describe 'the most famous person you've ever fucked' and Mark begins to relate a bizarre event that allegedly occurred in a London nightclub. Robbie is immediately irritated by this elaborate and scarcely plausible fantasy and the scene develops into a battle of wills between the two of them with Robbie constantly seeking to undermine Mark's narrative with sceptical interruptions. Undeterred, Mark asserts his independence by completing the anecdote. The miasma of fantasy and truth carefully illustrates the inability of the characters in the play as a whole to make sense of their world, as well as the questionable blurring of sexual boundaries that causes them such confusion.

It was 1984 or 1985, possibly in Annabel's or 'Tramp', and Mark was tripping. Desperately needing the toilet, he finds himself followed into the Gents by a woman dressed up as a WPC who appears eager for action. Mark then graphically describes the encounter: 'So I'm in there. I'm in and kneel. I pay worship. My tongue is worshipping that pussy like it's God.

And that's when she speaks. Speaks and I know who she is'.[15] The woman is identified as Princess Diana. In the London production of July 1997, this mixture of irreverence, improbability and direct language provoked much mirth and the laughter further increased when a second woman entered the cubicle and was identified by her ginger hair as Sarah Ferguson, the Duchess of York.

On 31 August 1997 Princess Diana was killed in a car crash. I witnessed the performance of *Shopping and F***ing* in Leeds two days later. As this scene approached, the audience, hardly any of whom are likely to have either witnessed a previous production or read the published script, became nervous. Some people are likely to have been disconcerted by the play as a whole, but most clearly feared that the as yet unidentified woman in the toilets might turn out to be the woman for whom many in the entire country were in united and grief-stricken mourning. I was unsure as to whether the script would be changed. It would have been in keeping with the work's desire to disconcert to leave things unamended. It would also undoubtedly have provoked a mass walkout or even – and this is no mere hyperbole – a verbal or literal invasion of the stage if the fantasy had been unadapted. As the audience began to speculate as to the woman's name, the tension rose. Mark uttered the speech printed above and added 'I recognise the voice. Get a look at the face. Yes. It's her'. The probable effect of the revelation that it was Diana was almost too much to endure. The atmosphere was both tense and appalled. Then the moment of catharsis was reached. The woman possessed a 'ginger minge', had lost weight and had formerly been a member of the Royal Family. She could safely be confirmed as Fergie, the Duchess of York. The sense of relief was overwhelming, although it might have been dissipated by Mark's announcement that a second policewoman 'squeezes her way in. With blonde hair', were it not for the timely intervention of Robbie who screamed, 'SHUT UP. SHUT THE FUCK UP'. I have never witnessed such a convincing demonstration of the power of theatre to aggravate, move and alarm (in a way to which the cinema can never aspire), nor been so grateful for such crude, emotive and vulgar language to disrupt the flow of a scene. It was a revelatory moment.

Continuity and Change: Institutions 4

The West End: Sclerosis, 1987

The West End of the late eighties continued to be characterised by a timidity born of economic stringency and, to a degree, the authoritarianism of the government. Few commercial producers could risk staging experimental works that did not promise a guaranteed return on their investment. This inevitably led to an increasing reliance on a popular market product, the musical, on well-known playwrights such as Stoppard and Ayckbourn, whose fame minimised the risk of failure, and on works that dispensed with large casts and complex, costly sets. The subject-matter of plays was similarly anaemic. The gradual withdrawal of funding from politically provocative companies such as Joint Stock and the English 7:84 company had signalled the Arts Council's disapproval of drama that interrogated the administration in power, and the West End continued to take this implicit censorship as a sign that the theatre-going public no longer enjoyed any taste for intellectually stimulating fare. It is ironic, then, that the finest West End play of 1987 was the Royal Court transfer of Caryl Churchill's *Serious Money*. A compelling denunciation of the greed, ruthlessness and selfishness of the financial markets (values that were applauded by the archetypal devotees of Thatcherite free enterprise, the yuppies), the play's West End success was partly due to the enthusiasm of those very jobbers whom the work satirised. Many theatre-lovers, however, were simply relieved that a play was at last being staged in the West End which questioned the ethos of Thatcherism and that Churchill had refused to be cowed by the need to keep one's head down – a point reinforced by the government's claim in 1985 that the paucity of the drama grant had been partly due to the public opposition to its policies by professionals such as Peter Hall.

Serious Money also highlighted the trend for new writing that gained force by integrating works from the past – the play includes a scene from *The Volunteers, or The Stockjobbers* (1692) by Thomas Shadwell – as well as plays that sharpened their didacticism through self-reflexivity and meta-drama (such as Timberlake Wertenbaker's *Our Country's Good* (1988)). The vibrancy and sophistication of the satire was viewed as a break from the more sanctimonious forms of political theatre of the seventies, allowing Michael Billington, who was by now becoming the conscience of left-of-centre drama lovers, to commend the work for attacking 'the City's greed and fear with zest rather than self-righteousness'.[16]

Steven Berkoff's *Decadence* (1981) had been an equally popular satire of eighties attitudes. Ever since the formation of the London Theatre Group in 1968, Berkoff had been intriguing audiences with his versatility, be it with his performance of the antennae-fingered Gregor Samsa in an adaptation of Kafka's *Metamorphosis* (1975), or the sexual brutishness of his own plays, *East* (1975), *West* (1983) and *Greek* (1979). By the mid-eighties, it was signifcant that this performance-centred artist, admired for his demonstrations of mime, athleticism and physicality, should also give expression to the growing political dissatisfaction with the governing party in a virulently anti-Tory piece, *Sink the Belgrano!* (1986).

Serious Money's commercial success followed its transfer from the Royal Court, a pattern that continued to breathe life into the impoverished heart of London's theatreland. Of nearly fifty new productions of serious works in the West End in 1987, less than half a dozen originated in that sector, and it was rapidly becoming comparable to Broadway as a home for musicals, farces, thrillers and one-man shows by star performers. Projects of some prestige enjoyed brief flourishings – Kenneth Branagh's Renaissance Theatre Company was established in 1987 with the royal blessing of Prince Charles, and the Peter Hall Company took up a successful residence in 1988 at the Haymarket and lured Dustin Hoffman to play Shylock in a 1989 *The Merchant of Venice* at the Phoenix – but elsewhere the picture was of tired, safe programming. Although continually under threat from meagre funding (in spite of an election year grant increase of eleven per cent in 1987), it was the subsidised sector that took the risks and produced the most exciting work over the next few years. Almost fifty years after the principle of subsidy had been established, its value was now self-evident to all but the funding authorities.

The National Theatre: Peter Hall 1979–1988

The most vociferous proponent of subsidy, Peter Hall, having ushered the NT into its new home in 1976, was to continue to direct the company for most of the eighties. The decade began auspiciously with Howard Brenton's adaptation of Brecht's *The Life of Galileo*, a play which has always been viewed as a modern classic that is immensely difficult to bring off in production. One scene in particular stands out. Having been tortured by the Catholic Church, which fully realises the threat that the scientist's discovery poses to its power, Galileo publicly recants his assertion that the earth revolves around the sun. In a moment of unbearable tension, Galileo's disciple, Andrea, rebukes his master for disowning the truth (which might have convinced people of the fallibility of church rule), with the bitter line, 'Unhappy the land that has no heroes'. Galileo, now broken and cowed, shuffles painfully towards his disgusted pupil and poses the inevitable Brechtian dialectic in his reply: 'No, unhappy the land where heroes are necessary'. This is one of the clearest examples of verbal Verfremdung.

For the actor playing Galileo, there are a number of challenges to which he has to rise. Aside from needing to age rapidly, he must at times be both selfish and generous, capricious and charming, appetitive and ascetic and courageous and cowardly. Michael Gambon was cast as the scientist in John Dexter's production and rose triumphantly to the task, earning this notice by John James in the *Times Educational Supplement* (that was echoed by other critics): 'Gambon gives a performance which places him at the height of his profession: a richly detailed characterisation, layer on layer of fallibly fleshed humanity using every twisting compromise to stay alive, at once justifying and castigating Galileo'.[17] Such was the demand to witness this bravura performance that the production ran in the Olivier theatre for over a year.

A second play by Brenton in the same year drew publicity of a different kind and illustrated several previously undetected deficiencies in the drafting of the 1968 Theatres Act. Fired by the continued involvement in Northern Ireland of the British Army, which he viewed as an army of occupation, Brenton wrote *The Romans in Britain* (1980), a work that sought to draw an analogy between the subjugation of the druids by the Romans and the position of the British in Ireland. The first-night critics were alienated either by the depictions of extreme violence or the provocative political analysis, with Michael Billington amongst the most sceptical:

> there is such a vast disproportion between the extravagance of the form and the banality of the thesis that one is reminded of the dotty Bavarian monarch who built a complex subterranean machine simply in order to have his dinner-table rise up through the floor.[18]

It was the reaction of the leader of the Greater London Council, however, which provided a grant for the National Theatre, that started the publicity bandwagon. Offended by the play's deliberate brutality, Sir Horace Cutler quickly threatened censorship through withdrawal of funding when he stated that he was 'not prepared to see rates and taxes spent to support plays which in my view have no artistic merit'.[19] An even more sinister threat was quickly posed by the chairman of the Viewers and Listeners Association, Mary Whitehouse. This self-appointed defender of public morality complained to Scotland Yard about a specific scene where a group of Roman soldiers chance upon three druids, kill two and attempt to rape a third. The casual and horrifying nature of their aggression was deliberately shocking (Brenton stated that the memory of My Lai was in his mind when he wrote the work) and a clear allegory in the playwright's view of the rape of Ireland by the British.

Under the 1968 Theatres Act a prosecution for obscenity could only be brought with the consent of the Attorney General. After some deliberation, he declined to permit this, but, undeterred, Whitehouse instructed her solicitor, the urbane Mr Ross Cornes, to prosecute the play's director, Michael Bogdanov, under the Sexual Offences Act for 'procuring an act of gross indecency'.

From a distance the whole affair now seems steeped in farce. Mary Whitehouse had never even seen the play in question and had simply relied on reports of the scene, the actors were merely pursuing mimesis and simulating buggery, and the production enjoyed receipts in excess of original expectations as the public were drawn by the whiff of scandal; but the ramifications were far from comic. For over twelve months the possibility of a two-year prison sentence hung over Bogdanov. His wife and children were abused in the street and the police eventually had to mount a surveillance operation. Critics of subsidy were given succour by the debate that raged around the acceptability of public funding for such politically inflammatory drama and the indecisive nature of the trial set an uncomfortable legal precedent that still hangs over the British theatre today. Although the case (held at the Old Bailey, no less) was terminated after three days when Whitehouse was forced to withdraw her suit in the face of the recognition that there was a distinction between a simulated depiction of an act on the stage and the real thing, the fact that the trial judge had initially ruled that there was a case to answer set a potentially disastrous legal precedent. The immunity from prosecution for simulating events that performers had always held to be sacrosanct was now thrown into doubt, and to this day no one has dared to stage *The Romans in Britain* again professionally for fear that the case might once more be tested. The people who drafted the 1968 Theatres Act had not envisaged this possibility.

The whole of Hall's tenure at the National in the eighties would be marked by a succession of similar crises and triumphs. On the debit side were problems that were partly self-inflicted, but more often than not these were a result of outside forces. One undoubted financial and critical success was Richard Eyre's production of *Guys and Dolls* (1982) which remained in repertoire for almost three years, transferred to the West End in 1985 for 370 performances and recouped almost a million pounds, helping to keep the institution afloat during a period of financial anxiety. Fired by this successful exercise in the most popular genre of the moment, Hall then agreed to mount a new American musical based on the life of Jean Seberg. This rags-to-riches figure had emerged from obscurity to star in Otto Preminger's film about St Joan, enjoy a career in the movies, but finally commit suicide after a series of depressing set-backs. Rather lacking the obligatory upbeat dimension, the musical was doomed from the start and tales of backstage rows, artistic differences and contractual stipulations that favoured the American backers over the National added to the atmosphere of impending catastrophe. The ludicrous nature of the book – Jean relates the story as a series of flashbacks from the night of her suicide – meant that notices such as Bernard Levin's conviction that it represented 'one of the most frightful stages of junk ever seen in London' were actually superfluous to the swift closure of the show. What compounded the folly was the fact that the vibrant *Guys and Dolls* had been removed from the repertoire to permit the still birth of *Jean Seberg*. Little wonder that Simon Callow describes the whole production as 'a lame and gormless experience'.[20]

Besides leaking sets and the closure of the Cottesloe there were also difficulties with the acoustics of the Olivier and the Lyttleton auditoriums. Even encouraging developments were often accompanied by depressing constraints. The Cottesloe had by this time gained a reputation for innovative studio work and regularly played to near-capacity audiences, but its seating capacity of approximately 300 (the exact number depended on the configuration of the stage) meant that it could never generate enough money from box-office income alone to cover its running costs. Similarly, the National as a whole was by now covering the expense of putting on its plays, but found it impossible to tackle its accumulated start-up costs. The choices it faced were partial closure, the seeking of sponsorship for individual productions and the soliciting of more corporate donations – strategies all reluctantly embraced from the mid-eighties onwards.

In spite of these persistent financial difficulties, on-stage the National was moving into adulthood. Gambon's Galileo was complemented thematically by Christopher Hampton's account of Brecht's exile from the Nazis in America, *Tales from Hollywood* (1983). Judi Dench gave another indication that the National was helping to launch a renaissance in acting with an interpretation of Lady Bracknell in *The Importance of Being Earnest* (1984) in which she reclaimed the role from Edith Evans, and Ian McKellen confirmed this with a trilogy of fine performances as Platonov in Chekhov's *Wild Honey*, Jaffier in Otway's *Venice Preserv'd* and the eponymous role in *Coriolanus*. This last production, directed by Hall, mirrored Dench's achievement in breathing new life into a part dominated by memories of an earlier 'definitive' interpretation, in this instance, Olivier's. In McKellen's case, what was remarkable was the decision to offer an equally athletic performance, but to make his own particular refinements. By holding in his mind the behaviour of the temperamental tennis player John McEnroe, McKellen produced a 'titanic study in arrogance'[21] that is now regarded as one of the classic performances of this difficult role.

The year 1985 was to prove a climactic one for the National Theatre. Prior to the Cottesloe's enforced closure, Tony Harrison's version of the medieval Corpus Christi plays, entitled *The Mysteries*, was produced in the studio space. Harrison possessed great experience as a literary adaptor, having created amongst other things the script for Hall's *The Oresteia* (1981), full of dissonant Anglo-Saxon lines. A vast undertaking, ten years in the devising and running for a full twelve hours when staged in its entirety, *The Mysteries*, in its re-animation of earlier, canonical works, seemed to justify the National's very raison d'être. Its utilisation of North Country dialectics helped create an appropriate mood of otherness and Bill Bryden's direction, which allowed the audience either to sit in the galleries or to promenade around the main space, reminded critics of the dusty phrase 'total theatre', rarely employed since the departure of Peter Brook to France. The critic of *The Times*, Bernard Levin, was rapt:

> In the uncanonical story of Mak the bad shepherd, Mak is caught steal-ing the sheep, and is sentenced to the pillory. The pillory is one of those seaside joke-photograph devices; the actor puts his head through a hole; and the children in the audience (there are many of them) are invited to pelt him with wet sponges. Many of them enter into the game with zest, but one or two hang back. 'Come on', says Mak encouraging them; then he mutters 'You won't get a chance like this at *Coriolanus* I can tell you.'
>
> It is this welding of the actor, audience, play and story into one whole that gives the performance its unique quality – and I wish there were another word for performance, for it diminishes the thing that has been created, which far transcends any idea of a theatre as a place which we visit to see a play, and of a play as that which we visit a theatre to see.[22]

It should be noted, however, that a significant minority were concerned that the production diminished the worth of medieval drama. Darryll Grantley encapsulated this view when he observed that

> What it all adds up to is a slick, comic, musical spectacle which, for the most part, ignores the serious artistic and didactic qualities of the medieval religious cycles. In its insistence on quaintness and 'merrie England' jolliness the production implicitly restates ideas about medieval drama which have for some time been outdated: that it was a rather simple-minded drama performed by unsophisticated men. Much of the laughter generated was not through the text at the foibles of mankind, but effectively through the production at the plays; what it amounted to was a parody of medieval drama.[23]

This debate about the nature of 'authentic' productions would become crystallised around the creation of Shakespeare's Globe on the South Bank by Sam Wannamaker.

When the Cottesloe closed, *The Mysteries* was required to move to the

Lyceum, but there was more innovation to come in the Olivier when fine writing and great acting coalesced in Howard Brenton and David Hare's *Pravda* (1985).

'Pravda', meaning 'truth' in Russian, was the title of the Soviet Union's chief propaganda broadsheet that offered anything other than an objective view of the world. By employing this word ironically as the title of their play about British newspapers in the eighties, Hare and Brenton were swiftly signalling that the edge of their satire had not been dulled by Thatcherism. The work charts the transmutation of Lambert Le Roux from a ruthless South African newspaper proprietor into an international press baron, media mogul and multi-faceted businessman. Bearing striking similarities to the two media magnates Rupert Murdoch and Robert Maxwell (who had both come to Britain from abroad), Le Roux first infiltrates the British press by purchasing the *Leicester Bystander* from its ineffectual owner, Sir Stamford Foley, who requires capital to purchase a one-eighth share of a race-horse for breeding. This withering parody of the anachronistic lifestyle of the British upper classes sets the tone for the play. Le Roux swiftly moves on to purchase the *Victory* (a synonym for *The Times*, which Murdoch had recently acquired) and we then encounter a series of characters either directly analogous to real-life figures or recognisable as types in British society. They are all bound together by their impotence in the face of Le Roux's crude, aggressive and pseudo-Darwinian method of operating which he defines in his portentous opening speech:

> What I do is a natural thing. There is nothing unnatural about making money. When you are born, you do have a feeling for nature. What I admire is – animals, birds, plants, they fucking get on with it and don't start complaining all the time.[24]

The verisimilitude of the work is deliberately striking. Elliott Fruit Norton, the dispossessed editor of the *Victory*, brings to mind William Rees-Mogg, a scion of the establishment, former editor of *The Times* and the then chairman of the Arts Council. In an act that adumbrates the 'cash for questions' scandal that rocked the Major government in 1996, Le Roux purchases the influence of the supine Member of Parliament, Michael Quince, who venally represents Le Roux's interests above those of his constituents. Le Roux also employs the services of the England Cricket Captain to endorse the products of his sporting franchise and provide some public gloss to his activities, reminding the audience of both Murdoch and Maxwell's recognition of the potency and marketing possibilities of popular sport.

The inability of Le Roux's opponents to organise themselves effectively, the refusal to confront his methods with equally ruthless tactics, and the complicity of the ruling administration in the behaviour of this acceptably right-wing businessman, are all seen as responsible for the elimination of truth from reporting, the advancement of vested interests and the corruption of public life. In the final scene, Le Roux announces his decision to merge the tabloid *Tide* with the broadsheet *Victory* – 'I've decided to combine the two newsrooms, I'll cut both papers in half. Up market, down market, it's all the same stuff. And we do the same things to it' – but to achieve his ends, Le Roux requires a willing readership, eager for his product, and it is for the compliant masses that the playwrights reserve their greatest scorn:

> What on earth is all this stuff about truth? Truth? Why, when everywhere you go people tell lies. In pubs. To each other. To their husbands. To their wives. To the children. To the dying – and thank God they do. No one tells the truth. Why single out newspapers? 'Oh! A special standard!' Everyone can tell lies except newspapers. They're the universal scapegoat for everybody else's evasions and inadequacies. It is a totally unworkable view of the world!

In Brenton and Hare's view, manipulators of public opinion such as Le Roux can only flourish through the consent of the manipulated.

Pravda proved to be the most popular straight play that the National had staged thus far, running for over two years. This was in part due to the dynamism of its Epic structure – newsrooms are swiftly constructed and dismantled, reporters charge across the stage in pursuit of their prey, celebrities complain of intrusion but crave publicity – as well as to the prescience of its satire. It should be remembered that this was a period when the press barons had access to Downing Street, apartheid was still functioning in South Africa, there was no effective political opposition (the Labour Party was in disarray) and materialism was condoned by central government. Its disturbing accuracy, however, was enormously sharpened by the magnetic performance of Anthony Hopkins, which was both sinister and amusing. His humorous ability to outwit his foes bore echoes of Volpone and the difficulty in condemning him outright proved both unsettling and a tribute to his elusive interpretation. *Pravda* marked the beginning of Hare's 'State of the Nation' plays for the National and is now seen as a telling indictment of one facet of mid-eighties life – as the critic of *City Limits*, Lyn Gardner, shrewdly predicted at the time:

> *Pravda* (a kaleidoscopic cartoon look at the 'Street of Shame' and a

hugely enjoyable satire ranking alongside Jonson's *Volpone*) is the funniest play in London. In South African newspaper proprietor Lambert Le Roux (Anthony Hopkins gives the performance of a lifetime, scuttling about like a wily cockroach and squeezing malicious pleasure from every Afrikaans vowel) Brenton and Hare have created a monstrous monument to the single-minded greed that besets our age.[25]

Such was the appeal of *Pravda* that the National ended the 1985/6 season in profit on productions, but this did not obviate the need to find alternative sources of income. In 1986, sponsorship of individual productions began with Citicorp/Citibank supporting *The Threepenny Opera* in the Olivier and quickly mushroomed to include sponsorship of the Cottesloe, Sideshow Sponsors, Special Project Sponsors and Business Entertainment Evening Sponsorship. A Corporate Contributors Scheme was also launched to support the work in the NT Studio which was based in the Annexe of the Old Vic, generously provided rent free by the Mirvish family. Peter Hall's own finances were put under the spotlight when the *Sunday Times* alleged in June 1986 that both he and Trevor Nunn had used their positions as artistic directors of the NT and RSC respectively to launch productions through their subsidised theatres and transfer them, if successful, for lucrative commercial runs from which they would personally benefit. The substance of the allegation and the figures quoted were untrue, but the resultant controversy, which Hall wondered might have been politically motivated, given his open hostility to government policy, was viewed by him as a disconcerting irritant. It now seemed inevitable that after fifteen years of graft to establish the National at the South Bank, Hall would retire in 1988 when his present contract had expired.

In the twilight of his reign, more excellent work was produced and the standard of acting remained enviably high. Michael Gambon was eulogised for his role as Eddie Carbone in Arthur Miller's *A View from the Bridge* (1987), directed by another playwright, Alan Ayckbourn, and Ayckbourn's own *A Small Family Business* (1987), depicting 'a grasping society where goodness is boring and corruption sexy',[26] signalled a darker, less comfortable view of middle-class society than in his previous works and added to the National's growing reputation for staging thoughtful new writing. Hall, too, returned to form in his last full season by directing Judi Dench and Anthony Hopkins in *Antony and Cleopatra* (1987). With its emphasis on precise expression – 'the most intelligently spoken Shakespeare I have heard in years'[27] – charismatic acting – '[Hopkins'] is a performance whose power and passion is matched by Judi Dench's towering spit-fire Cleopatra'[28] – and acceptable directorial control – 'The huge spans of the action tense up, arch and unfold like great symphonic movements, and the poetry of this sensuous athletic text tolls with burnished conviction',[29] the production provided a salutary reminder of the practical skills of Hall as a director that coexisted with his talents as an administrator and propagandist. The greatest achievement of his amorphous career was to leave the National in such good shape for his successor, Richard Eyre.

The National Theatre: Richard Eyre 1988–1997

'Seats for all prices,' is the familiar message at West End theatre box offices. But not at the National Theatre. There, six of the eight plays in repertory are sold out every night, playing to audiences that average more than 90%. You could call it the one non-musical theatre that is making money. Ironically so, since until recently the view in high political circles was that subsidy was a dubious exercise for putting on plays not enough people wanted to see.[30]

Four years after his accession, it was evident that Richard Eyre was making the National Theatre work. There was no reason to alter this judgement upon his departure from his post in 1997, a confirmation of the sense of quiet evolution that Eyre brought to the South Bank. Whether it was in encouraging a policy of touring in the regions ('I realised the danger of becoming a parody if the National didn't live up to its name'[31] ensuring a balance that was popular at the box office between musicals such as *Carousel* (1992) and weightier fare including Stoppard's *Arcadia* (1993), or in reducing the number of occasions that the National featured on the news as opposed to the arts pages of the papers, his tenure as director provided a welcome period of stability and growth after the turbulence that surrounded the Hall years. In many ways, Hall fought the necessary battles and Eyre capitalised on their success.

Like Hall, Eyre was an accomplished director, already noted for his NT productions of *Comedians* and *Guys and Dolls*, and he, too, endured a comparably shaky start to his directorship. To mark the silver jubilee of its foundation, the National was accorded the status of a Royal title in 1988, but Eyre's first three productions of *The Changeling* (1988), *Bartholomew Fair* (1988) and *Hamlet* (1989) did little to celebrate this accolade. The production of *Hamlet*, a rite of passage for incoming NT directors, initially seemed particularly inauspicious. Daniel Day-Lewis, the charismatic actor who had recently finished filming *My Left Foot*, for which he was to earn an Oscar, was recruited to play the Prince. His performance was full of nervous energy, tension and unpredictable bursts of emotion, which both attracted the public and perturbed the critics (as often seems to be the case with this play), who complained of uneven performances, imprecision and inaudibility. The run proceeded until the sixty-fifth performance, when real-life drama aped the events on the stage. Day-Lewis, increasingly disturbed by the parallels between Hamlet and Old Hamlet and himself and his own father, the former Poet-Laureate, Cecil Day-Lewis, froze on stage when he encountered the ghost and fled to the wings in terror. For a profession whose unofficial rallying cry is 'the show must go on', this was a near disaster, but this nadir proved to be not just a turning-point in the production but an early illustration of how Eyre would enjoy more good fortune than was allotted to his two predecessors. Day-Lewis's successor in the role was Ian Charleson, whose performance was both mesmerising and highly affecting, and the press regarded the whole episode as an illustration of how victory could be snatched from the jaws of defeat. Few knew at the time, though, that this actor's performance was truly heroic, given his recent discovery that he was HIV positive. Seldom can an actor have given a performance of Hamlet in such a certain conviction of his own mortality. Charleson was to die of AIDS in 1989.

Eyre's first big appointment had been as the artistic director of the Nottingham Playhouse in 1973 and it was here that he encountered David Hare, then the theatre's literary manager. Their working collaboration at the RNT over the next few years was to produce a series of significant plays that continued in the tradition (initiated by *Pravda*) of analysing various British institutions. *The Secret Rapture* (1988) takes as its title the phrase describing the moment when a nun expects to be reunited with Christ, in other words, the moment of her death, and its melancholic associations indicate that in this and subsequent works, Hare enriches his critiques of society with depictions of personal pain and feelings of loss. Two sisters, Marion, a junior minister in a Tory government and Isobel, a designer in a small-scale firm who rejects her sibling's espousal of Thatcherism, are reunited by the death of their father. Their nervous relationship is scrutinised under the twin strains of the alcoholism of their stepmother and the takeover of Isobel's firm by Marion's husband, Tom, the President of Christians in Business. Again, as in *Pravda*, Hare refuses to condemn in a simplistic fashion those who embrace Marion and Tom's values, as if the rejection of a creed of greed and selfishness requires little more than the exercise of a little moral fibre. Instead, he portrays what might have to be sacrificed by such a self-centred attitude. Isobel's partner, Irwin, agrees to the take-over of the firm and sees his salary doubled. Prospering materially, the business expands and he discards the humanism which he had previously so fiercely cherished. He also loses the love that he and Isobel enjoyed and it is this destruction of the relationship that

Hare posits is the price that must be paid for substituting the material for the emotional and the spiritual.

Hare's future work continued to stress the indivisibility of the public and the private worlds. His much admired trilogy of *Racing Demon* (1990), *Murmuring Judges* (1991) and *The Absence of War* (1993) observe the Church of England, the judiciary and the Labour Party respectively, but in the broad sweep of their analysis of entrenched institutions the individual's potential to suffer is never lost. This is particularly true of *The Absence of War*, which is loosely based on the figure of Neil Kinnock, the leader of the Labour Party who had the misfortune to lead his party to two successive General Election defeats in 1987 and 1992. As with Kinnock, Hare's protagonist, George Jones, is a man of immense conviction, powerful oratory (though with a tendency towards loquaciousness) and an innate handicap, not necessarily of his own making: no matter how much the public may like him, they do not trust him to be Prime Minister. The play, premièred a year after the devastating blow to the left of John Major's surprise General Election victory in May 1992, was aptly described by John Peter, the critic of the *Sunday Times*, as being 'a lament by a left-wing romantic rebel who has the rebel's dislike of power and the romantic's despair that his party will ever get it'.[32] That Hare could once again place his hope in the party that writers of his persuasion had written off for being too right-wing in the seventies illustrates how desperate non-Conservatives had become by the early nineties.

The National began to get into its stride under Eyre's directorship in 1990 with an eclectic mixture of productions that set the precedent for the rest of his tenure. Intelligent new writing, spectacular shows, magnificent acting, the best of world drama, technically superb musicals, innovative directorial approaches and visiting productions from new, experimental groups all meshed to create a stunning year. Tony Harrison's *The Trackers of Oxyrhyncus*, which incorporated the fragment of a satyr play by Sophocles, proved a challenging work and a surprising success. The graphically erect phalluses attached to the satyrs provided a memorable talking point, but the play's debate about the nature of high and low art was also applauded for being intellectually stimulating. An even greater hit was an imaginative adaptation by Alan Bennett of Kenneth Grahame's *The Wind in the Willows*. Its full utilisation of the Olivier's little-used multi-level revolving stage to transform the set into the river-bank setting for Rat's domain and the ostentatious grandeur of Toad Hall drew applause from the audience, and the employment of well-known television actors including Griff Rhys Jones (as Toad) and Richard Briers (as Rat) helped broaden the play's appeal.

Richard Eyre himself transformed *Richard III* into a study of tyranny that resonated with twentieth-century analogies. Ian McKellen's depiction of the hunch-backed king drew strongly on Adolf Hitler and Oswald Mosley, but it also employed an iconography that allowed the work to appeal to post-communist audiences throughout Europe, where it toured during 1991. The production of Brien Friel's *Dancing at Lughnasa* (1990) illustrated the RNT's continued commitment to opening up the South Bank to world theatre and was notable not just for being a demonstration of Friel's Chekhovian talents but for the liberating dance of ecstasy that the five sisters undertook to a reel being played on the radio. Stephen Pimlott's production of Sondheim's *Sunday in the Park With George* (1990) was another foreign import hailed for providing enlightenment about a genre in which the British theatre was now claiming pre-eminence. Based on the work of the French impressionist, Seurat, James Lapine's book proved that musicals need not be feasts for the eyes and ears alone, but could induce thought and reflection. Michael Billington, not normally a fan of musicals, was particularly aware of the challenges that this particular example set its audience: '*Sunday in the Park* makes you work. But it demands and repays the closest attention since it is a genuine pathfinder that proves the musical can not only deal with ideas but illuminate the mystery of creation itself'.[33]

Two further productions completed this momentous year. The talented director, Deborah Warner, who had made her name with a gory and moving *Titus Andronicus* for the RSC in 1988, continued her collaboration with Fiona Shaw, which had already resulted in a version of Sophocles' *Electra* (1988). Shaw's depiction of Shen Te/Shui Ta in Brecht's *The Good Person of Setzuan* (1989) finally proved the genius of this work to sceptical British audiences and earned her a series of acting awards. *Fuente Ovejuna* (1989) by Lope de Vega similarly attracted new talent to the National. The fringe company, Cheek By Jowl, founded by Declan Donnelan and the designer, Nick Ormerod, reinvigorated the Lyttleton theatre and was also showered with awards. A new wave of performers was emerging and the RNT was proving an hospitable home.

By 1993, Eyre was having to respond to an unusual charge to be levelled against the director of the National Theatre:

> I've been accused of pursuing a policy of hits. My response is: where on earth is the breadbin that you get the hits from? I personally can't follow the Thatcherite line of supplying just what the public wants. It's more a question of marking a course between second-guessing your audience and following your instincts. Instincts are all we've got.[34]

In his policy of pragmatism and popularism Eyre was following New

Labour principles at the very time that the concept was being devised – Tony Blair was elected leader of the Labour Party in 1994 – and it would prove just as successful. The list of achievements embraces musicals (*Carousel* (1992), *City of Angels* (1993), Eyre's revived production of *Guys and Dolls* (1996)); auspicious visiting productions (Théâtre de Complicité's interpretation of Dürrenmatt's *The Visit* (1991), Robert Lepage's mudbath version of *A Midsummer Night's Dream* (1992)); invigorating revivals of modern classics (Priestley's *An Inspector Calls* (1992) directed by Stephen Daldry, Tennessee Williams' *The Night of the Iguana* (1992), Sophie Treadwell's *Machinal* (1993)); inspirational interpretations of Shakespearean drama (Phyllida Lloyd's *Pericles* (1994), Deborah Warner's *Richard II* with Fiona Shaw playing an asexual king (1995)); new, indigenous writing of quality (Pinter's *Mountain Language* (1991), Bennett's *The Madness of George III* (1991), Stoppard's *Arcadia* (1993), Hare's *Skylight* (1995) and *Amy's View* (1997), Patrick Marber's *Closer* (1997)); and new world writing of importance (Tony Kushner's *Millennium Approaches* (1992) and *Perestroika* (1993)).

Eyre had been blessed with more luck than Hall but he had used it well. His legacy to Trevor Nunn, who succeeded him in 1997, was of a confident, respected institution, at last fulfilling the hopes invested in it over thirty years earlier.

The Royal Shakespeare Company: 1979–1997

Casting an eye back over an equally exciting thirty years of work at the RSC, Benedict Nightingale summarised its achievement as having rid 'the British theatre of the accretions of tradition [and], without distorting their essentials, [having] made the classic plays our contemporaries'.[35] This had been undertaken by means of a policy of constant evolution, no better illustrated than in what was proving to be a climactic year for Britain, 1997. Whilst perhaps not the theatrical equivalent of Tony Blair's landslide defeat of the Tories in May, Adrian Noble's decision to vacate the Barbican for half of the year was a notable shift of strategy. Depending on a point of view it represented either a bold, adventurous attempt at decentralisation or a precipitous, self-imposed exile that too swiftly forgot the battles fought in the sixties to secure a permanent base in the capital. Noble himself, who had succeeded Terry Hands as artistic director in 1991, had little difficulty in justifying this radical move. The decision reflected a nationwide desire in the late nineties for cultural and political decentralisation away from the metropolis of London (borne out by the votes in favour of Scottish and Welsh devolution in September 1997). The RSC needed to expand its commitment to its regional residencies, such as the annual season at the Theatre Royal, Newcastle, which had been running since 1976, as well as to its international tours. As an organisation with an annual turnover in excess of £30 million and claiming a total £8.5 million in subsidy from the Arts Council and the Corporation of London, the RSC needed to reach out to theatre-goers and taxpayers throughout the country. And, crucially, the transplantation of more activities back to its Stratford base would reinvigorate creative energies. Noble might also have added that actors disliked the working conditions at the Barbican with its cramped back-stage facilities and absence of natural light.

Immediate practical consequences of the announcement were the addition of a four-week residency at Plymouth, a coastal city in the south-west of England, 29 productions for the 1997/8 season of which 17 were new (including 3 world and 2 British premières) and an imaginative application for Lottery funding to rebuild Collins Music Hall on Islington Green as a venue for Stratford transfers to be shared with both Manchester's Royal Exchange theatre and Max Stafford-Clark's Out of Joint company. Whilst the potential of these plans looks exciting, their wisdom remains to be tested. However, their innovatory nature continues a leitmotif evident in the company's work of the eighties and nineties.

The first Aldwych season of the eighties is a characteristic illustration of the RSC's uncanny ability to transform adversity into triumph. In spite of accepting the embrace of sponsorship, the RSC was only able to fund three productions in its London space in 1980, so it was decided to mount two 'super-shows', which later were seen as initiating a new form of production termed 'event-theatre'. In other words, spectacular shows that were grandiose both in conception and execution. John Barton's *The Greeks* continued the company's tradition of rewriting classic texts and eliding old and new sections into a seamless whole. Ten plays, including seven from Euripides and a forty-minute piece devised by Barton himself, formed three central episodes – The War, The Murders and The Gods – which telescoped the main Greek myths, the fall of Troy, the murder of Agamemnon and the retribution that followed. Lasting ten hours, the entire project spoke of a group supremely confident in its own artistic merit in spite of uncongenial external factors. Michael Billington was moved to write of 'a marvellous narrative and a healing myth: something that exposes the sore of human conflict but that finally resolves it in a plea for balance, harmony and order'.[36]

David Edgar's eight-and-a-half-hour adaptation of Dickens' *Nicholas Nickleby* exuded similar self-belief. A cast of forty-five, a visually arresting set designed by John Napier and Dermot Hayes, consisting of a catwalk, sloping bridges and Victorian ironmongery, and charismatic performances from Roger Rees (Nicholas), Edward Petherbridge (Newman Noggs) and

Bob Peck (Mulberry Hawk) all drew critical and popular admiration for the ambition of the enterprise. In this, it adumbrated *Les Misérables* (1985), also directed by Trevor Nunn. Opening at the Barbican, the production was mounted in association with the commercial management of Cameron Mackintosh and has now become one of the most enduring successes of all time.

At the start of the twentieth century, Frank Benson, the then director of the original Shakespeare Memorial Theatre, outlined his aims: 'to train a company, every member of which would be an essential part of a homogenous whole consecrated to the practice of the dramatic arts and especially to the representation of the plays of Shakespeare'.[37] As the century drew to a close, the company was still adhering closely to this vision. The joint artistic directorship of Trevor Nunn and Terry Hands, which lasted from 1978 to 1986, continued to expand upon the company's heritage by securing further space to perform. In addition to the opening of the Barbican in 1982, a third Stratford venue was built within the shell of the first Memorial Theatre that had been destroyed by a fire in 1926. The Swan, as it was named, is a galleried playhouse with a thrust stage, and its construction proved possible only through a large, initially anonymous donation, from an American benefactor, Frederick R. Koch. Dedicated to staging classics, new plays and the drama of neglected playwrights, including Shakespeare's contemporaries, the Swan quickly became the most popular of all the RSC's venues, appreciated for the close proximity of the seating to the stage, its intimate atmosphere and the potential for audience interaction. It is not unusual in Swan productions for actors to be placed within the audience, only to reveal themselves at strategic and unexpected moments. In its approximation of an Elizabethan playhouse and its resurrection of works not seen for 300 years, the Swan, together with the reconstructed Globe, has contributed to the revived interest in the conditions of Elizabethan and Jacobean performance.

Major new acting talent began to emerge from the RSC in the eighties to grace these new stages. Antony Sher's lithe, sinewy Fool to Michael Gambon's Lear (1982) alerted critics to his potential and was followed by Martin Glass in David Edgar's *Maydays* (1983) and an interpretation of Richard III (1984) that evoked comparisons with Olivier's 1946 Old Vic performance:

Mr Sher ... presents an astonishing image. On his first entry ... he seems small, dark and jovial. But, as he tells us he is not shaped for sportive tricks, he levers himself forward in giant leaps on two crutches that descend from his arms. These crutches not only make him the fastest mover in the kingdom, they become a staff to beat Lady Anne's attendants, a phallic symbol to probe under her skirt, incisors to grip Hastings' threatened head, a sword to frighten recalcitrant children with, and a cross to betoken Richard's seeming saintliness.[38]

Sher's sinister dexterity with his crutches produced one of the most chilling theatrical images of the decade and he has continued to inspire audiences with lead roles in plays as diverse as *The Torch Song Trilogy* (in the West End, 1985), *The Resistible Rise of Arturo Ui*, (for the National, 1991), *Tamburlaine* (1992), *Cyrano de Bergerac* (1997) and *The Winter's Tale* (1998), as well as writing novels, staging exhibitions of his painting (RSC 1985, RNT 1989), directing plays (notably a South African *Titus Andronicus* (1996)) and becoming a respected film actor (*Mrs Brown* (1997)).

Kenneth Branagh has proved similarly versatile. During his association with the RSC he played a self-deprecating, uncertain Henry V (1984) and a declining athlete in Louise Page's *Golden Girls* (1984), before directing his own production of *Romeo and Juliet* (1986) and performing in a work which he himself had written, *Public Enemy* (1987). The following year he bravely broke free from the institution to create his own Renaissance Company, ostensibly to escape a perceived domination by directors of Shakespearean drama, a move that bore echoes of the rebellion in the seventies. Its opening season at the Phoenix in 1988 saw three productions of Shakespearean classics directed by actors – Derek Jacobi, Geraldine McEwan and Judi Dench – with the latter's *Much Ado About Nothing*, featuring Branagh as Benedick. For Sheridan Morley in *Punch* this represented a welcome breath of fresh air:

> They are young and a little raw around the edges, but the verse speaking is crystal clear, and there is a lyrical amiability about the staging which makes one realise for how many years Shakespearean comedies have been shrouded in the darkness that usually comes from a director trying to tell us something about them. What we have here is not exactly Shakespeare for schools, but it does seem to me to mark a shift of emphasis and an absolute faith in the line-by-line qualities of the text, one which points up, albeit unintentionally, the desperate gimmickry and intellectual exhaustion of the current RSC *Much Ado* at Stratford.[39]

Following the auspicious launch of Renaissance, Branagh, too, moved into film, directing and starring in notable versions of *Much Ado About Nothing*, *Henry V* and *Hamlet*.

Irrespective of whether one subscribed to Branagh's views on directorial domination at the RSC, his departure ironically served to highlight the continual ability of the company to recruit new, talented members. Actors were frequently prepared to sacrifice more profitable employment else-where for the opportunity to train and work in a renowned ensemble with the security of a contract that ran for at least a season. Thus, Terry Hands, who became the sole Artistic Director and Chief Executive in 1986, presided over the emergence of the actresses Juliet Stevenson and Harriet Walter, directors Nicholas Hytner, Sam Mendes and Deborah Warner and designers David Fielding, William Dudley and Bob Crowley. Hands also adhered to the tradition of offering Shakespearean productions that were in tune with the times: the first *Coriolanus* for twelve years in 1989, with Charles Dance as the lead, gave a reading of the play that viewed it as nei-ther right-wing nor left-wing, and, following in Peter Hall's footsteps, epic versions of groups of plays were staged (for example Adrian Noble's *The Plantagenets* (1988), which ran for nine hours). New writing included Tim-berlake Wertenbaker's *The Love of a Nightingale* (1989) which utilises a Greek performance of the myth of Tereus and his rape of Philomel to incorporate a direct plea to break our silence and overcome our intoler-ance of minority groups.

Hands' successor in 1991, Adrian Noble, has continued this policy of evolution, not revolution, at least until 1997. Examples of 'event theatre' productions number *The Strange Case of Dr Jekyll and Mr Hyde* (1991) and Wertenbaker's translation of Sophocles' Oedipus trilogy, renamed *The Thebans* (1991). Richard Brome's *A Jovial Crew* (1992) and Carlo Goldoni's *The Venetian Twins* (1993) attested to the wisdom of the policy of reviving neglected plays in the Swan. The return of Branagh to Strat-ford in 1992 in a production of *Hamlet* directed by Noble led to the largest advance box-office ever, and, together with the Hands/Sher interpretation of *Tamburlaine* (1992), resulted in the company playing to houses that were eighty per cent full in 1993. The same year also witnessed an inter-esting recruiting policy, with several stars of the sixties, including Robert Stephens, Alec McCowen and Derek Jacobi, being reintegrated into the company. One beneficial consequence of this influx was Stephens' Lear in 1993.

Throughout the nineties acclaimed productions have vied with threat-ened financial crises for publicity, but with enormous sponsorship deals including the five-year agreement with Allied Domecq for £5.5 million of support, a world-wide reputation as the gold standard of Shakespearean productions, its role as a major contributor to Britain's invisible earnings through tourism and as a cultural ambassador for the nation (the company was awarded the Queen's Award for Export Achievement in 1986), the RSC appears in a more stable position than at any point in its history. Whether this stability will be threatened by the decision to leave London is one of the many intriguing questions for the company in the new millennium.

Yorkshire Born and Bred: Northern Broadsides

Lest one should think that the RSC has retained a cultural monopoly of
Shakespearean productions in the 1990s or that a London base is essential for critical success, it is important to consider the resilient Northern
Broadsides. The company was formed in 1992 by Barrie Rutter, an actor
who had become frustrated by what he felt to be the southern bias of the
RSC and RNT, where Received Pronunciation ('BBC English', as it is
sometimes termed) predominates. 'You can go to the RSC and see all
those bloody RP-speakers: and it's dead', Rutter claimed in 1993, and he
fiercely resented the fact that, as a Yorkshireman, he was 'kept in the basement of Shakespeare and only given the comic bits. I have a slow-burning
revenge against the people who have told me I can never play kings
because I don't have RP'.[40]

This indignation has been put to fine artistic use. Employing only northern actors, cherishing a Yorkshire sensibility and celebrating the region's
distinctive speech patterns, the company have toured Britain with much-
praised performance-centred productions of (mainly) Shakespeare in
venues that range from mills, warehouses and the Royal Armouries to
orthodox proscenium arch theatres in the large conurbations. Versions of
Richard III (1992), *The Merry Wives of Windsor* (1993) (with references to
Windsor itself expunged and the incorporation of a fat witch of Bradford),
A Midsummer Night's Dream (1994), *Antony and Cleopatra* (1995) and
Blake Morrison's adaptation of Kleist's *The Cracked Pot* (1995) have all
earned admiration for their effective ensemble playing, minimal use of
props and furious pace. The refreshing unpretentiousness of the performances that Rutter, as artistic director, elicits provides a salutary reminder
that challenging theatre can be staged as excitingly in dusty (and generally
chilly) rooms, as in state-of-the-art complexes.

The Royal Court: The National Theatre of New Writing

For all its travails since 1979, the subsidised sector has proved the power-
house of British theatre. The RSC and RNT have developed into organisations admired throughout the world, regional theatres – the most
vulnerable to cuts in funding – have ensured that drama has not been
over-centralised in London and state support, however diminished, has
helped counter the reluctance of commercial theatre to take the risk of
staging untested work, as well as providing the necessary help to permit
much new writing to flourish. Nowhere has the wisdom of this policy been

more apparent than at the theatre that initiated the new wave of theatrical writing in the fifties, the Royal Court.

The early eighties witnessed a flourishing of young women playwrights whose work was nurtured in the state sector. Sarah Daniels' *Ripen Our Darkness* (1981), *The Devils' Gateway* (1983) and, in particular, *Masterpieces* (1983) examined in an unflinching manner male violence against women. *Masterpieces*, which premièred at the Royal Exchange, Manchester, took as its theme the link between apparently innocuous misogynist jokes and exploitative male pornography. Tracing the growing awareness of the social worker, Rowena, of her subjugation by her husband and a world shaped by men, it culminates in two shocking scenes: Rowena pushes a man who had made demeaning and suggestive remarks under a tube train (for which she is later tried for manslaughter) and the play concludes with a description of a scene from a snuff movie where a woman is dismembered with a chain saw for the sexual gratification of the viewers. Daniels' attempt to portray the cause and effect of these two acts is seen variously as contentious and sensational or revelatory and courageous. Few plays of the eighties possess a similar power to split an audience.

Sharman MacDonald also took sexual appetite as a theme in *When I Was a Girl I Used to Scream and Shout* (1984), which won the *Evening Standard*'s Most Promising Playwright award, although her focus is on the emotional conflicts that are caused by the growing sexual awareness of an adolescent girl. Nell Dunn's *Steaming* (1981), originating from the Theatre Royal, Stratford East, which has been revived under the leadership of Philip Hedley, enjoys great popularity for its depiction of the solidarity engendered amongst a group of women when the public Turkish bath that they use is threatened with closure, and Caryl Churchill's *Top Girls* (1982) investigates the difficulties that aspiring women face in a world defined by men and provides a salutary reminder of how much more needs to be done to create conditions in which women can truly flourish.

Churchill's protagonist, Marlene, has recently been appointed the director of the Top Girls Employment Agency. To celebrate her promotion she invites an eclectic group of female achievers to a party. The guests include Pope Joan, who became pregnant whilst masquerading as a man; Isabella Bird, a Victorian traveller; Dull Gret, a figure from a nightmarish Breugel painting who had led a countercharge against her male oppressors; Lady Hijo, a courtesan at the Japanese imperial court who became a Buddhist nun to escape her exploitation; and Griselda, the personification of patient fortitude from Chaucer's *The Clerk's Tale*.

When Marlene raises a toast to the gathering she observes that '... we've all come a long way' and invites them to celebrate 'our courage and the way we changed our lives and our extraordinary achievements', but what strikes the audience is the extent to which the individual stories speak more of sacrifice and pain than attainment and emancipation. In Act Two, which charts Marlene's rise to power, a similar tale of power and exploitation is revealed, although this time it is Marlene who is rude, aggressive and particularly contemptuous of women who are not as adept at aping male practices as she is. The didactic call for a third way towards emancipation between feminine passivity and male aggression is clear and subtle, if less strident than that of works such as *Masterpieces*, and explains why Churchill's blend of time-shifts, overlapping dialogue and provocative plot has proved so enduring.

Top Girls was directed by Max Stafford-Clark at the Royal Court, before being transferred to Joe Papp's Public Theatre, New York, in a generous co-production arrangement that helped keep the Royal Court afloat in the early eighties. Indeed, the resilience of the Royal Court has led to the perverse argument that shoe-string budgets create an atmosphere of make-do-and-mend that is conducive to new writing, in that it slims down casts and focuses the writer's mind on a bare space. This nonsense received its widest currency in 1987 after the transfer of another Stafford-Clark/Churchill transfer, *Serious Money*. Max Stafford-Clark would doubtless be able to point to the enormous pile of scripts worthy of production but condemned to oblivion for lack of funds to rebuff this extreme form of cultural monetarism.

In spite of the scorched earth policy of the eighties, which saw the Theatre Upstairs go dark for nine months in 1989, Max Stafford-Clark continued to profile new writing at the Royal Court which was often deemed unstageable for commercial or artistic reasons elsewhere. It was a courageous and stoical policy that has led to a golden harvest in the nineties. In 1986 the political commitment of the theatre was emphasised by the production of Jim Cartwright's first play, *Road*. Produced as a promenade performance, whereby the audience was invited to mingle with the performers, the work denounced the contemporaneous social conditions of a decaying northern town, and gave, through a series of vignettes, a searing account of the debilitating effect of unemployment. The narrator, Scully, was immediately seen as a Jimmy Porter for the eighties and the gritty realism of the characters' language viewed as effectively confrontational (Louise, the reticent central figure, asks at one point 'Why is life so tough? It's like walking through meat in high heels'). *Road*'s searing portrait of a part of Britain generally shielded from the affluent south-east of England inevitably drew indignant criticism from sections of the right-wing press.

The Royal Court's biggest triumph of the eighties was a play that has since become a fixture of the British school curriculum, Timberlake

Wertenbaker's *Our Country's Good* (1988). Loosely based on Thomas Keneally's novel The *Playmaker*, it shows convicts preparing to stage the first theatrical production of Farquhar's *The Recruiting Officer* in Australia and affirms the civilising and educational benefits of drama. After a voyage from England of dreadful privations, the convicts and their gaolers, the soldiers of the First Convict Fleet, land in Botany Bay. The Governor, Arthur Phillip, conscious of both the need to quell any unrest over diminishing supplies and the possibility that the criminal activity for which they have been convicted could have been influenced by their poverty and suffering, empowers the Second Lieutenant, Ralph Clark, to rehearse a play. Phillip's defence of this decision to his sceptical and often hostile colleagues creates the basis of the work's dialectic:

> The theatre is an expression of civilisation. We belong to a country which has spawned great playwrights: Shakespeare, Marlowe, Jonson, and even in our own time, Sheridan. The convicts will be speaking a refined, literate language and expressing sentiments of a delicacy they are not used to. It will remind them that there is more to life than crime, punishment. And we, this colony of a few hundred will be watching this together, for a few hours we will no longer be despised prisoners and hated gaolers. We will laugh, we may be moved, we may even think a little.[41]

The brilliance of *Our Country's Good* lies in its refusal to supply simple dichotomies. The complexity of human motivations is stressed throughout. Clark's decision to direct, for example, is inspired less by a love of drama than by a desire for promotion. Only through the process of rehearsing does he recognise its inherent value. Phillip's intentions, too, are not as liberal as he himself believes. His view of theatre as an exercise in mimicry is immediately challenged by the audience's observation of the practical difficulties of the first rehearsals: Dabby cannot read, old enmities between Liz and Dabby threaten physical violence and the literary nature of Farquhar's text and elevated nature of the action are alien to the experience of most of the performers.

The importance of words and their ability to be misconstrued are important themes in the work and are most obviously centred on the character of Wisehammer. Marginalised from society by his Jewishness and adamant that he is innocent, he teaches Mary the power of language whilst she is copying out the text to create more scripts – a symbolic act in itself. Language can be painful –

You have to be careful with words that begin with 'in'. It can turn everything upside down. Injustice. Most of that word is taken up with justice, but the 'in' twists it inside out and makes it the ugliest word in the English language

– but it can also be tender and liberating:

WISEHAMMER: … Shy is not a bad word, it's soft.
MARY: But shame is a hard one.
WISEHAMMER: Words with two Ls are the worst. Lonely, loveless.
MARY: Love is a good word.
WISEHAMMER: That's because it only has one L. I like words with one L: Luck. Latitudinarian.
(*Mary laughs.*)
Laughter.

It all depends on the context in which it is used, and its consolatory effect is dependent on humans creating the conditions in which it can be received positively.

The play concludes with Clark recanting his previous opposition to the inclusion of Wisehammer's newly written prologue. When he observes that 'The theatre is like a small republic, it requires private sacrifices for the good of the whole', the audience recognises that he, too, has been educated by this exercise in tolerance, co-operation and understanding. The new prologue, full of irony and political comment, adds the prisoners' own individual stamp to the production and demonstrates that drama constantly evolves in order to survive and remain relevant:

From distant climes o'er wide-spread seas we come,
Though not with much éclat or beat of drum,
True patriots all; for be it understood,
We left our country for our country's good;
No private views disgraced our generous zeal,
What urg'd our travels was our country's weal,
And none will doubt but that our emigration
Has prov'd most useful to the British nation.

The audience only witnesses the first few lines of the opening speech of *The Recruiting Officer* before *Our Country's Good* comes to an end. By finishing her play at this point, Wertenbaker is stressing a fundamental fact about all drama productions: the preparatory rehearsal process is as important to the individual performers' personal and artistic development as the finished product.

The humanity of *Our Country's Good*, its poignant emphasis on rehabilitation as opposed to punishment (which contrasted with the government's belief in the efficacy of prison) and its utilisation of meta-drama created a box-office success, which has resonated ever since. At the Royal Court in 1988 it played in repertoire with *The Recruiting Officer*, and won the Laurence Olivier Play of the Year Award in the same year, before being transferred to the Garrick Theatre in 1989 and Broadway in 1991. To coincide with a revival and a tour to Australia in 1989, Max Stafford-Clark wrote a detailed account of the rehearsal process which he addressed to Farquhar, entitled *Letters to George*, and the drama has swiftly become a highly popular choice for amateur and school groups, not least for its preponderance of good female roles and its encouragement to cross-cast and thereby question gender stereotyping. A work rich in observations about theatre, politics, colonialism, rehabilitation and social interaction, *Our Country's Good* has already confirmed Wertenbaker as one of the most stimulating playwrights of the post-war period. Her ability to marry insight with theatricality was evident again in another Royal Court production, *Three Birds Alighting on a Field* (1991), which begins with the auction of a flat, unpainted canvas for £1.2m and proceeds to discuss the value and purpose of art.

As the eighties drew to an end with the collapse of communist regimes throughout Europe and the fall of the Berlin Wall, Stafford-Clark reaffirmed the Royal Court's commitment to political writing and new drama. This led to the *May Day Dialogues* in 1990 where short pieces were commissioned to explore the key political and social issues of the previous decade. Thus, Nicholas de Jongh's *Aids Memoir* asked whether the theatre had failed to recognise AIDS as a serious international emergency; Manfred Karge's *The Wall-Dog* (translated by Jane and Howard Brenton) reflected on the imminence of unemployment for an East German border guard and his dog and Jeanette Crowley's *Goodnight Siobhan* showed how the conflict in Northern Ireland sours potential personal relationships. The concept of rapidly produced political comment appealed more to commentators than the wider public, however, although the policy was more successful with the productions of Caryl Churchill's *Mad Forest* (1990), Tariq Ali and Howard Brenton's *Iranian Nights* (1989) and Ariel Dorfman's *Death and the Maiden* (1991). Churchill's work bore similarities to the *May Days* project in that it focused on the experience of two Romanian families living through the demise of the dictator, Nicolae Ceauçescu. *Iranian Nights* also arose from a specific event, namely the *fatwa* that was issued against the writer Salman Rushdie by the Ayatollah Khomeni following the publication of *The Satanic Verses* (1988). Ali and Brenton's play was a swift response to the intolerable situation that

Rushdie now found himself in, being forced to live in hiding and endure frequent changes of address and twenty-four-hour security. Termed a 'pin-prick for free speech', the authors suggested that the whole episode was a literary equivalent to the Falklands War, and that the issues about a writer's freedom of expression that arose from the affair were as disturb-ing as Rushdie's personal plight.

Ariel Dorfman's *Death and the Maiden* similarly drew broader conclu-sions from an individual incident. Paulina has been raped during the repressive rule of a Chilean regime. Having kidnapped a man whom she believes to be her interrogator and rapist, she proceeds to demand the man's confession. A compelling study of the revenge that is demanded when a dictatorship collapses, the work was hailed as a 'terrifying moral thriller which combines brilliant theatricality with clear thought and fierce compassion'[42] by John Peter of the *Sunday Times*, a verdict borne out by the public response to the work that ensured its transfer from the Theatre Upstairs (reopened following a seventeen per cent increase in the Royal Court's grant in 1990) to the main auditorium and then to the West End.

In 1992 the board of the Royal Court decided that they wanted a change of direction. Stafford-Clark's contract was due to expire at the end of March 1992, having been renewed at intervals since 1979. He was re-appointed artistic director from April 1992 for eighteen months, although it was simultaneously announced that Stephen Daldry was to be the direc-tor-designate scheduled to take over in 1994. The cumbersome nature of this arrangement and the peremptory treatment of Stafford-Clark drew some unfavourable criticism, although Daldry's appointment seemed innovative. Young and a rising star, he had made a name for himself as director of the fringe Gate Theatre in Notting Hill, where he had initiated several productions of neglected international works, in particular a highly successful season of Spanish Golden Age drama featuring works by Tirso de Molina and Caldéron in 1991, while his revival of J.B. Priestley's *An Inspector Calls* (1992) for the National Theatre was immediately seen as a masterful reinvigoration of a classic text. The shotgun collaboration of Daldry and Stafford-Clark seemed doomed to fail, but paradoxically from this inauspicious beginning there would emerge some of the most notable productions of the nineties.

The years 1992 and 1993 witnessed two American transfers at the Royal Court which confirmed Daldry's influence. John Guare's *Six Degrees of Sep-aration* (1992), directed by Phyllida Lloyd, was loosely based on fact, and told the story of how a black youth appeared in the apartment of a New York art dealer claiming to be the son of Sydney Poitier. Its mixture of com-edy, pathos and absurdity ensured that the Royal Court enjoyed a third hit following *Our Country's Good* and *Death and the Maiden*. This line was extended by David Mamet's controversial *Oleanna* (1993). A two-hander featuring David Suchet as a college professor and Lia Williams as his pupil, Carol, the work interrogates the dictums of political correctness, where 'An amiable, almost impersonal hug around the shoulder is read as sexual harassment [and] physically attempting to prevent you from leaving the room becomes attempted rape'.[43] The work's chilling intensity and the fact that the director was Harold Pinter heightened public interest, and Terry Johnson's new work, *Hysteria* (1993), and a revival of John Arden's *Live Like Pigs* (1993) concluded a memorable final year for Stafford-Clark.

Daldry's first production as artistic director was a revival of Arnold Wesker's *The Kitchen* (1994) which represented a triumphant debut. It was a mark of Daldry's confidence not only that he chose to restage this Royal Court classic from the fifties as his first play, but also that in doing so he should transform the actual theatre by removing the stalls to create a gleaming, oval-shaped kitchen area which was viewed from the circle and the galleries. As with his production of *An Inspector Calls* (which was still running in the West End in 1997), Daldry here reinvested a work from an earlier era with contemporary significance, leading Benedict Nightingale in *The Times* to observe: 'A period play about a few exemplary individuals suddenly implicates civilisation itself. How many other directors could achieve so much?'[44] Notices such as this and a seating capacity reduced from 395 to 250 made tickets for *The Kitchen* the hottest property in town.

The rest of the year also witnessed some notable firsts at the Royal Court. As with so many theatre institutions in the eighties and the nineties, change was accompanied by continuity. Max Stafford-Clark proved that his obituaries ('No producer displayed a noticeably sharper nose for untried talent in the barren eighties'[45]) were premature by founding with Sonia Freedman, in 1993, a new theatre company, Out of Joint, whose aim was 'to create and produce new writing for the stage and to tour this work both nationally and internationally'.[46] Ironically, Out of Joint's home would prove to be Stafford-Clark's old base. Its first productions echoed the practice of alternating *Our Country's Good* and *The Recruiting Officer* in 1988, with the twinning, in 1993, of the revived *Road* and a new comedy by Sue Townsend, *The Queen and I*. Although the latter play, about the fate of the Royal Family after being forced by a Republican government to move into a council house, was thin fare, the rationale of the company was a welcome development. Its second pairing of Etheredge's *The Man of Mode* and Stephen Jeffrey's new work *The Libertine*, which covered the life of the pornographic poet, the Earl of Rochester, allegedly the model for Dorimant, was much more harmonious and the policy of alternating works continued in 1995 with Timberlake Wertenbaker's *The Break of Day* and Chekhov's *The Three Sisters*.

Although Daldry arrived at the Royal Court expressing the desire to see more international works produced, it has actually been the showcasing of new British writing that has been the defining mark of his tenure. *My Night with Reg*, directed by Roger Michell, premièred in the Theatre Upstairs in 1994, before its transfer to the Criterion. *Babies* (1994) continued in the tradition of Jonathan Harvey's *Beautiful Thing* by basing a comedy on gay life in south-east London. Jez Butterworth's *Mojo* explored in a sub-Tarantino manner gangland life in 1958 and *Blasted* by Sarah Kane enveloped the theatre in the type of press interest that had last been seen following the staging of Edward Bond's *Saved* in 1965. Containing scenes of masturbation, rape and oral sex, not to mention the consumption by the soldier of Ian's eyes or the polishing off of the remains of Cate's dead baby, the play is clearly not for the faint-hearted. Headlines such as 'You pays your money and they eat their eyes' helped fan the media circus, but not everybody saw the work as gratuitously offensive. Benedict Nightingale, whilst conceding its repulsiveness, felt that the work had much to say about violence and elemental human behaviour: 'Artfully constructed and distressingly watchable, its unmitigated horrors and numbing amorality leave a sour taste in the mind'.[47] Up until the production of *Blasted*, Daldry had frequently been mentioned as the front runner to succeed Richard Eyre as the Director of the National Theatre. Trevor Nunn, rarely acknowledged as being in the running, was eventually named as Eyre's successor. One can only speculate whether Daldry's uncompromising defence of the production caused the governors of the National Theatre to overlook him.

An eventful 1995 for the Royal Court ended with the theatre being awarded an enormous grant from the National Lottery of £16 million to allow the building that had been constructed in 1888 to be redeveloped over a period of eighteen months. That the structure needed attention was undeniable – the understage and stalls were regularly flooded, the stage was crumbling and access for the disabled was virtually impossible – but the question now was what would happen to the company when the theatre closed. The answer was both sensible and ironic. The subsidised company would move into the Duke of York's and Ambassadors theatres in the West End. The symbolism of this transplantation should not be underestimated. The diversity of works produced in 1996 – a season of Royal Court Classics including Ron Hutchinson's *Rat in the Skull* about the troubles in Ireland (first performed in 1984), David Storey's *The Changing Room* and Terry Johnson's *Hysteria*, and new work by Harold Pinter (*Ashes to Ashes*), Martin McDonagh (*The Beauty Queen of Leenane*) and Mark Ravenhill (*Shopping and F***ing*) – provided a reminder from the very heart of the other sector's territory that subsidised theatre was again the home of innovative new writing that was commercially popular. Commercial theatre, with the exception of musicals, was the poor relation now, a total transformation from the period immediately following the war.

In 1997 Daldry announced his intention to leave the Royal Court to pursue an interest in making films. His reign had been brief and exhilarating, creating a 'Theatre of Urban Ennui' and promoting plays that provoke thought, such as Ayub Khan-Din's *East is East* (1997) about racism and ethnicity, as well as works that revelled in their ability to sensationalise and disturb, most recently Jim Cartwright's dialogue between Man and Slag, enticingly called *I Licked a Slag's Deodorant* (1997). By the end of the century, the Royal Court had rediscovered the cutting edge it had possessed between 1956 and 1962.

Blurred Parameters: the Fringe, the West End and the Subsidised Sector

The announcement of Daldry's successor as Ian Rickson yet again underlined the Royal Court board's capacity for surprise. Although he had been the director of Jez Butterworth's *Mojo*, which earned him the Most Promising Newcomer in the Evening Standard Awards of 1995, Rickson was little known outside the organisation (of which he had been an associate director since 1994). Early signs were promising, however, with his consummate productions of Conor McPherson's scrutiny of Irish rural life, *The Weir* (1997), at the Royal Court Theatre Upstairs and Kevin Elyot's examination of gay middle-aged life, *The Day I Stood Still* (1998) at the National.

What is significant about Rickson's accession for the history of post-war British theatre is the way that his rise can be seen as emblematic of the reorientation of theatre that has been occurring since 1945. For example, it is possible to read his career thus far in the following manner: born in South London to an 'aspiring working class family'[48] (theatre is now less class-bound than in Rattigan's day), Rickson did not see his first play until he was fifteen (other media now compete with drama for our leisure time). The first play in question was Harold Pinter's *The Caretaker* (a cornerstone of the post-war canon), and starred the comedian Max Wall (a performer of both post-war classics by writers such as Beckett and popular culture). Educated at Essex University (non-Oxbridge), Rickson was inspired by its writer-in-residence, Edward Bond (an iconic figure), and he was later to work with Bond as an actor (directors no longer remain aloof from the process of theatre as a whole). Rickson's directorial work has mainly been with new writers and companies such as Paines Plough and the pub theatre the King's Head (the London fringe acts as both a source of material and a valuable conscience for the West End), although he has also directed plays in the subsidised powerhouses of the Royal Court and the National (important nurturers of new writing).

This eclectic curriculum vitae illustrates how by the end of the twentieth century distinctions between the Fringe, the subsidised sector and the West End have begun to collapse. Off-West End venues have proved vital training grounds for the subsequent young Turks of the subsidised sector – witness how Giles Croft ran the Gate before becoming the literary manager of the National Theatre; Stephen Daldry created 'design-spectaculars'[49] at the same venue and Ian Rickson cut his teeth at the King's Head – and the very term 'Fringe' no longer connotes agitprop or political confrontation but implies less commercially safe and slightly more daring work than certainly the West End and probably the Royal Court and the National produce. This has led to higher profiles for the Almeida, Hampstead, Cockpit, Tricycle, Gate and Bush theatres, which attract loyal audiences, although some playgoers lament what they perceive to be the loss of a socially-critical cutting edge. Whether this process of homogenisation will ultimately prove beneficial is difficult to predict: the only certainty is that unpredictability has been the leitmotif of the past fifty years.

Towards the Millennium and Beyond

As the millennium approaches, British theatre is defined by its contradictions. The robustness of the Royal Court contrasts with the continuing struggle of regional theatres to balance their budgets. (The Crucible, Sheffield, had in 1998 an accumulated deficit of almost £1 million.) The commercial West End shows little sign of shaking off Benedict Nightingale's withering description of it as a 'gaudy graveyard bereft of new plays',[50] although its ever proliferating list of mega-musicals continues to draw in the audiences. New writing occasionally flourishes outside the triumvirate of the RSC, RNT and Royal Court, but successes such as Harold Pinter's *Moonlight* (1993) at the Almeida, Islington (his first full-length play since *Betrayal* in 1978) are generally notable as exceptions to the rule. The reconstruction of the Globe Theatre on the South Bank and the early productions by Mark Rylance's company have been fascinating to observe, but raise awkward questions about the advisability of staging 'authentic productions' given the constantly evolving nature of drama. Whilst women playwrights are gradually achieving greater prominence (although nowhere near equality of access to stages), female directors such as

Phyllida Lloyd and Deborah Warner are earning increasing acclaim, and female administrators are running dynamic institutions (such as the West Yorkshire Playhouse), female performers continue to earn considerably less than their male counterparts. A survey by the actors' union, Equity, in 1992 revealed that whilst average annual earnings for men were £36,843, women received a mere £11,431.[51]

The backward-looking nature of the Conservative administration's attitude to the arts, symbolised by the creation of a Department of National Heritage, has been replaced in 1997 by a government claiming to be a greater believer in the importance of the arts in national life, yet aside from creating a Department of Culture it is hard to see how extra money can be generated for theatre given Labour's election pledge to retain the Conservative's spending plans for the first two years of its office. Even the advent of the National Lottery, which has provided large grants for capital expenditure, has again illustrated how the British nation prefers to invest in buildings rather than people. Attempts were being made by the Arts Council through their A4E scheme in 1997 to channel money into programming, but amendments to the original Lottery legislation are still needed to make this a far-reaching source of additional funding.

But these contradictions need not be a source of despondency. Conflict has always been the essence of British drama and a simple comparison between the centralised activity of 1945 and the multiplicity of productions in 1997 provides a testimony as much to the resilience of the theatre profession as to its dynamism and innovation. Seldom has the British theatre been in such a period of regeneration. The Royal Opera House in Covent Garden is currently undergoing structural enlargement and restoration ready to welcome back the Royal Opera and Ballet and there are signs that this will serve a less elite society, Sadlers Wells, that other survival from the Baylis years, is being entirely rebuilt on the old site, the National Theatre (now a Grade 2 listed building) is having its first face-lift ready for the next century, money has been made available to improve the facilities of the Royal Court, fine new regional theatres like the West Yorkshire Playhouse in Leeds have been built and impressive arts complexes planned, as in Salford, the old London Lyceum has been restored to its splendour, even though temporarily, one hopes, surrendered to the hypes of Lloyd-Webber, smaller venues such as the Donmar, the Greenwich, the Orange Tree, and the Place in London and the Citizens in Glasgow offer rewarding fare and, throughout the country, successful regional tours by professional companies now take quality theatre to the local authority theatres put up during the wave of creative optimism which followed the end of the war. We have a Theatres Trust to watch-dog theatrical provision, a Theatre Museum to record and preserve its history, a Society established during the period under question to study seriously its history and progress, and greatly improved facilities for training in a number of University Drama departments and several Drama Schools.[52]

In January 1997, The Peter Hall Company took up residency at the Old Vic, which had benefited throughout the eighties from having over £26m ploughed into it by David and Ed Mirvish. Although its first three months of repertory productions incurred heavy losses, Hall's company drew much favourable comment for re-establishing first rate repertory theatre in the capital, in particular Granville Barker's *Waste*, Chekhov's *The Seagull* and Beckett's *Waiting for Godot*, and it soon began to recoup its losses. This latter production, starring Alan Howard and Ben Kingsley, was completely sold out, bound for a Broadway transfer and, by the summer of 1997, helping to ensure that the theatre was playing to a healthy 68 per cent capacity. Just as the company was beginning to establish itself artistically and financially, however, the Mirvishes announced in August 1997 that they could no longer sustain the financial burden of the building and would be putting the Old Vic up for sale at a cost of £7.5 million. Once again, uncertainty surrounded the fate of this venerable institution, as it has done for much of the twentieth century. As so often since 1945, financial imperatives had thwarted artistic excellence, but out of disaster there emerged a glimmer of optimism. Peter Hall had already planned a new season and it was expected that the great survivor would transfer to a West End theatre at the end of his Old Vic tenure in December – a mixture of resilience and vision so characteristic of the history of British Theatre since 1945.

Notes

Chapter 1: 1945–1954

1. Anthony Quayle, *A Time to Speak*, (London, Barrie & Jenkins, 1990), p.302.
2. Henry Pelling, *A Short History of the Labour Party*, (Basingstoke, Macmillan, 1986), p.94.
3. See Harold Hobson, 'Long West End Runs', *Sunday Times*, 8/7/1945.
4. See Angus Calder, *The People's War*, (London, Jonathan Cape, 1969), p.367.
5. See Harold Hobson, 'London Theatres Filled Now But See Big Boom With Peace', *Christian Science Monitor*, 24/3/1945.
6. Harold Hobson, 'Number of Houses Reduced By 12 Per Cent Since 1939', *Christian Science Monitor*, 24/11/1945.
7. Ibid.
8. See Harold Hobson, 'Later Theatre Scheme Fails', *Sunday Times*, 30/12/1945.
9. George Rowell, *The Old Vic Theatre: A History*, (Cambridge, CUP, 1993), p.138.
10. Ivor Brown, 'Henry IV Part One', *Observer*, 30/9/1945; insertion mine.
11. Ivor Brown, 'Henry IV Part Two', *Observer*, 7/10/1945.
12. Rowell, 1993, p.137.
13. See Donald Spoto, *Laurence Olivier*, (London, Harper Collins, 1991), p.166.
14. Kenneth Tynan, *Oedipus Rex* in *A View of the English Stage*, (London, Methuen, 1984), p.27.
15. Author: Interview with Jack Reading, Vice-President of the Society for Theatre Research, 6/6/1996.
16. See Michael Sanderson, *From Irving to Olivier*, (London, Athlone Press, 1985), p. 263.
17. See Anthony Jackson and George Rowell, *The Repertory Movement: A History of Regional Theatre in Britain*, (Cambridge, CUP, 1984), p.97.
18. Ibid., p.81.
19. See Richard Huggett, *Binkie Beaumont: Eminence Grise of the West End Theatre 1933–1973*, (London, Hodder & Stoughton, 1989), p.323.
20. Ibid., p.325.
21. John Osborne, *Almost a Gentleman*, (London, Faber and Faber, 1991), p.20.
22. See Vivien Leigh's contract for *A Streetcar Named Desire*, 'Papers Relating to H.M. Tennent', RP 95/2363, Theatre Museum, London.
23. William Conway, the General Manager of H.M. Tennent's wrote to Barbe-Weste on 21 October 1949 to announce that, following sell-out performances, her salary would be increased to £10 per week from the 24th. The actress was delighted, replying on 22 October 1949: 'many thanks for your kindness regarding my salary'. It is hard to avoid the feeling that this correspondence is akin to an exchange between master and serf. Both letters and Barbe-Weste's

original contract are in 'Papers Relating to H.M. Tennent', RP 95/2363, Theatre Museum, London.

24. See 'Papers Relating to H.M. Tennent', RP 95/2363, Theatre Museum, London.

25. Kenneth Tynan and Cecil Beaton, *Persona Grata*, (London, Allan Wingate, 1953), 'Foreword', p.vi.

26. Ibid., pp.15–6.

27. In John Johnston, *The Lord Chamberlain's Blue Pencil*, (London, Hodder & Stoughton, 1990), pp.63–4.

28. The Lord Chamberlain's Papers are kept in the Department of Manuscripts at the British Library, London.

29. This comment is contained in a handwritten note added by the Lord Chamberlain to the reader's report on Reginald Beckwith's suppressed work, *No Retreat*, in 1957. British Library.

30. Reader's Report on *First Thing*, 1945, British Library.

31. Reader's Report on *Patricia English*, 1946, British Library.

32. Reader's Report on *Getting a Flat*, 1946, British Library.

33. A description applied to *House of the Red Lamp* in its Reader's Report, 1950. British Library.

34. Reader's Report on *Street Girl*, 1950, British Library.

35. Reader's Report on *If He Came*, 1948, British Library.

36. Reader's Report on *Our Ladies Meet*, 1952, British Library.

37. Note attached to Reader's Report on *The Rosenberg Story*, 1953, British Library.

38. See Colin Chambers, *The Story of the Unity Theatre*, (London, Lawrence & Wishart, 1989), p.335.

39. See Richard Findlater, *Banned*, (London, Panther, 1967), p.197.

40. Reader's Report on *Strangers in the Land*, 1953, British Library.

41. See Sally Beauman, *The Royal Shakespeare Company*, (Oxford, OUP, 1982), p.171.

42. Anonymous, *The Times*, 29/4/1946.

43. See Beauman, 1982, p.177.

44. Ibid., p.189.

45. J.C. Trewin, *Observer*, 26/5/1946.

46. See Spoto, 1991, p.173.

47. Harold Hobson, 'Mr Olivier's Lear', *Sunday Times*, 29/9/1946.

48. Ivor Brown, 'King Lear', *Observer*, 29/9/1946.

49. John Russell Taylor writes that 'If ever a revolution began with one explosion it was this', *Anger and After*, (London, Eyre Methuen, 1969), p.14. The term 'Kitchen-Sink' was applied in the London theatre (often pejoratively) to plays that eschewed drawing-room settings for working-class environments following John Osborne's *Look Back in Anger* (1956) and Arnold Wesker's *The Kitchen* (1959). 'New wave' is a less subjective term to describe the work of the post-1956 generation of British dramatists.

50. Harold Hobson, *Indirect Journey*, (London, Weidenfeld and Nicolson, 1978), p.211.

51. J.C. Trewin, 'Queens of the Castle', *Observer*, 16/2/1947.

52. See Harold Hobson, 'A French Actor', *Sunday Times*, 12/9/1948.

53. Harold Hobson, 'French Visitors', *Sunday Times*, 17/10/1948.

54. Harold Hobson, 'Black Magic', *Sunday Times*, 13/3/1949.

55. Harold Hobson, 'Visitors', *Sunday Times*, 30/9/1951.

56. Harold Hobson, 'Partage de Midi, *Sunday Times*, 7/10/1951.

57. Harold Hobson, 'London Survey', *Sunday Times*, 30/3/1952.

58. Max Wilk, *OK! The Story of Oklahoma!*, (New York, Grove Press, 1993), p.76.

59. 'Nothing … has more struck the imagination of Londoners than the dances. These dances are not the work of the accomplished principals. They consist of a multitude of solos, fitted into an elaborate pattern which makes a satisfying and unusual whole.' Harold Hobson, '*Annie Get Your Gun* in London', *Christian Science Monitor*, 7/7/1947.

60. Wilk, 1993, pp. 257–8.

61. J.C. Trewin, 'Morning Glory', *Observer*, 4/5/1947.

62. 'Papers Relating to H.M. Tennent',

95/2363, Theatre Museum, London.
63. See Huggett, 1989, p. 418.
64. See 'Papers Relating to H.M. Tennent', RP 95/2363, Theatre Museum, London.
65. Ibid.
66. 'Aldwych Theatre', *The Times*, 13/10/1949.
67. Anthony Cookman, *Tatler*, 20/10/1949.
68. J.C. Trewin, 'Rough Riding', *Observer*, 16/10/1949.
69. Quoted in Huggett, 1989, p.420.
70. Quoted in 'State Patronage of the Theater', *Christian Science Monitor*, 7/1/1950.
71. *Southwark Cathedral Magazine*, 1949.
72. 'Papers relating to H.M. Tennent, 95/2363, Theatre Museum, London.
73. A.P. Herbert, *No Fine on Fun*, (London, Arts Council, 1957), p.16.
74. See Simon Trussler, *The Cambridge Illustrated History of British Theatre*, (Cambridge, CUP, 1994), p.303.
75. See Kitty Black, *Upper Circle*, (London, Methuen, 1984), p.154.
76. Ibid., p.153.
77. Ivor Brown, 'Cash and Colour', *Observer*, 2/11/1947.
78. *Hansard*, (London, H.M.S.O., 1949), p.2086.
79. See Black, 1984, p.233.
80. Hugh Hunt, Kenneth Richards, John Russell Taylor, *The Revels History of Drama in English Volume VII: 1880 to the Present Day*, (London, Methuen, 1978), p.50.
81. John Russell Taylor, 1969, p.17.
82. Charles Duff, *The Lost Summer – The Heyday of the West End Theatre*, (London, Nick Hern Books, 1995), p.xii.
83. Kenneth Tynan, 'West-End Apathy', *Observer*, 31/10/1954.
84. Ivor Brown, 'Up from the Liverpool Theatre', *Observer*, 2/2/1947.
85. Ivor Brown, 'Assorted Fruits', *Observer*, 28/11/1945.
86. Ivor Brown, 'Plots and Finery', *Observer*, 24/10/1948.
87. Harold Hobson, 'The Theatre Justified', *Sunday Times*, 30/1/1949.
88. Harold Hobson, 'Henry IV', *Sunday Times*, 8/4/1951.
89. Phyliss Hartnoll, ed., *The Oxford

Companion to the Theatre*, (Oxford, OUP, 1990), pp. 579–80.
90. Ivor Brown, 'The Star-Lit Steppers', *Observer*, 1/5/1949
91. Ibid.
92. J.C. Trewin, 'Windy and Wuthering', *Observer*, 14/3/1948.
93. Black, 1984, p.233.
94. Ivor Brown, 'High Fantastical', *Observer*, 22/1/1950.
95. Ibid.
96. Ivor Brown, 'Handling the Text', *Observer*, 19/2/1950.
97. Ivor Brown, 'Gin and Falernian', *Observer*, 7/5/1950.
98. Trevor R. Griffiths and Carole Woddis, eds., *The Bloomsbury Theatre Guide*, (London, Bloomsbury, 1991), p.120.
99. J.C. Trewin, 'Mixed Double', *Observer*, 12/9/1948.
100. J.C. Trewin, 'Old Acquaintance', *Observer*, 23/7/1950.
101. Ivor Brown, 'Very Blue Waters', *Observer*, 23/7/1950.
102. Harold Hobson, 'Derivations', *Sunday Times*, 11/3/1951.
103. John Elsom, *Post-War British Theatre Criticism*, (London, Routledge & Kegan Paul, 1981), p.39.
104. I am indebted to George Rowell's excellent *The Old Vic Theatre: A History*, (Cambridge, CUP, 1993) for this section, and in particular pp. 137–48.
105. Henry Pelling, *Modern Britain: 1885–1955*, (London, Nelson, 1965), pp.187–8.
106. Ivor Brown, 'Trips to the Moors', *Observer*, 22/4/1951.
107. Ivor Brown, 'The Lass Unparalleled', *Observer*, 13/5/1951.
108. Ivor Brown, 'In Gay Bohemia', *Observer*, 1/7/1951.
109. Ivor Brown, 'Greater and Less', *Observer*, 23/9/1951.
110. For a consideration of whether Hester was originally Hector, see Geoffrey Wansell, *Terence Rattigan*, (London, Fourth Estate, 1995), pp.216–20.
111. Ivor Brown, 'Greene Fields', *Observer*, 19/4/1953.
112. Ivor Brown, 'French and English',

Observer, 5/11/1950.

113. Ivor Brown, 'Guessing Game', *Observer*, 11/4/1954.
114. Anon., 'Profile: The Lord Chamberlain', *Observer*, 10/2/1952.
115. Kenneth Tynan, 'Ins and Outs', *Observer*, 5/9/1954.
116. Kenneth Tynan, 'The Second Rate', *Observer*, 19/9/1954.
117. Kenneth Tynan, 'The Lost Art of Bad Drama', *A View of the English Stage*, (London, Methuen, 1984), p.149.
118. Kenneth Tynan, 'Mixed Double', *Observer*, 26/9/1954.
119. 'Separate Tables', in Tynan, 1984, pp. 145–6.
120. Kenneth Tynan, 'West End Apathy', *Observer*, 31/10/1954.
121. Kenneth Tynan, 'Dead Language', *Observer*, 21/11/1954.
122. Kenneth Tynan, 'Pogrom Notes', *Observer*, 14/11/1954.
123. Kathleen Tynan, *The Life of Kenneth Tynan*, (London, Methuen, 1988), p.116.
124. Peter Roberts, *The Best of Plays and Players, Volume One: 1953–1968*, (London, Methuen, 1988), p.42.

Chapter 2: 1955–1962

1. Eugène Ionesco, 'The Playwright's Role', *Observer*, 29/6/1958.
2. Letter to Susan Manning, 16/4/1953, held at the Harry Ransome Humanities Research Center, Austin, Texas.
3. Lawrence Graver, *Waiting for Godot*, (Cambridge, CUP, 1989), p.13.
4. Samuel Beckett, *Waiting for Godot* (London, Faber and Faber, 1965), p. 48. The quotations from this play that follow are from ibid., pp. 50, 91, 92, 93, 18, 75, 11, 33, 48, 5 and 69.
5. Harold Hobson, 'Tomorrow', *Sunday Times*, 7/8/1955.
6. Peter Bull, *I Know the Face, But ...*, (London, Peter Davies, 1959), pp.169–70.
7. Milton Shulman, 'Duet For Two Symbols', *Evening Standard*, 4/8/1955.
8. Stephen Williams, 'Stephen Williams at the Theatre', *Evening News*,

4/8/1955.
9. David Lewin, 'Nothing happens, it's awful (it's life), *Daily Express*, 4/8/1955.
10. W.A. Darlington, 'An Evening of Funny Obscurity', *Daily Telegraph*, 4/8/1955.
11. Samuel Beckett, letter to H.O. White, 10/10/1955, referred to in Deidre Behr, *Samuel Beckett: A Biography*, (London, Cape, 1990), p.480.
12. Kenneth Tynan 'Waiting for Godot', *Observer*, 7/8/1955.
13. Terence Rattigan in the *New Statesman*, 4/3/1950.
14. Quoted in Geoffrey Wansell's *Terence Rattigan*, (London, Fourth Estate, 1995), p. 241.
15. Rattigan, 'Aunt Edna Waits for Godot', *New Statesman*, 15/10/1955.
16. See, for example, Stephen Lacey, *British Realist Theatre*, (London, Routledge, 1995), p.17.
17. For a more in depth study of Hobson's career, see Dominic Shellard, *Harold Hobson: Witness and Judge*, (Keele, Keele University Press, 1995) and *Harold Hobson: The Complete Catalogue 1922–1988* (Keele, Keele University Press, 1995).
18. In my account of the early genesis of the ESC, I am indebted to Irving Wardle's *The Theatres of George Devine*, (London, Eyre Methuen, 1979), pp.161–174.
19. Ibid., p.161.
20. A. Alvarez, ed., *The New Poetry* (Harmondsworth, Penguin, 1962), p. 21.
21. T.S. Eliot in A. Alvarez, 1962, p.21.
22. Ibid., p.25.
23. See Lacey, 1995, p.42.
24. George Devine, letter to Tony Richardson, 14/4/1954, quoted in Philip Roberts, 'George Devine, Tony Richardson and Stratford', *Studies in Theatre Production*, No 12, Dec 1995, p. 126.
25. See Devine, quoted in Wardle, 1979, p.169.
26. Quoted in Wardle, 1979, p.170.
27. Ibid., p.171.
28. Analysis of the production costs by Gillespie Brothers and Co. (Accoun-

tants), 17/1/1959, in 'Papers Relating to H.M. Tennent', RP 95/2363, Theatre Museum, London.

29. 4/4/1956, quoted in Wardle, 1979, p. 67.
30. 21/4/1956, quoted in ibid., p. 67.
31. 15/4/1956, quoted in ibid., p. 71.
32. These putative titles all appear on the Autograph Manuscript Notebook for *Look Back in Anger*, held at the Harry Ransome Humanities Research Center, Austin, Texas.
33. See John Osborne, *A Better Class of Person*, (Harmondsworth, Penguin, 1982), p.274.
34. Richardson in Wardle, 1979, p.181.
35. 'Carry On Up The Zeitgeist – *Look Back in Anger*', BBC Radio 4, broadcast on 3 April 1992.
36. John Osborne, *Look Back in Anger*, (London, Faber and Faber, 1986), p.15.
37. Ibid., Act One, p.20.
38. Ibid., p.17.
39. Ibid., p.35.
40. Ibid., Act Three, p.84.
41. 'Carry On Up The Zeitgeist – *Look Back in Anger*'.
42. Rattigan, quoted in Wansell, 1995, p.270.
43. Patrick Gibbs, 'A Study of an Exhibitionist', *Daily Telegraph*, 9/5/1956.
44. John Barber, 'This Bitter Young Man – Like Thousands', *Daily Express*, 9/5/1956.
45. Colin Wilson, 'This actor is a great writer', *Daily Mail*, 9/5/1956.
46. Milton Shulman, 'Mr Osborne Builds A Wailing Wall', *Evening Standard*, 9/5/1956.
47. Osborne, 1991, p.22.
48. Ibid., p.11.
49. Osborne, 1986, Act One, p.11.
50. Ibid., p.13
51. Osborne, 1991, p.22.
52. Ibid., p.23.
53. John Osborne, 'They Call it Cricket' in *Declaration*, ed. T. Maschler, (London, Macgibbon & Kay, 1959), p.74.
54. Lacey, 1995, p. 21.
55. See Osborne, 1991, p.23.
56. Letter to Philip Whitehead, 29/8/1956, Harry Ransome Humanities Research Center, Austin, Texas.

57. Lord Chamberlain's Papers, British Library.
58. Tynan on *Variation on a Theme*, in Wansell, 1995, p.296.
59. Ibid., p.278.
60. This view may, in part, stem from John Russell Taylor's snap-shot book of 1962 – *Anger and After: A Guide to the New British Drama* (1962) – in which he writes of Theatre Workshop's 'wandering on-and-off sort of life on tour in Wales, the industrial north and elsewhere', prior to its arrival in the East End of London in 1953 (Russell Taylor, 1983, p.119). His implication that solid achievement is attained through a permanent London base is inescapable – a centralising view of British life that many of the playwrights cited in his work sought to challenge.
61. Ewan MacColl in Howard Goorney, *The Theatre Workshop Story*, (London, Methuen, 1981), p.2.
62. Ibid., p.5
63. Joan Littlewood, *Joan's Book*, (London, Methuen, 1994), p.68.
64. Quoted in Goorney, 1981, p.11.
65. Littlewood, 1994, p.158.
66. Goorney, 1981, p.50.
67. Ibid.
68. MacColl in Goorney, 1981, p. 50.
69. Quoted in Goorney, 1981, p.214.
70. Howard Goorney, quoted in Littlewood, 1994, p.448.
71. Ibid., p.518
72. Goorney, 1981, p.98.
73. Ibid., p.94.
74. Ibid., p.98.
75. Harold Hobson, 'Richard II', *Sunday Times*, 23/1/1955.
76. Ibid.
77. Harold Hobson, 'East, West', *Sunday Times*, 18/3/1956; insertion mine.
78. Littlewood, 1994, p.468.
79. Ibid.
80. Goorney, 1981, p.105.
81. Littlewood, 1994, p.470.
82. Kenneth Tynan, *A View of the English Stage*, (London, Methuen, 1984), p.180.
83. See Littlewood, 1994, p.471.
84. Goorney, 1981, p.105.
85. See Littlewood, 1994, p.472.

86. Jack Reading, Letter to the author, 10/10/1997.
87. Harold Hobson, 'Try Again', *Sunday Times*, 3/7/1955.
88. Kenneth Tynan in Kathleen Tynan, *The Life of Kenneth Tynan*, (London, Methuen, 1988), p.118.
89. Kenneth Tynan, 'Dead Language', *Observer*, 12/12/1954.
90. Kenneth Tynan, *Observer*, 6/1/1955.
91. In Kathleen Tynan, 1988, p.118.
92. Bertolt Brecht, translated by John Willett as *Brecht on Theatre*, (London, Methuen, 1986), p.283.
93. See Tynan, 1984, p.196–8.
94. Ibid., p.197.
95. Ibid., pp.197–8.
96. George Devine, letter to Brecht, 22/12/1955, in the Osborne archive at the Harry Ransome Humanities Research Center.
97. Information contained in the Osborne archive; phone call logged as 11/1/1956.
98. Osborne, 1991, p.28.
99. George Devine, 'The Berliner Ensemble' in *New Theatre Voices of the Fifties and Sixties*, ed. Charles Marowitz, Tom Milne and Owen Hale, (London, Methuen, 1981), pp.14–18.
100. Harold Hobson, 'Bertolt Brecht', *Sunday Times*, 4/11/1956.
101. W.A. Darlington, 'Dame Peggy Saves Dull Brecht Play', *Daily Telegraph*, 1/11/1956.
102. Bertolt Brecht, *The Good Woman of Setzuan* in *Parables for the Theatre*, trans. Eric Bentley (Harmondsworth, Penguin, 1982), p. 26. Further quotations from this play that follow are to be found at ibid. pp. 31, 104 and 107–8.
103. There is no direct translation of 'Verfremdung' into English. It is best simply to utilise the German term and retain a sense of its etymology. The prefix 'Ver' means 'to make', whereas 'fremd' is the German adjective 'strange'. To make things appear strange, or rather, the familiar to appear unfamiliar is the business of 'Verfremdung'.
104. Michael Patterson, 'Brecht's Legacy' in *The Cambridge Companion to Brecht*, ed. Peter Thomson and Glendyr Sacks, (Cambridge, CUP, 1994), p.277.
105. Michael Billington, quoted in his celebratory piece, 'Brecht', *Guardian*, 10/2/1998.
106. Kenneth Tynan, 'The Court Revolution', *Observer*, 6/4/1958.
107. The following poetry recitals took place: Stephen Spender (10/3/1957), Edith Evans (2/11/1958), Sybil Thorndike and Lewis Casson (8/3/1959).
108. Olivier, quoted in Spoto, 1991, p.226.
109. Ibid, p.227.
110. Olivier, quoted in Richard Findlater, *At the Royal Court*, (London, Amber Lane Press, 1981), p.40.
111. John Osborne, *The Entertainer* (London, Faber and Faber, 1990), 'Number Seven', p. 59.
112. Ibid., 'Number Five', p. 42.
113. Kenneth Tynan, *Observer*, 14/4/1957.
114. Harold Hobson, 'A Magnificent Week', *Sunday Times*, 14/4/1957.
115. Rex Harrison, *Daily Mail*, 20/9/1960.
116. 30/7/1959.
117. Balance sheet of *My Fair Lady*, in H.M. Tennent archive RP95/2363, Theatre Museum.
118. J.H. Whitney to B. Beaumont, 16/12/1958, in H.M.Tennent archive, RP95/2363.
119. Anthony Jackson, 'Young People's Theatre (Britain)', in *The Cambridge Guide to World Theatre*, ed Martin Banham, (Cambridge, CUP, 1990), pp.1087–8.
120. Information for this paragraph comes from 'Civic Theatre', *The Oxford Companion to the Theatre*, p.158.
121. W.A. Darlington, 'Mad Meg and Lodger', *Daily Telegraph*, 20/5/1958.
122. Harold Hobson, 'Vagaries of the West End', *Sunday Tines*, 31/1/1960.
123. Harold Hobson, 'The Screw Turns Again', *Sunday Times*, 28/5/1958.
124. William Gaskill, *A Sense of Direction*, (London, Faber and Faber, 1988), p.35.
125. Martin Esslin, *The Theatre of the Absurd*, (Harmondsworth, Penguin, 1961; Third Edition, 1982), p.234.

126. Harold Pinter, *The Room* in *Pinter Plays: One* (London, Methuen, 1987), p. 101.
127. *The Birthday Party* in ibid., p. 27.
128. Harold Hobson, 'The Screw Turns Again', *Sunday Times*, 25/5/1958.
129. Peter Hall, *Making an Exhibition of Myself*, (London, Sinclair-Stevenson, 1993), pp.189–90.
130. N.W. Gwatkin, letter to Gerry Raffles, 24/10/1958, in the Albery papers at the Harry Ransome Humanities Research Center.
131. See Simon Masters, *The National Youth Theatre*, (London, Longmans Young Books, 1969), p.7.
132. Tynan, 1984, p.274.
133. See Hall, 1993, p.135.
134. Harold Hobson, 'Helping Shakespeare', *Sunday Times*, 7/7/1957.
135. Hall, 1993, p.146.
136. See Peter Lewis, *The National: A Dream Made Concrete*, (London, Methuen, 1990), p.97.

Chapter 3: 1963–1968

1. Robert Stephens, *Knight Errant*, (London, Hodder & Stoughton, 1995), pp.27–8.
2. See, for example, *British Theatre in the 1950s*, ed. D.M. Shellard (Sheffield, Sheffield Academic Press, 1999).
3. Stephens, 1995, p.59.
4. Tim Goodwin, *Britain's Royal National Theatre*, (London, NT/Nick Hern Books, 1988), p. 5.
5. Ibid., p.6.
6. Ibid, p.9.
7. Harold Hobson, 'Danger Threatens the Theatre', *Sunday Times*, 6/7/1958.
8. Tynan, quoted in Lewis, 1990, p.4.
9. Olivier, letter to Tynan, 21/8/1962, Kenneth Tynan Archive, British Library.
10. See Lewis, 1990, p.7.
11. See Fiona Kavanagh Fearon, 'Continental Drama on the Stage of the National Theatre' draft of PhD thesis, Chapter 2.
12. Olivier, quoted in Lewis, 1990, p.8.
13. See Stephens, 1995, p.62.
14. Harold Hobson, 'The Peerless Uncle Vanya', *Sunday Times*, 3/11/1963.
15. Robert Cushman, quoted in Goodwin, 1988, p.30.
16. William Gaskill, 1988, p.55.
17. Gaskill, programme notes for *The Recruiting Officer*, quoted in Goodwin, 1988, p.31.
18. Harold Hobson, 'Farquhar for all souls', *Sunday Times*, 15/12/1963.
19. See Stephens, 1995, p.70.
20. Tynan, letter to George Devine, 31/3/1964, Kenneth Tynan Archive.
21. Stephens, 1995, p.65.
22. George Devine, signed letter to Tynan, 9/4/1964, Kenneth Tynan Archive.
23. Olivier signed letter to Devine, 12/4/1964, Kenneth Tynan Archive.
24. See Spoto, p.283.
25. Ronald Bryden, quoted in Goodwin, 1988, p.32.
26. Franco Zeffirelli, quoted in ibid, p.32.
27. Tony Richardson, quoted in Lewis, 1990, p.17.
28. Jack Reading, in a letter to the author (20/10/1997) has an interesting view of this production: '... it surprised me at the time, and has since, that no-one compared or related it to the [Ralph] Richardson/Olivier *Othello* which they played at the Old Vic in the 1937/8 season. In this he, as Iago, ruthlessly upstaged Richardson at every point in the play – probably encouraged or at least condoned by the producer, [Tyrone] Guthrie. There was a climax to this which came at the end of Act III Scene iii when both men declare their allegiance to each other, and their trust. Othello kneels to make his declaration: then Iago, too, kneels. Both men are centre stage:

 O: ... Now art thou my lieutenant.
 I: ... I am your own for ever!

Olivier used this for one of his bravura deliveries on a rising inflection, soaring to the top of the gallery where he had fixed his eye, as if on heaven. It was an awesome moment which I can still recall vividly and, obviously intended as such, because it was made for the break for the Interval.

When he came to play Othello himself it was very obvious to me that he had determined to use his remembrance of his Iago to make sure that poor Frank Finlay never had a chance to upstage him. At every point he was as ruthless in this aim as he had been to score over Richardson, so I was keenly anticipating how he would succeed when his own climactic moment came. What did he do? He had directed the scene so that Finlay said the line, with his back to the audience exiting through a door at back stage. If ever a director-actor had shown a mean-jealousy that was a prime example'.

29. See Spoto, p.289.
30. See *Kenneth Tynan Letters*, ed. Kathleen Tynan, (London, Weidenfeld & Nicolson, 1994), pp.306–8.
31. Quoted in Huggett, 1989, p.339.
32. See Lewis, 1990, p.20.
33. See Stephens, 1995, p.20.
34. Bernard Lewin, quoted in Goodwin, 1988, p.33.
35. Herbert Kretzmer, quoted in Goodwin, 1988, p.33.
36. Ronald Hayman, *British Theatre Since 1955*, (Oxford, OUP, 1979), pp.52–3.
37. Stephens, 1995, p.75.
38. Ibid., p.74.
39. See Lewis, 1990, p.21.
40. Kretzmer, quoted in Goodwin, 1988, p.35.
41. Stephens, 1995, p.91.
42. Hall, 1993, p.167.
43. See David Addenbrooke, *The Royal Shakespeare Company: The Peter Hall Years*, (London, William Kimber, 1974), p.231.
44. See Stephen Fay, *Power Play: The Life and Times of Peter Hall*, (London, Hodder & Stoughton, 1995), p.129.
45. Ibid., p.133.
46. Ibid., p.135.
47. Olivier, letter to Hall, quoted in Fay, 1995, p.137.
48. Hall, 1993, p.174.

49. See Fay, 1995, p.155.
50. Ibid., p.156.
51. Hall, 1993, p.176.
52. Hall, 1993, p.177.
53. Ibid., p.178.
54. Bernard Levin, quoted in Fay, 1995, p.159.
55. Peter Weiss, *Marat/Sade*, trans. Geoffrey Skelton (London, Marion Boyars, 1991), pp. 14–15. The following quotations from this work are to be found at ibid., pp. 82, 108–9 and in the Introduction by Peter Brook.
56. See Hall, 1993, p.199.
57. Peter Brook, Introduction to Weiss, 1991, pp.5–7.
58. Quoted in Fay, 1995, p.186.
59. Harold Hobson, 'The Aldwych affair', *Sunday Times*, 30 August 1964.
60. Harold Hobson, 'Dazzling, purifying, profound', *Sunday Times*, 23/8/1964.
61. Hall, 1993, p.190.
62. Harold Hobson, 'Controversial Hamlet', *Christian Science Monitor*, 22/8/1965.
63. Hall, 1993, p.188.
64. Colin Chambers, *Peggy: The Life of Margaret Ramsay, Play Agent*, (London, Nick Hern Books, 1997), p.91.
65. Ann Jellicoe, quoted in Chambers, 1997, p.99.
66. Peggy Ramsay, quoted in Chambers, 1997, p.121.
67. Ibid., p.146.
68. Ibid., p.154.
69. Joe Orton, *Entertaining Mr Sloane* in *Orton – The Complete Plays* (London, Methuen, 1987), pp. 148–9.
70. Both letters are reproduced in *The Orton Diaries*, ed. John Lahr, (London, Methuen, 1987), p.283.
71. Joe Orton, *Loot*, in Orton, 1987, p. 197. The quotations that follow from this play are in ibid., pp. 197, 205–6, 245–6, 274, 275, 232–3 and 243.
72. Peggy Ramsay, quoted in Chambers, 1997, p.181.
73. See Huggett, 1989, p.512.
74. Hall, 1993, p.180.
75. Goorney, 1987, p.116.
76. Littlewood, 1994, p.581.
77. Littlewood, quoted in Goorney, 1981, p.124.

78. See Littlewood, 1994, p.669.
79. Harold Hobson, 'Business is business', *Sunday Times*, 31/3/1963.
80. See Goorney, 1981, p.127.
81. Littlewood, 1994, p.707.
82. See Michelene Wandor, *Drama Today: A Critical Guide to British Drama 1970–1990*, (London, Longman, 1993), p.2.
83. See *Make Space!*, (London, Theatre Design Umbrella, 1994), p.18.
84. Michael White, *Empty Seats*, (London, Hamish Hamilton, 1984), pp. 77–8.
85. Penelope Gilliat, in Peter Daubeny, *My World of Theatre*, (London, Jonathan Cape, 1971), p.325.
86. Lib Taylor, 'Early stages: Women Dramatists 1958–68' in *British and Irish Women Dramatists Since 1958*, ed. Trevor R. Griffiths and Margaret Llewellyn-Jones, (Buckingham, Open University Press, 1993), p.25.
87. Sydney Newman, quoted in George Brandt, *British Television Drama*, (Cambridge, CUP, 1981), p.16.
88. White, 1984, p.88.
89. See Shellard, 1995, p.196.
90. See Tynan, 1984, pp.366–7.
91. 'The Censorship', *Sunday Times*, 11/4/1965.
92. John Osborne, *A Patriot for Me* in *The Plays of the Sixties* (London, Methuen, 1985), p. 340.
93. Reader's Report for *A Patriot for Me*, 30/8/1964, in the Lord Chamberlain's Papers, British Library.
94. See Wardle, 1979, p.275.
95. See 'The Censorship', *Sunday Times*, 11/4/1965.
96 Lord Chamberlain's Papers, British Library'.
97. Quoted in Nicholas De Jongh, *Not in Front of the Audience*, (London, Routledge, 1992), p. 118.
98. Gaskill, quoted in Philip Roberts, *The Royal Court Theatre 1965–1972*, (London, Routledge, 1986), p.16.
99. Ibid., p.17.
100. Edward Bond, *Saved*, in *Plays One*, (London, Methuen, 1995), p. 38. References to *Saved* in this chapter are from ibid., pp. 55, 70, 81 and 82.
101. Ibid, p.36.
102. Edward Bond, 'Author's Note', *Plays One: Saved*, (London, Methuen, 1995), p.13.
103. Bond quoted in Roberts, 1986, p.39.
104. C.D. Heriot, Reader's Report on *Saved*, 30/6/1965, in the *Saved* file, Lord Chamberlain's Papers, British Library.
105. Gilliatt, *Observer*, 7/11/1965.
106. Irving Wardle, 'Saved', *The Times*, 4/11/1965.
107. See Roberts, 1986, p.24; insertion mine.
108. Leo Gradwell, quoted in Gaskill, 1988, p.69.

Chapter 4: 1969–1979

1. The *Hair* File, Lord Chamberlain's Papers, British Library.
2. Kenneth Tynan in Kathleen Tynan, 1988, p.277.
3. Wardle, quoted in ibid., p.294.
4. See Wandor, 1993, p.2.
5. I am indebted in this section to John Bull's *New British Political Dramatists*, (Basingstoke, Macmillan, 1984), particularly Chapter 1.
6. David Hare, interview in *New Theatre Voices of the Seventies*, ed. Simon Trussler, (London, Methuen, 1981), p.112.
7. Gaskill, 1988, p.135.
8. For further details about the Joint Stock Method, see Rob Ritchie, *The Joint Stock Book*, (London, Methuen, 1987), pp.11–32.
9. Gaskill, 1988, p.136.
10. Howard Brenton, *Times*, 10/8/1976.
11. Hare, in Trussler, 1981, p.114.
12. Michelene Wandor repeats this charge in *Drama Today*, 1993.
13. Bull, 1984, p.19.
14. McGrath in Trussler, 1981, p.105.
15. Lizbeth Goodman, *Contemporary Feminist Theatres*, (London, Routledge, 1993), p.75.
16. Christopher Innes, *Modern British Drama 1890–1990*, (Cambridge, CUP, 1992), p.451.
17. De Jongh, 1992, p.153.
18. Michael Billington, 'Bent'. *Guardian*,

4/5/1979, in *One Night Stands: A Critic's View of British Theatre from 1971–1991*, (London, Nick Hern Books, 1993), p.134.

19. John Barber, quoted in De Jongh, 1992, p.154.
20. *Equity Journal*, September 1996, p.15.
21. Goodman, 1993, pp.36–7.
22. Ibid., p.69.
23. See Innes, 1992, p.450.
24. See Lewis, 1990, p.35.
25. See Lewis, 1990, p.40.
26. Billington, 'Long Day's Journey into Night', *Guardian* 1/9/1972, in Billington, 1993, p. 18.
27. Lewis, 1990, p.66.
28. Billington, 'The Sickness of London Theatreland', *Guardian*, 12/10/1979, in Billington, 1993, p. 141.
29. James Fenton, quoted in Lewis, 1990, p.139.
30. John Barber, quoted in Tim Goodwin, *Britain's Royal National Theatre*, (London, NT/Nick Hern Books, 1988), p.61.
31. Billington, 'Amadeus', *Guardian*, 5/11/1979, in Billington, 1993, p.146.
32. Simon Callow, *Being an Actor*, (Harmondsworth, Penguin, 1995), p.116.
33. *The Times*, 15/10/1974.
34. Frank Marcus, quoted in Goodwin, 1988, p.49.
35. See Goodwin, 1988, p.20.
36. Alan Ayckbourn, *The Norman Conquests*, (Harmondsworth, Penguin, 1977), 'Preface', pp.10–11.
37. Ibid.
38. Ayckbourn, quoted in Michael Billington, *Alan Ayckbourn*, (London, Grove Press, 1983), p.19.
39. Alan Ayckbourn, *Relatively Speaking* (London, Evans Plays, 1976), p. 26.
40. Ibid., p.168.
41. Billington, 'Semi-Monde', *Guardian*, 12/9/77, Billington, 1993, p. 107.
42. Adrienne Scullion, 'The Scottish Theatre Archive', *Theatre Papers*, (Northern Group of the Society for Theatre Research), Issue 1, May 1997.
43. See Jackson and Rowell, 1984, pp.92–3.
44. Ibid., p. 89.
45. John Neville, interview with Emrys Bryson, *Nottingham Evening Post*, 2/6/1967.
46. See Jeffrey Wainright, 'Exit stage left: the big cheese of people's theatre', *Independent*, 25/2/1998.
47. Clive Barnes, quoted in Sally Beauman, *The Royal Shakespeare Company*, (Oxford, OUP, 1982), p.303.
48. Ibid., p.304.
49. Ibid., p.309.
50. See Billington, 1993, p.1.
51. Billington, 'Macbeth', *Guardian*, 10/9/1976, in Billington, 1993, p. 87.
52. Billington, 'Henry VI', *Guardian*, 17/4/1978, in Billington, 1993, p. 121.

Chapter 5: 1980–1997

1. Margaret Thatcher, *The Path to Power*, (London, Harper Collins, 1995), p.308.
2. See Laura Cumming, 'Nobody loves the Arts Council', *New Statesman*, 25 July 1997, pp.38–40.
3. Thatcher, 1995, p.632.
4. See Billington, 1993, p.248.
5. Billington, 'Subsidised Theatre', *Guardian*, 5 July 1986, in Billington, 1993, p. 261.
6. Figures from Billington, 'The Cork Report', *Guardian*, 27/9/1986, in Billington, 1993, pp. 270–2.
7. Quoted in Billington, 1993, p.273.
8. See Richard Morrison, 'Rescued, but it's a lottery', *The Times*, 24/1/1992.
9. Billington, 'Starlight Express', *Guardian*, 28/3/1984, in Billington, 1993, p. 211.
10. Billington, 'Richard III', *Guardian*, 21/6/1984, in Billington, 1993, p. 219.
11. Sheridan Morley, *Our Theatre in the Eighties*, (London, Hodder & Stoughton, 1990), p.98.
12. Quoted in Caroline Lees, 'Critics clash as gay plays invade the West End', *Sunday Times*, 2/10/1994.
13. John Peter, 'The love that dares speak', *Sunday Times*, 17/4/1994.
14. Quoted in Lees, 2/10/94.

15. Mark Ravenhill, *Shopping and F***ing* (London, Methuen, 1997), p. 73.
16. Billington, 'Serious Money', *Guardian*, 30/3/1987, in Billington, 1993, p. 276.
17. John James quoted in Goodwin, 1988, p.62.
18. Billington, 'The Romans in Britain', *Guardian*, 17/10/1980, in Billington, 1993, p. 160.
19. Quoted in Lewis, 1990, p.144.
20. Simon Callow, *The National: The Theatre and its Work 1963–1997*, (London, NT/Nick Hern Books, 1997), p.60.
21. Jack Kroll, quoted in Goodwin, 1988, p.78.
22. Levin, in Goodwin, 1988, p.79.
23. Darryll Grantley, 'The National Theatre's Production of *The Mysteries*: Some Observations', *Theatre Notebook*, Number 2, Vol XL, 1986.
24. Howard Brenton and David Hare, *Pravda* (London, Methuen, 1995), p. 27. The following quotations from the play can be found at ibid., pp. 113 and 103–4.
25. Lyn Gardner, in Goodwin, 1988, p.80.
26. Jane Edwardes, in Goodwin, 1988, p.88.
27. Billington, 'Antony and Cleopatra', *Guardian*, 11/4/1987, in Billington, 1993, p. 279.
28. Clive Hirschhorn, quoted in Goodwin, 1988, p.87.
29. John Peter, quoted in Goodwin, 1988, p. 87.
30. Peter Lewis, 'Grand National', *Sunday Times*, 5/7/1992. In 1992, productions were touring for 30 weeks of the year.
31. Ibid.
32. John Peter, *Sunday Times*, 3/10/1993.
33. Billington, 'Sunday in the Park With George', *Guardian*, 17/3/1990, in Billington, 1993, p. 332.
34. James Woodall, 'A mild eminence', *Sunday Times*, 21/3/1993.
35. Benedict Nightingale, 'Why Lady Macbeth was to become the Prime Suspect', *The Times*, 16/9/1997.
36. Billington, 'The Greeks', *Guardian*, 4/2/1980, in Billington, 1993, p. 147.
37. Programme for *The Merry Wives of Windsor*, Stratford, 1996/7 season.
38. Billington, *Guardian*, 21/6/1984, in Billington, 1993, p. 218.
39. Morley, 1990, p.198.
40. Quoted in Andy Lavender, 'The Bard as spoken up north', *The Times*, 14/12/93.
41. Timberlake Wertenbaker, *Our Country's Good* (London, Methuen, 1988), p. 21. The following quotations from this play are from ibid., pp. 39, 40 and 89.
42. John Peter, 'Timely plays for today', *Sunday Times*, 24/11/1991.
43. John Peter, 'All present and correct', *Sunday Times*, 10/1/1993.
44. Benedict Nightingale, 'How to spice up a leftover polemic', *The Times*, 24/2/1994.
45. Benedict Nightingale, 'Right man, right time, but wrong direction?', *The Times*, 11/11/1991.
46. Mission statement in *Shopping and F***ing*, (London, Methuen, 1997), Preface p.v.
47. Benedict Nightingale, 'Shocking scenes in Sloane Square', *The Times*, 20/1/1995.
48. Dalya Alberge, 'Royal Court appoints "unknown" as director', *The Times*, 14/8/97.
49. Kate Bassett, 'Last exit from Notting Hill', *The Times*, 3/3/95.
50. Benedict Nightingale, 'All too quiet on the western front', *The Times*, 2/2/1994.
51. 'Actresses stage protest over pay', *The Times*, 3/3/1992.
52. I am indebted to Jack Reading for his suggestions for this paragraph.

Select Bibliography

Addenbrooke, David, *The Royal Shakespeare Company: The Peter Hall Years* (London, William Kimber, 1974).

Ayckbourn, Alan, *The Norman Conquests* (Harmondsworth, Penguin, 1977).

Beauman, Sally, *The Royal Shakespeare Company* (Oxford, OUP, 1982).

Beckett, Samuel, *Waiting for Godot* (London, Faber, 1965).

Behr, Deidre, *Samuel Beckett: A Biography* (London, Cape, 1990).

Billington, Michael, *Alan Ayckbourn* (London, Grove Press, 1983).

——, *One Night Stands: a Critic's View of British Theatre from 1971–1991* (London, Nick Hern Books, 1993).

Black, Kitty, *Upper Circle* (London, Methuen, 1984).

Bloomsbury Theatre Guide, ed. Griffiths, Trevor R. and Woddis, Carole (London, Bloomsbury, 1991).

Bond, Edward, *Plays One: Saved* (London, Methuen, 1995).

Brandt, George, *British Television Drama* (Cambridge, CUP, 1981).

Brecht, Bertolt, *Brecht on Theatre*, trans. Willett, John (London, Methuen, 1986).

British and Irish Women Dramatists Since 1958, ed. Griffiths, Trevor R., and Llewellyn-Jones, Margaret (Buckingham, Open University Press, 1993).

Bull, John, *New British Political Dramatists* (Basingstoke, Macmillan, 1991).

——, *Stage Right*, (London, Methuen, 1994).

Bull, Peter, *I Know the Face, But ...* (London, Peter Davies, 1959).

Calder, Angus, *The People's War* (London, Cape, 1969).

Callow, Simon, *Being an Actor* (Harmondsworth, Penguin, 1995).

——, *The National: the Theatre and its Work 1963–1997* (London, RNT/Nick Hern Books, 1997).

Cambridge Companion to Brecht, The, ed. Thomson, Peter and Sacks,

Glendyr (Cambridge, CUP, 1994).

Cambridge Guide to World Theatre, The, ed. Banham, Martin (Cambridge, CUP, 1990).

Cave, Richard Allen, *New British Drama in Performance on the London Stage 1970–1985* (Gerrards Cross, Colin Smythe, 1987).

Chambers, Colin, *The Story of Unity Theatre* (London, Lawrence & Wishart, 1989).

——, *Peggy: The Life of Margaret Ramsay, Play Agent* (London, Nick Hern Books, 1997).

Cottrell, Tony, *Evolving Stages* (Bristol, The Bristol Press, 1991).

Coveney, Michael, *The Aisle is Full of Noises* (London, Nick Hern Books, 1994).

Daubeny, Peter, *My World of Theatre* (London, Jonathan Cape, 1971).

Declaration, ed. Maschler, T. (London, Macgibbon & Kay, 1959).

De Jongh, Nicholas, *Not in Front of the Audience* (London, Routledge, 1992).

Drama Criticism Since Ibsen, ed. Hinchliffe, Arnold P. (Basingstoke, Macmillan, 1979).

Duff, Charles, *The Lost Summer – The Heyday of the West End Theatre* (London, Nick Hern Books, 1995).

Elsom, John, *Post-War British Theatre Criticism* (London, Routledge & Kegan Paul, 1981).

Elsom, John, and Tomalin, Nicholas, *The History of the National Theatre* (London, Routledge & Kegan Paul, 1978).

Esslin, Martin, *Brecht, a Choice of Evils: a Critical Study of the Man, his Work and his Opinions* (1959; fourth, rev. edn, London, Methuen, 1984).

——, *The Theatre of the Absurd* (1962; third edn, Harmondsworth, Penguin, 1982).

Fay, Stephen, *Power Play: The Life and Times of Peter Hall* (London, Hodder & Stoughton, 1995).

Findlater, Richard, *Banned* (London, Panther, 1967).

——, *At the Royal Court* (London, Amber Lane Press, 1981).

Gaskill, William, *A Sense of Direction* (London, Faber, 1988).

Goodman, Lizbeth, *Contemporary Feminist Theatres* (London, Routledge, 1993).

Goodwin, Tim, *Britain's Royal National Theatre* (London, NT/Nick Hern Books, 1988).

Goorney, Howard, *The Theatre Workshop Story* (London, Methuen, 1981).

Graver, Lawrence, *Waiting for Godot* (Cambridge, CUP, 1989).

Hall, Peter, *Peter Hall's Diaries* (London, Hamilton, 1983).

——, *Making an Exhibition of Myself* (London, Sinclair-Stevenson, 1993).

Harrap's Book of 1000 Plays, ed. Fletcher, Steve, and Jopling, Norman (London, Harrap, 1989).

Hayman, Ronald, *British Theatre Since 1955* (Oxford, OUP, 1979).

Herbert, A.P., *No Fine on Fun* (London, Arts Council, 1957).

Hobson, Harold, *Indirect Journey* (London, Weidenfeld & Nicolson, 1978).

Hodgson, Terry, *The Batsford Dictionary of Drama* (London, B.T. Batsford, 1988).

Huggett, Richard, *Binkie Beaumont: Eminence Grise of the West End Theatre 1933–1973* (London, Hodder & Stoughton, 1989).

Hunt, Hugh, Richards, Kenneth and Russell Taylor, John, *The Revels History of Drama in English Volume VII: 1880 to the Present Day* (London, Methuen, 1978).

Innes, Christopher, *Modern British Drama 1890–1990* (Cambridge, CUP, 1992).

Itzin, Catherine, *Stages in the Revolution* (London, Eyre Methuen, 1980).

Johnston, John, *The Lord Chamberlain's Blue Pencil* (London, Hodder & Stoughton, 1990).

Kott, Jan, *Shakespeare Our Contemporary* (London, Routledge, 1990).

Lacey, Stephen, *British Realist Theatre* (London, Routledge, 1995).

Leeming, Glenda, *Poetic Drama* (Basingstoke, Macmillan, 1989).

Lewis, Peter, *The Fifties – Portrait of an Age* (London, The Cupid Press, 1989).

——, *The National: A Dream Made Concrete* (London, Methuen, 1990).

Littlewood, Joan, *Joan's Book* (London, Methuen, 1994).

Make Space! (London, Theatre Design Umbrella, 1994).

Masters, Simon, *The National Youth Theatre* (London, Longmans Young Books, 1969).

Morley, Sheridan, *Our Theatre in the Eighties* (London, Hodder & Stoughton, 1990).

New Poetry, The, ed. A. Alvarez, (Harmondsworth, Penguin, 1962).

New Theatre Voices of the Fifties and Sixties, ed. Marowitz, Charles, Milne, Tom, and Hale, Owen (London, Eyre Methuen, 1981).

New Theatre Voices of the Seventies, ed. Trussler, Simon (London, Methuen, 1981).

Orton Diaries, The, ed. Lahr, John (London, Methuen, 1987).

Osborne, John, *A Better Class of Person* (Harmondsworth, Penguin, 1982).

——, *Almost a Gentleman* (London, Faber and Faber, 1991).

——, *Look Back in Anger* (*c* 1957; London, Faber and Faber, 1996).

Oxford Companion to the Theatre, The, ed. Hartnoll, Phyllis (Oxford, OUP, 1990).

Pelling, Henry, *Modern Britain: 1885–1955* (London, Nelson, 1965).

——, *A Short History of the Labour Party* (Basingstoke, Macmillan, 1985).

Plays and Players. The Best of Plays and Players, Volume One: 1953–1968, ed. Roberts, Peter (London, Metheun, 1988).

Plays and Players. The Best of Plays and Players, Volume Two: 1969–1983, ed. Roberts, Peter (London, Methuen, 1989).

Quayle, Anthony, *A Time to Speak* (London, Barrie & Jenkins, 1990).

Ravenhill, Mark, *Shopping and F***ing* (London, Methuen, 1997).

Ritchie, Rob, *The Joint Stock Book* (London, Methuen, 1987).

Roberts, Peter, *The Old Vic Story* (London, W.H. Allen, 1976).

Roberts, Philip, *The Royal Court Theatre 1965–1972* (London, Routledge, 1986).

Rowell, George, *The Old Vic Theatre: A History* (Cambridge, CUP, 1993).

Rowell, George, and Jackson, Anthony *The Repertory Movement: A History of Regional Theatre in Britain* (Cambridge, CUP, 1984).

Russell Taylor, John, *Anger and After* (London, Eyre Methuen, 1969).

——, *The Second Wave* (London, Methuen, 1971).

Sanderson, Michael, *From Irving to Olivier* (London, Athlone Press, 1985).

Shellard, D.M., *Harold Hobson: Witness and Judge* (Keele, Keele University Press, 1995).

——, *Harold Hobson: The Complete Catalogue 1922–1988* (Keele, Keele University Press, 1995).

Spoto, Donald, *Laurence Olivier* (London, Harper Collins, 1991).

Stephens, Robert, *Knight Errant* (London, Hodder & Stoughton, 1995).

Thatcher, Margaret, *The Path to Power* (London, Harper Collins, 1995).

Theatre Papers, (Sheffield, Northern Group of the Society for Theatre Research, 1997), Issue 1.

Trussler, Simon, *The Cambridge Illustrated History of British Theatre* (Cambridge, CUP, 1994).

Tynan, Kathleen, *The Life of Kenneth Tynan* (London, Methuen, 1988).

Tynan, Kenneth, *A View of the English Stage* (London, Methuen, 1984).

——, *Kenneth Tynan Letters*, ed. Tynan, Kathleen (London, Weidenfeld & Nicolson, 1994).

Tynan, Kenneth and Beaton, Cecil, *Persona Grata* (London, Allan Wingate, 1953).

Wandor, Michelene, *Drama Today: A Critical Guide to British Drama 1970–1990* (London, Longman, 1993).

Wansell, Geoffrey, *Terence Rattigan* (London, Fourth Estate, 1995).

Wardle, Irving, *The Theatres of George Devine* (London, Eyre Methuen, 1979).

——, *Theatre Criticism* (London, Routledge, 1992).

Weiss, Peter, *Marat/Sade* (London, Marion Boyars, 1991).

White, Michael, *Empty Seats* (London, Hamish Hamilton, 1984).

Wilk, Max, *OK! The Story of Oklahoma!* (New York, Grove Press, 1993).

Willet, John, *The Theatre of Bertolt Brecht: a Study from Eight Aspects* (1959; third, rev. edn, London, Eyre Methuen, 1977).

Index